From the Critics

The Oakland Press
Dolly Moiseeff, Assistant Managing Editor

"Think you know vacation spots in Michigan pretty well? Bet the 'Michigan Vacation Guide' can steer you to a couple of places you've never heard of. It's a dandy paperback that is a guide to cottages, chalets, condos and B&Bs throughout Michigan.

A couple a years ago, my family followed the recommendation to a listing at Spider Lake near Traverse City, and it was everything the guide had promised. Even if you're like me and have had a lifetime of vacations in Michigan, this book is loaded with good ideas and enough information to make vacation plans."

The Detroit Free Press
Gerry Volgenau, Travel Editor

"Think spring and plan a Michigan trip...Michigan Vacation Guide: Cottages Chalets, Condos, B&B's ... [will help you] find a more interesting place than the Holiday Inn."

Midwest Book Review

"The Michigan Vacation Guide a truly first-rate and highly recommended resource ..."

HOW TO USE THIS BOOK

Welcome to the Seventh Edition of *The Michigan Vacation Guide to Cottages, Chalets, Condos, B&B's*. This simple to use publication, arranged by region and alphabetically by city, is designed to assist you with one of your first vacation priorities...where to stay. Our intention is to offer some interesting alternatives to the usual hotels/motels. We hope our Guide helps you find your perfect vacation lodging as quickly and effortlessly as possible.

Understanding Special Notes:

Editor's Note   Our staff has not had the opportunity to visit every listed property in this book. Descriptions have been supplied by owners. When we have visited a lodging, the Editor's Note reflects our overall impression of the property. If (based on photographs supplied by owners) a newly added property looks interesting or major updates have been made at an existing property, an Editor's Note will be added to provide our readers with relevant information.

Editor's Choice   Indicates places our staff have visited which, in our opinion, meet or exceed the basic requirements of comfort, cleanliness, location and value for the area.

Reviews   This edition of the MVG features all new reviews never published in previous editions of our guide. All comments are solely the opinion of our staff and do not necessarily reflect the opinions of others.

Whenever possible, prices have been included. However, prices frequently change or fluctuate with the seasons. We recommend calling to verify rates when making reservations. If the owner requires an advance deposit, verify refund policies (if any). **As a renter, be sure you understand the terms of the rental agreement.**

VISIT OUR OFFICIAL WEBSITE
www.MiVG.com
-or-
www.michiganvacationguide.com

Join Us at our Website

www.MiVG.com

Also accessed via ... **www.michiganvacationguide.com**

*Join us on-line as we continue
our journey through Michigan*

➡ Use our **Advanced Accommodations Search** to quickly find the property best suited to your interests and needs.

➡ **Join in our Interactive Forum.** It's fun and informative, so come on in! Ask a question...give an answer. Share your recent Michigan adventure or a great new restaurant... or just chat a bit.

➡ Sign-up for our **Email List** and receive late-breaking news on our MVG discoveries. Plus, **information on area events, discounts or other specials** our property owners are offering.

➡ Access our **Newsletter** and find out about our most recent discoveries and late-breaking news.

*Discover the Beauty of Michigan and
Your Home Away From Home
at the new ... www.MiVG.com!*

Michigan

Let me take you to the land once called "Michigania"

across flat planes to ever increasing slopes, hills and

mountains; through virginal forests and crystal lakes,

dotted by cottages resting on sugar white sand.

Where falls are painted by an artist's brush

and winters are blanketed in white.

Here are the forests and

wildlife, quaint cities and

great cities, museums and

shipwrecks,

and so much more.

I am your dream maker ...

the great outdoors ...

the vacation land for all

seasons.

by C. Rydel

Table of Contents

REGIONAL DIVISIONS

Selecting an Accommodation

Staying at a cottage, condo or bed and breakfast is truly a unique and enjoyable experience. However, it is **different** than staying at a hotel or motel. Rental owners may forget to provide certain information about their property/room that are important to you. Below is a brief overview of the questions you may want to ask. Also in this chapter is information on the distinguishing differences between rental properties to help you understand and appreciate their differences.

The Basics

Questions to ask the property owner/manager:

- Understand the *House Rules* (the do's and don'ts the property owner/ manager asks that you abide by).

- Number of bedrooms/bathrooms.

- Housekeeping policies. Is daily room cleaning provided? Who's in charge of making sure the property is clean before your arrival.

- Determine your contact (and their availability day or night) if there is a problem.

- If a "king-size bed" is included, ask if the king-size bed is really king-size or two twin beds placed together.

- Furnishing and bedding ... when was the lodging last redecorated and did that include new carpeting, mattresses, are linens provided, etc.

- If the property is described as "beach front", find out if it's truly beach front or is there a road that separates the beach, etc. You may also want to ask about the condition of the beach (i.e., is it a safe swimming area, is the base mostly sand, a mix of pebbles/sand or rocky).

- If the property is described as having a "lake view", determine if it's a direct lake view or obstructed.

- Miscellaneous questions may include the property location ... is it off a busy main road or intersection, is there any construction nearby, etc.

Always be sure you understand the terms of the rental agreement. Determine advance deposit and cancellation/refund policies.

Clean up after yourself. Please be courteous and leave your lodging in the same condition in which it was found.

9

Terminology

Fully Equipped Kitchens. Includes stove, refrigerator, pots, pans, dishes, eating utensils and sometimes (not always) microwaves, toasters, automatic coffeemakers, dishwashers.

A/C and CATV. A/C refers to air conditioning (may or may not be central air conditioning); CATV refers to color cable television.

Modern Cottage. Does not mean new. It refers to electricity and indoor plumbing (private bath, hot water, etc.). Most of today's cottages are considered modern.

On the Water. Refers to a lodging which fronts water. It does not necessarily mean the property has a swimming beach (see below) or a place to dock your boat.

Swimming Beach. A water area with gradual incline, no surprise drop-offs, no strong currents. It may or may not be a smooth, sand beach.

Full Breakfast. Beverages, main course and, sometimes, dessert.

Continental Breakfast. Beverages with breads and/or pastries.

American Plan Resorts. All meals included in the price.

What Are the Differences?

While it's impossible to give a single description for each type of lodging, there are certain traits that make each distinctively different:

RESORT COTTAGES:

Atmosphere: Most resorts were built in the 1950s-60s with some dating back even further. Resort environments are family-friendly.

While there is a rising number of cottage resorts that our updating their lodgings with luxury in mind, most still remain simple in comfort and amenities. You may find a ceiling fan but only a few have air conditioning. Furniture is sometimes a collection of older, second-hand items. A fireplace in your cabin is not uncommon and wood is usually provided. Resorts generally do not provide daily maid service.

Features: Many resorts offer on-site activities for the family. For example, those by the water often have a safe swimming area with a canoe or rowboat as part of the rental price. You can usually bring your own boat (not all allow high speed motors). There may be a children's play area, badminton, basketball or tennis courts. Game rooms may include pinball, video arcades, etc.

Many rent motors, paddle or pontoon boats and other watercraft. Nature/ snowmobile trails, chartered fishing along with planned daily group activities, or American Plan programs may be available.

Rates/Rental Policy: Resorts often provide the most economically priced lodging, especially those not located on the water. A few begin renting as low as $450 weekly with several exceeding $2,000. During prime season, most require weekly rentals (Saturday to Saturday). Advance deposits are generally asked with refund policies varying.

What to Bring: Towels, linens, pillows, cleaning and paper products.

PRIVATE COTTAGES & CHALETS:

Atmosphere: These accommodations offer a private vacation. Whether overlooking the water, woods or ski slopes, this place will seem like your own private retreat.

Since these cottages are used by the owners, interior decor will vary greatly. Some are small and simply furnished while others are spacious, contemporary and luxurious.

Please note, privately owned cottages or homes may or may not have a 'cleaning service' and many have special 'house rules'. Also very important, ask who your contact is should there be any problems while you're there.

Features: You usually won't have all of the outdoor amenities found at resorts, such as basketball/ tennis courts or video game rooms. However, interiors tend be more comfortable. Private cottages may have fireplaces, but you'll probably have to supply your own wood. Other extra features may include ceiling fans, air conditioning, hot tubs, stereos, TVs, VCRs and kitchens with dishwashers.

Rates/Rental Policies: Owners frequently need to be contacted during evenings or weekends when they're not working. During prime season, most will rent weekly (Saturday to Saturday) some will agree to a 2-day minimum stay. Prices may be a little higher than resorts with average rates from $800 to over $3,000. Most require up front deposits with varying refund policies.

What to Bring: See "Cottage Resorts".

CONDOMINIUMS:

Atmosphere: For those who enjoy the anonymity and comfort a hotel/motel provides but also want the added convenience of a full kitchen, living room, etc., condos are a good choice. While there are a few older condos, most were built in the last 5 to 20 years. You will generally find the interior furnishings newer with matching sofa, chairs, tables and decor.

Features: Air conditioning is often available. Rooms may have Jacuzzi tubs and wet bars. Condo "resorts" frequently feature championship golf courses, heated swimming pools, tennis and health clubs.

Rates/Rental Policies: Units are rented by private owners or associations with more flexible policies (not all require week long rentals). Weekly rentals prices are similar to private cottages from $800 to over $3,000. Advance deposits are required with varying refund policies.

What to Bring: See "Cottage Resorts".

BED & BREAKFASTS:

B&B's and inns provide a quiet, relaxing atmosphere and are equally enjoyed by business and vacation travelers alike. While some establishments welcome well behaved children, most cater to the adult traveler. A bed and breakfast is not the place for loud parties. However, with notice, many cater to small group gatherings.

Proprietors take great pride in decorating and maintaining their lodgings in a style which will welcome their guests and provide a comfortable, inviting setting. As a result, courtesy and respect of property is expected.

Features: These establishments can be very diverse in features and amenities. Some may be small homes in subdivisions with private or shared bath. Others may be large historical estates or contemporary with 10 or more guest rooms. These accommodations are frequently decorated with antiques and/or authentic reproductions. Additional features may include in-room Jacuzzi and fireplace, air conditioning.

Price/Rental Policies: Prices vary greatly with averages between $75 to $100 daily and a few luxury suites exceed $200. Most bed and breakfasts rent daily and may offer special week or weekend package rates. Advanced deposits are generally requested, refund policies vary.

What to Bring: Just your clothes and a smile.

Breakfasts: Breakfasts are part of every B&B package (those categorized as inns may not include breakfast). Breakfasts vary from continental to full. Ask the owner about serving times. Some establishments encourage guests' mingling at a common table during breakfast. Others may provide private tables or will bring breakfast directly to your room. Many innkeepers are happy to accommodate special dietary needs but will need to be told in advance.

Just remember, if you're not sure about something ...
ASK THE OWNER.

Featured Property Reviews

Crews' Lakeside Resort
Caseville, Michigan

Reservations: 989-856-278 6
Email: info@crewslakesideresort.com
Website: www.crewslakesideresort.com

Owners:	Larry & Julia Crews
Accommodations:	Resort, 7 cottages on Lake Huron
Extras:	CATV, private balconies, equipped kitchens with microwave and traditional perk coffeepots. Also includes two full baths, ceiling fans, two fireplaces (one in master bedroom). Swimming beach. Tennis and basketball court, shuffleboard. Swing set for toddlers. Outdoor bonfire. Bring linens.
Rates/Payment:	Weekly $848-$1,113. Checks accepted.
Miscellaneous:	No pets.
Open:	May through September.

Crews' Lakeside Resort is not new to the cozy lakeside community of Caseville. For more than 37 years travelers driving around Michigan's Thumb have passed this quiet family resort on Pt. Austin Drive. Few, however, will

Crews' Lakeside rests along a sandy stretch of Lake Huron.

recognize it today. Fully rebuilt, this former traditional cottage resort is now one of Caseville's most appealing family accommodations.

Resting vertically along 61 ft. of Lake Huron beach, the resort's seven, two-level cottages (Larry and Julia prefer to call them detached condos) are a rather spacious 1,400—1,600 sq. ft. Each offers two bedrooms (queen beds) with a pull-out sofa bed and is more than comfortable for 4-6 people.

Completely renovated, you'll enjoy spacious lakefront comfort. First floor design combines living with kitchen and dining areas.

1 of 2 upstairs bedrooms, the master bedroom (pictured here) features gas-log fireplace and enclosed balcony.

The first floor design is open, combining kitchen, dining and living areas into one large room. A gas-log fireplace warms the main room that is comfortably furnished and includes a cable TV. Kitchens are clean and nicely equipped. The first floor bathroom is just off the kitchen. We were particularly impressed with the screened sun porches to the back of the dining/kitchen area. Comfortably furnished, they are bright, cheerful and a lovely space to enjoy your morning coffee or relax after a busy day on the lake.

Perhaps the most impressive changes are in the upstairs bedrooms. Completely new, they are beautifully designed. Much like a welcoming bed and breakfast, they are furnished with bright quilts, appealing decor with an immaculate, spacious bathroom. Their large master bedroom has a chalet-styled ceiling and includes cozy gas-log fireplace and cable TV. Some also have a private walk-out balcony. The master bedrooms are a wonderful place for adults to have a little quiet time after the kids are asleep.

If you're like most of us, you'll be spending a good part of each day at the resort's private Lake Huron beach that has a light mix of sand and stone. There's nothing quite like waking up to the sparkling light of sunrise, enjoying the cool waters during the heat of the day, then settling down to a beautiful sunset to make a vacation memorable .

For those times when you need a 'lake-break', there are a number of activities in the area. Just down the road is miniature golf (what family vacation would be complete without one). Also nearby is an 18-hole professional course. Not far is Sleeper State Park and Historic Caseville with bicycle trails and nature walks. Drive to the surrounding communities of Caseville, Oak Beach or Historic Grindstone City and explore their museums and unique shops,

Crews' Lakeside Resort is a welcoming resort and one of our happiest rediscoveries in Michigan's thumb region. We suggest making reservations early.

Dale's Lakefront Cottages
Caseville, Michigan

Reservations: 888-681-6565; 989-874-5181
Email: dlfc102@avci.net
Website: www.daleslakefrontcottages.atfreeweb.com

Owner:	Dale Ignash
Accommodations:	Seven homes/cottages, 2-4 bedrooms (sleeps 5-10) on Saginaw Bay.
Extras:	Most have fully equipped kitchen, microwave, and CATV. Other amenities vary, including: VCR, fireplace, washer/dryer, ceiling fans, private porches, BBQ, furnished decks and 100 ft. sandy swimming beach.
Rates/Payment:	Weekly $800 and up. Checks.
Miscellaneous:	Over 20 homes/chalets/cottages/condos in the Caseville area. No smoking. Ask about pet policy. Some handicapped friendly.
Open:	Year around.

Traveling to Michigan's Thumb is one of our favorite adventures because we always seem to discover something new. Just a couple of hours from Metro Detroit, it's a great area for a weekend or week-long getaway. On this particular trip we met with Dale Ignash, a well-known property manager in the region, who has acquired a diverse selection of rental properties in Caseville.

Several of Dale's cottages and rental homes are located lakeside.

From spacious lakefront homes to cozy cottages, Dale's has a lodging and price to meet your needs in Caseville.

We met Dale on a sunny spring day at one of his properties, Dale's Lakefront Resort. Fronting the blue water of Saginaw Bay, these seven one and two-story cottages sit perpendicular to the water on a 600x100 ft. lot. This is not a typical resort but, rather, several private rentals on the same grounds, making it great for single families, reunions or corporate retreats. Units 1, 2 and 3 are closer to the water and have the best view of the Bay with units 4, 5, 6 and 7 closer to the road.

Fresh wood and paint emphasize the new or renovated row of cottages and larger two-story homes. Each has a furnished porch or deck to enjoy the cool summer evenings, while watching the boats in the bay. As we discuss the characteristics of these cottages, it should be noted that three of them are less than 10 years old. The remaining four are older with the interiors reflecting a vintage design.

Inside, the homes tend to have spacious living rooms with a contemporary mix of furnishings. Walls are light or paneled with carpeting throughout.

Dale's larger home can easily accommodate 10-15 people.

Oak trim accents stairs and windows in some of the new rentals providing a nice touch. The smaller cottages can comfortably accommodate four adults, with a deck offering a bay view. Large windows and door walls make it easy to enjoy the scenery or lake. Some living rooms and bedrooms include ceiling fans for those occasional warm evenings.

Kitchens are up-to-date with new Formica counters and light wood cupboards. All are well equipped with plenty of dinnerware and storage space. Eating

Bedrooms vary in size and decor.

areas can be cozy and casual or large and formal, depending on the size of the cottage. The same goes for bedrooms, which also vary in size.

Dale's largest and most impressive lodging is his two-story, three-bedroom 2,500 sq. ft., home. With vaulted ceilings in the bedrooms, large windows and bright walls, the home is particularly appealing. Of particular interest, the second floor has a good-size gathering/meeting room setup to handle corporate meetings or large family gatherings. With lighted worktables in the center of the room, 10-15 people can easily be accommodated.

The view of the bay from the two large wooded decks was wonderful. These tree covered community decks provide a great area to gather for a little chit-chat or to simply relax with a good book. Strolling down to the beautiful stretch of sandy beach, we could imagine spending the day there.

Besides swimming, Saginaw Bay is popular for recreational sports, including boating, skiing and fishing. As an interesting side note, Saginaw Bay is an outlet for America's largest contiguous freshwater wetland system. The water shed, nearly 9,000 square miles, supports the many rich agricultural, wildlife and tourist resources the region offers.

Dale's diverse selection of rentals offers something for everyone. Maybe it's time for you to rediscover the Thumb and beautiful Saginaw Bay.

Lake Vista Motel & Cottage Resort
Port Austin, Michigan

Telephone: 989-738-8612
Email: lakevista168@yahoo.com
Website: www.lakevistaresort.com

Owners:	Ronald and Mary Gottschalk
Accommodations:	Cottages, suites and motel on Saginaw Bay.
Extras:	Cottages/Suites: equipped kitchen, microwave, A/C, ceiling fans, CATV. Motel Units: AC, ceiling fans, CATV. Laundry facility. Grounds include two gazebos, boardwalk, heated pool, stairs down to water, lawn chairs, BBQ, picnic tables, play area, fishing/hunting supplies and licenses. Snacks and ice available.
Rates/Payment:	Weekly beginning at $615; Nightly beginning at $82. Major credit cards, checks.
Miscellaneous:	No smoking/pets. Towels, toiletries not included.
Open:	April through November.

Michigan's "Hidden Gold Coast", Port Austin, rests at the top of the thumb with over 90 miles of unspoiled shoreline. This quaint, unassuming town is home to Lake Vista Motel & Cottage Resort and has been welcoming guests for over 25 years. Owned and operated by Ronald and Mary Gottschalk, it's located on M-25 where Van Dyke (M-53) meets Saginaw Bay.

Picturesque gardens and beautifully maintained grounds.

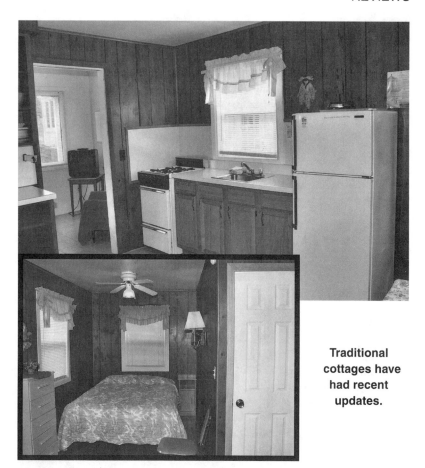

Traditional cottages have had recent updates.

The resort features picturesque grounds with lovely garden walls, fountains, flowerbeds along with brick walking paths, well manicured lawns and tall shade trees. Two gazebos make great places to meet fellow vacationers. There are also charcoal grills, picnic tables, and lawn chairs on the grounds. A boardwalk surrounds the heated in-ground pool that overlooks the Bay. Stairs lead you to the small beach with a mix of sand and stone.

Lake Vista Motel & Cottage Resort has three distinct types of accommodations that include traditional-styled cottages, standard motels units and luxury suites. Their bright and contemporary suites were our favorite and made an excellent new addition to the resort. They're long design with high vaulted ceilings and skylights offer a spacious feel. Glistening white walls contrast nicely against the deep green carpet and colorful bedspreads. Each one-room unit contains two queen beds positioned along one long wall. Furnishings consist of sofa, chair, and table for meals or evening games. Opposite from

We were most impressed with Lake Vista's newest luxury suites.

the beds, a kitchenette with refrigerator, microwave, coffee pot and toaster should comfortably handle your light meals and snacks. At the back of each suite is a rather spacious bathroom with tub/shower. Another nice feature is the large windows that draw you outside for a direct view of the lake. If you want to get closer to nature, sit out on the deck and watch ships pass on the water's horizon.

The cottages at Lake Vista are consistent with styles built 20 to 40 years ago. Ron and Mary spend a lot of time maintaining these popular cottages to keep them ready for guests. Characteristic traits would be the dark paneled walls, smaller bedrooms and bathrooms with showers. Kitchens are fully equipped. Carpet, linoleum or wood cover the floors and the furniture is a mix of styles. While we were there, we noted a couple of cottages had new installed ceramic tile floors. The two larger cottages have nicely furnished sunrooms. Two features not often found at resorts, air conditioning and cable TV, are available in all of the cottages, motel rooms and suites.

The simple motel units have comfortable furnishings, light walls and carpeted floors and more space than your average motel room. Each has one or two beds with a dining

Pool overlooks scenic Lake Huron.

table large enough to easily handle a family. Another plus besides the size is the mini-frig and microwave in each unit.

Yet another nice feature at the resort is its fantastic heated swimming pool. An expansive boardwalk surrounds the area and overlooks the Bay. Nearby stairs lead you to the small beach with a mix of sand and stone.

Port Austin is surrounded by Caseville on the west and Grindstone City to the east. A simple nostalgic area of the state where life is relaxed, townsfolk know each other and welcome visitors. It is often thought of as a water wonderland with great beaches, fishing and underwater shipwrecks, but let's not forget its other offerings. There are some great restaurants, golf courses, mini-golf, little boutiques and antique shops to enjoy.

Regardless of your vacation plans, Lake Vista is ideally located in the center of it all. Why not give them a call...we recommend their new luxury suites.

Lodge at Oak Pointe B&B And Cottage
Caseville, Michigan

Reservations: 989-856-3055
Email: oaklodge@avci.net
Website: www.oakpointelodge.com

Innkeepers:	Robert & Becky Dorfman
Accommodations:	Bed and Breakfast. 5 guest rooms/private baths; 1 bedroom cottage.
Extras:	Continental plus breakfast. Central A/C. Gas fireplaces, 2-person whirlpool tubs, queen beds, screened porches with scenic views. Cottage with full kitchen.
Rates/Payment:	Daily $79-$110. Major credit cards, checks.
Miscellaneous:	30 acres with nature trails. Wildlife safehaven. No phones/TV's in guest rooms. Call about pet policy. Well-behaved children welcome. Handicap access.
Open:	Year around.

Located in the laid-back community of Caseville in Michigan's thumb, is the rustically elegant Lodge at Oak Pointe. You'll enter The Lodge grounds through a quiet driveway just off M-25 (Port Austin Road). Like a secret soon to be revealed, the grounds open to a fantastic scene of lush lawns and

Picture-perfect setting of the Lodge at Oak Pointe.

Interior styling celebrates "The Hunt"

sparkling pond waters reflecting the surrounding trees, sky and log inn. Keep your camera handy because we're certain you'll want to capture this picture for your memory book.

Robert and Becky Dorfman, amiable innkeepers, have created a wonderful retreat for travelers seeking a romantic getaway. Interior styling of The Lodge celebrates 'The Hunt', which begins in the spacious main gathering room.

Guest rooms include open-canopy bed, sitting area and 2-person whirlpool tub.

The Cottage is wonderful for those seeking a little more privacy.

This impressive 30'x30' room features a sweeping cathedral ceiling, warm and inviting wood-paneled walls. Comfortable burgundy and blue plaid chairs and sofas are offset by the fireplace and entertainment center, which is equipped with satellite TV and full surround-sound.

The library is an excellent place to curl up with a book or chat with friends by the fireplace. This two-story loft room offers a scattering of tables, sofa and chairs on the first level. The loft offers an assortment of books from which guests may select. If you start reading a book you simply can't finish, you're welcome to take it home. You can return it on your next visit.

Of course, our main attention was focused on the Lodge's immensely comfortable and well-designed guest rooms. Each includes a romantic canopied queen bed and small sitting area with two glider-rocking chairs near the cozy gas-log fireplace. The private bath is comfortably sized and features a spacious, two-person whirlpool tub. Building on the romantic ambiance of each room is the absolutely lovely view. A doorwall leads to a private sun porch with direct view of the reflecting pond and grounds. A wonderful site where one could easily spend time just taking in the calm beauty of nature.

Speaking of nature, there are groomed walking trails on the 30-acres of surrounding woodland. Being a safe haven for wildlife, it's not uncommon to find raccoon, deer, rabbits and a variety of birds as you stroll along the trails.

In the morning, you'll awake to a tasty continental plus buffet setup in the small kitchen/serving area along the 100 ft. guest dining hall. Each morning's buffet includes a choice of cereals, bagels, freshly baked pastries along with juices, milk, coffee and tea that you may take to your room or setup on the cozy, two-seat dining table just outside your room.

Their small cottage rental wasn't available for us to see during our visit. It's just steps from the Lodge and is nestled along the treed grounds. This little bungalow features private bath with oversized shower, queen bed, gas log fireplace, rocker recliners and large private deck overlooking the pond. It also includes coffeemaker, microwave and refrigerator. A spiral staircase takes you to the loft sitting room. A deluxe continental breakfast is also included for cottage guests.

After you've finished that last cup of coffee, it's time to explore Huron County. If it's beaches you crave, you're in the right spot. Huron County is home to over 90 miles of Lake Huron shoreline. In fact, some of Michigan's best swimming beaches can be found along Lake Huron and Saginaw Bay. One of the area's noted public beaches is at Caseville's Sleeper State Park. The Pinnebog River flows through Sleeper and attracts canoe, pontoon, power boaters and fishing enthusiasts. In the winter, head toward Sleeper or the Wagener County Parks to take advantage of their cross-country ski trails.

Enjoy the scenic shoreline drive along M-25, take advantage of the area's excellent beaches, fishing and nature centers. And, at the end of a busy day, you'll find the quiet, relaxing comforts at The Lodge at Oak Pointe a wonderful way to unwind and relax with the one you love.

Chickadee Guesthouse
East Tawas, Michigan
Reservations: 989-362-8006
Email: info@east-tawas.com
Website: www.east-tawas.com

Owners:	Don and Leigh Mott
Accommodations:	Private cottage, two bedroom, 1 bath. Recommended for 4 but can accommodate up to 7.
Extras:	Central A/C. Equipped kitchen with microwave. Electric fireplace, CATV, ceiling fans, enclosed porch. Outdoor furnishings, gas grill and freestanding wood burning firepot.
Rates/Payment:	Weekly $1,050 and up; Nightly $165 and up. Rates based on 4 people. Checks.
Miscellaneous:	No pets/smoking.
Open:	Year around.

We were particularly happy to chat with Leigh Mott on a bright and sunny spring morning. She had just completed her new 'pet' project, the complete renovation of an 1800's cottage. Being one of East Tawas Junction Bed and Breakfast's charismatic owners and former interior designer, we were really looking forward to seeing the magic Leigh had performed.

As we walked down the quiet back street leading from the bed and breakfast

Beautifully renovated 1860's home.

to the Chickadee Guesthouse, Leigh talked about the unique challenges she faced in restoring the old place. Though in need of major repair, Leigh realized the home's potential and eagerly took on the challenge using her expert design and renovation skills.

The changes could be seen immediately upon approaching the grounds. The front yard, previously a mix of weeds and dirt, had been replaced with freshly seeded lawn and small plantings. Broken walkways were replaced. New siding was enhanced with finely crafted stonework. On the property's treed side lot was a large birdfeeder attracting the area's diverse bird populations including, of course, chickadees.

We entered through the cheerful ceramic tiled, glass-enclosed porch. Comfortably furnished with chairs, rocker and coffee table to one side and a trundle day bed on the other. The surrounding windows provided a quiet view of the front and side yards.

Bright and inviting sunroom.

Stepping into the home from the porch, Leigh's real surprise was quickly revealed. Freshly painted walls, wood-beamed ceiling, refinished wood floors along with very homey furnishings, were immediately inviting and welcoming. The main room combined living and dining areas. The living room held a recliner, cottage-country sofa and chair. An electric fireplace added a cozy ambiance. There was also the all-important cable TV, so you won't miss the 'big game'.

Open design combines living with dining areas.

A dining table (comfortably seating four) separated the living room and kitchen. Placed before a good-sized window, it overlooked the treed side yard and the Chickadee's famous birdfeeder. An excellent way to watch the cottage's namesakes enjoy their breakfast as you enjoy yours.

Immaculate and well equipped kitchen.

Those who are particularly sensitive about cleanliness in kitchens need not fear. The refinished kitchen is immaculate and equipped with all the basics including full-size refrigerator and stove, microwave and coffeemaker.

Equally inviting is the Chickadee's two, newly carpeted bedrooms. The master bedroom is furnished with queen-sized bed, sitting chair and single, folddown chair bed. The theme is floralfresh with light gray and hunter green accents. The second bedroom

Chickadee has two bedrooms. The one pictured above has a queen bed the other has two twins.

has two twin beds with cottage-country styling. Ceiling fans in both bedrooms and kitchen definitely help keep the cottage comfortable during warmer summer days and nights.

The home has a single bathroom with glass-enclosed shower. Though somewhat small, Leigh has given particular attention to adding special touches in décor to make it inviting.

The Chickadee is conveniently located. Just down the road and across the street is East Tawas Park and Lake Huron. Beautiful sugar sand beach, playground and picnic areas are nearby. Just a few blocks away is an assortment of unique shops and restaurants. Golf courses, miniature golf, horseback riding and water sports are within a few miles. Certainly, while in the area, you'll want to enjoy a leisurely drive along the River Road National Forest Scenic Byway. Also, with the AuSable River not far away, you may want to rent a canoe for a day-long exploration of this well-known canoeing river.

We couldn't have been more pleased with the overall comfort, styling and cleanliness of The Chickadee Guesthouse. With a great deal of patience and money, the home was transformed into a delightfully cozy and abundantly comfortable little treasure. But, of course, with Leigh in charge of the renovation and design, how could it be otherwise?

Miller's Guest House on Burt Lake
Burt Lake, Michigan

Reservations: 231-238-4492
Email: jemil@ncmc.cc.mi.us
Website: www.upnorthlakes.com

Owners:	Jess and Pam Miller
Accommodations:	Private cottage/guest house on Burt Lake.
Extras:	Full kitchen, microwave, TV/VCR, radio, ceiling fan, BBQ grill, lawn furniture, hammock, sandy swimming beach, use of canoe and pedal boat.
Rates/Payment:	Weekly $550 to $950 (seasonal). Checks.
Miscellaneous:	No pets/smoking, bring linens and towels.
Open:	Year around.

As a child, I remember going up to the room my neighbors had over their garage. It was magical and one of my favorite spots. Miller's Guest House holds much of the same charm. It was magical and turned out to be one of our favorite accommodations in the area.

Jess and Pam Miller have taken the room over their garage and turned it into a simply charming lodging. It looks brand new, even though the Guest House is over 12 years old. Large windows and light walls make it bright and cheerful

A charmingly updated lodging above the Miller's garage.

Living room has a TV/VCR. Bunk beds offer additional sleeping space.

with contemporary furniture, TV/VCR, ceiling fan and a bunk bed along one wall comfortably arranged.

The kitchen offers lots of cupboards and plenty of space to move around. It's also stocked with all the necessary

View from the Guest House doorwall.

eating and cooking utensils with a formal dining table. Behind the kitchen, a nice sized bedroom with matching furniture and queen size bed is waiting for you. With bunk beds and sleeper sofa in the living room, the cottage comfortably holds four adults or a couple with two to four children. We were also happy to see their updated bathroom was fresh and appealing with a shower.

A sofa in front of the door wall makes for the perfect spot to watch the morning sunrise reflect off the water. Standing out on the deck you can hear waves splashing along the sandy shore and the distant whir of an occasional

Immaculate, updated kitchen includes small dining area.

motorboat. A hammock rests under the trees, inviting a little nap after a busy day. Of course, who wants to sleep when Miller's beautiful sandy beach and lake are calling you.

The water is pretty shallow going out for over 100 ft. and would be great for family water fun. Don't be surprised if the Miller's family-friendly dog, who loves to swim, joins you. The way she enjoyed the water when we were there, you'd have thought she might have been a fish disguised as a dog.

Miller's Burt Lake beach is great for swimming.

In addition to the hammock, there's also lawn furniture and a picnic table setup near the beach. The serene setting is perfect for an evening bonfire. Burt Lake is fairly large and surrounded by trees. We could see sleepy little cottages poking through here and there but, for the most part, its shoreline remained unbroken. Because the lake is so appealing, why not take advantage of the canoe and pedal boat that Pam and Jess have available for guests.

Burt Lake is part of the area's Inland Waterways. This 38-mile route connects several lakes and rivers that end at Lake Huron. It's a popular tourist destination for boating. There are several marinas near Miller's for you to store your boat. The Inland Waterways are noted for some unique shops and wonderful casual dining along the route. The Burt Lake region is teaming with wildlife and is an excellent fishing lake, sporting over 17 species of fish including trout, pike, bass, perch and walleye. Miller's prime location puts it just a half hour from the Mackinaw Bridge and approximately two hours from Traverse City.

The Guest House is a great year around escape. For your winter getaway, it's close to more than 500 miles of groomed snowmobile trails, down hill and cross-country skiing.

We really like Miller's Guest House because the grounds lend to a relaxing vacation, the beach is wonderful and the price is reasonable. Additionally, they are centrally located to all the fun that the UP and Northwestern Lower Peninsula have to offer. Give them a call well in advance of your next vacation.

Bay View at Mackinac
Mackinac Island, Michigan

Reservations: 906-847-3295
Email: bayviewbnb@aol.com
Website: www.mackinacbayview.com

Innkeepers:	Doug & Lydia Yoder.
Accommodations:	Bed and Breakfast/Inn. 17 guest rooms/3 suites. Private baths. All rooms with lake views.
Extras:	Full breakfast. A/C, TV with VCR (free movie library). In-room phones. Afternoon refreshments/evening desserts. Suites with whirlpool/Jacuzzi tubs. Balconies.
Rates/Payment:	Daily $95-$375. Credit cards, checks.
Miscellaneous:	No pets/smoking.
Open:	May to October.

We left the boat ferry on a cool October morning, delighted to return to one of our favorite Michigan travel destinations, Mackinac Island. Since motorized vehicles are not permitted from spring through fall, the street sounds that greet us are particularly unique. The quiet clip clop of horses and whir of bicycles mingled with the cheerful tones of people as they meandered along the shop-lined streets. Actually, the Island is remarkably quiet at this time of year with only a few people strolling about. Certainly a big differ-

Historic Bay View, a delightful B&B with a Victorian theme.

ence from the summer when shops and restaurants are bustling with visitors from across the globe.

On this trip, we had reservations at Bay View at Mackinac. A delightful Victorian bed and breakfast overlooking the harbor on the outskirts of town. As we picked up our few pieces of luggage, the ferryman asked if we'd like a carriage. On this bright morning, however, we opted for the several-block walk allowing us to enjoy the town sites.

Stepping onto the streets of Mackinac Island will take you back to the 19th Century.

Stepping onto the Island's main street is like walking right into the 19th Century. Well-maintained period buildings, balconied hotels along with an assortment of gift emporiums including the famous Mackinac Island fudge shops lined the street.

Passerbys on bicycles and horse-drawn wagons waived cheerfully as we approached the rising bluff and our first impressive glimpse of Fort Mackinac. This well-preserved, historic fort hosts craft

demonstrations and mock military events with costumed interpretive guides to help give a real sense of what life was life between 1780 and 1895. The fort is a popular island attraction and one that should not be missed during your visit.

Passing the fort, we looked ahead to the welcoming, sun-bright yellow exterior of Bay View. What a beautiful picture it made against the deep blue waters of

Bay View's Executive Suites are spacious and beautifully designed with in-room whirlpool tubs, mini-kitchens and sitting areas.

the lake and clear sky. Its double-gabled roof and Victorian styling blended perfectly with the Island's ambiance. It is the only inn on Mackinac Island that directly fronts the lake and, with all rooms offering a water view, gives Bay View its reputation as a "Room With A View".

The inn's charismatic office manager greeted us. In between checking-in new guests and helping others with questions about the Island, she managed to provide us with a brief history of the home.

Built in 1891, Bay View was to have been home to the Armour family. As it turned out, the Armours decided not to move-in and sold the shoreline home to Matthew Bailey, son of Dr. John R. Bailey who was the highest ranking officer and surgeon at the now restored Historic Fort Mackinac. Well-known on the Island, Matthew was the first pharmacist and founder of Bailey's Drug

Store which is now owned by Doug and Lydia Yoder, and operates as Murdick's Fudge Shop. Throughout the generations the home remained in the family with its current owner, Doug Yoder, being the great-grandson of Matthew Bailey and the great-great grandson of Dr. John R. Bailey. In the 1990's Doug's wife, Lydia, applied her skillful interior design touches and the home was completely refurbished to period with much of its original Victorian architecture intact.

Standard rooms significantly vary in size with Victorian themes.

Guest rooms are located throughout the home's three-levels (no elevators), with room size varying significantly. The newest and most luxurious rooms are their executive suites. These lovely suites include mini-kitchens, Jacuzzi tubs, sitting areas and more spacious bathrooms. Of course, even Bay View's smallest room is tastefully styled with Victorian prints and period antiques. All rooms include A/C, private telephone,

TV and VCR. As an added note, since many of Bay View's private baths originally served as closets, space may be a bit tight.

A wonderful part of the Bay View experience is the very roomy third-floor open deck that overlooks the lake, nearby marina and town. This rare, panoramic view is one you'll not soon forget. You can sit at a private table; sip some of Bay View's famous coffee while enjoying the beauty of the lake.

Of course, what Mackinac Island vacation would be complete without temptation of the palate? And your palate will definitely be tempted at Bay View, thanks to Head Chef, Rose Grant. Of Jamaican decent, Rose's cheery island disposition

Full breakfasts and evening, sit-down desserts are served in the bright and airy sunroom. Be prepared to be spoiled by Chef Rose!

along with her perfectly prepared gourmet breakfasts served in the window-lined veranda will absolutely dissolve the possibility of having a bad morning.

Menus sometimes come from old family recipes passed down through Doug or Lydia's family. One favorite is the southern-style Peach French Toast originating from Lydia's Georgian family. In the evenings, homemade desserts are served. Throughout the day you can stop by the veranda for fresh-baked chocolate chip cookies, muffins, cinnamon rolls and a cup of the Yoders' special Bay View blend coffee.

In between your breakfast and the Yoder's wonderful, seated evening dessert, you may want dinner (who would think it possible). Doug or Lydia will happily recommend the best places and, if needed, arrange for a carriage. That night we decided on the French Outpost, noted for their incredible Trapperburgers. We opted this time for their Pan Seared Great Lakes Salmon, and were not disappointed. It was delicious. After dinner, we sipped our wine while listening to the melodic tunes of a guitar balladeer.

It was getting late as our small group boarded the carriage taking us back to our various destinations. On this brisk October evening, with a warm woolen blanket covering our laps, we chatted amiably with the other passengers sharing our Mackinac Island experiences. Though we hated to end the evening, it was a real pleasure to come back to the warmth of Bay View and the comfort of our room (we did snatch one of Rose's yummy chocolate chip cookies before going upstairs). It was a wonderful way to end a perfect day on Mackinac Island.

Lakebluff Condos at Stonecliff
Mackinac Island, Michigan

Telephone: 800-699-6927 • 888-847-0487
Email: marianneoneil@mindspring.com
Website: www.yesmichigan.com/lakebluff

Owners:	Mark and Marianne O'Neill; Patricia Held
Accommodations:	Two one room suites and one/two/three bedroom condos.
Extras:	Varies and includes: Fireplaces, CATV/VCR, Jacuzzi, fully equipped kitchen or Kitchenette, microwave, wet bar, skylights, solarium, private balcony or patio.
Rates/Payment:	Nightly $135 to $475, depending on unit and season.
Miscellaneous:	No pets/smoking.
Open:	May 22 to October 15.

Today we were heading to Lakebluff Condos at Stonecliffe on the beautiful, secluded West Bluff of Mackinac Island. It was raining that afternoon so, instead of walking the 1.5 miles, we decided to take a carriage taxi. Our cheerful driver welcomed us on board. We were his only passengers on this trip; and we chatted amiably as the horse-driven carriage meandered along the streets, past the world-renowned Grand Hotel toward Stonecliffe.

Upscale condos are located on the secluded West Bluff of the Island.

The driver mentioned he had worked on the island for years and gave us some interesting background on the stables. During the peak summer months there are about 600 horses stabled on the island. They are given excellent care and only work four-hour shifts, unlike our driver who was finishing up his 12-hour day. In the winter the horses are boarded at farms on the mainland.

We continued our conversation as the horses picked up their pace. Our carriage passed several townspeople who called out greetings to us. We made a

Beautifully landscaped grounds in a serene setting.

couple of short stops, once for him to put on his heavy yellow rain slicker and a second time for him to change horses. While waiting, we pulled out a couple of wool blankets from an under seat trunk and wrapped ourselves in their warmth. Even though we were a little cold and wet, it made us realize just how people lived some 100 years ago and, believe it or not, it was fun.

Soon enough our carriage arrived at the west bluff of the island, which is much less populated and beautiful. The setting was serene, with large trees, gardens and a few private homes and summer cottages. Resting on top of a bluff overlooking Lake Huron and the Mackinaw Bridge, Lakebluff Condos at Stonecliffe reminds us of an 1800's mansion with dark wood and peaked roofs. Natural wood patios and decks help to blend the resort into its surroundings.

Entering these units, we were immediately brought back into the 21st century with an eclectic collection of casual luxury. Mark, Marianne and Patricia, in conjunction with Stonecliffe, have spared no expense or missed any details for your comfort. The major difference in the four units is primarily size. The

A diverse range of lodgings are available, from cozy one room to spacious, 3-bedroom loft. All have picturesque views.

Gardenview and Penthouse suites are cute, one-room units. Gardenview has a Jacuzzi, shower and kitchenette. The Penthouse includes cathedral ceiling, skylight, Jacuzzi and fireplace with full kitchen and our favorite feature, a solarium, overlooking Lake Huron and the Mackinaw Bridge.

The more spacious one and two bedroom condos include full kitchens, Jacuzzi, and fireplace. The two bedroom unit adjoins the Gardenview and can become a three bedroom by opening the connecting doors. Plush, dark carpeting greeted us as we moved through the living areas. Massive, contemporary floral or leather sofas and loveseats are centered in the living rooms opposite a fireplace. Light wood coffee tables and side tables have floral touches. Light, tastefully accented walls are brightened with vaulted, beamed ceilings, large windows and doorwalls.

One of our favorites was the solarium condo.

Kitchens or kitchenette are equipped with full appliances, microwave, coffee pot, toaster and plenty of cupboard space. Dining tables match interior furnishings so that the total experience is very esthetic. Bathrooms are large and include tub or shower with light features and vanity.

Queen size beds fill the spacious bedrooms surrounded with contemporary furnishings that frequently include a sitting area with table and chairs. Vaulted ceilings, oversized windows or doorwalls make these rooms appear very large. Each suite has a patio or balcony with a fabulous view of the gardens, grounds or water. They are all really quite wonderful.

Of course, as much as you may want to stay inside these lovely condos, the island draws you out. There are 175 acres of bike trails, walking trails and

You're surrounded in woodlands and gardens and will enjoy a private view of the Mackinac Bridge.

roads throughout and around the island. Downtown features numerous gift stores, clothing stores, fudge shops, ice cream parlors and restaurants. The Grand Hotel has recently completed the back 9 holes of their golf course at Stonecliffe and you can tee-off on the bluff while viewing the Mackinac Bridge and Lake Huron. By the way, the front 9 are on the hillside of Fort Mackinac.

After taking this all in, we had reservations at The Woods Restaurant. It's right on the grounds of Stonecliffe, maybe 100 yards from the condos. The Woods is a Grand Hotel restaurant that provided an experience we will never forget. We entered into a warm country gentleman atmosphere, with dark woods, leather appointments and deep blues, greens and browns. A crackling fire, impeccable service and sumptuous food rounded out the evening.

There is so much to do on the island, just be sure to take some time to walk the shoreline and enjoy the magnificent views. After all, Mackinac Island is only nine miles around. Lakebluff Condos at Stonecliffe are fabulous condos and suites for a one-of-a-kind vacation spot. Mark, Marianne and Patricia have seen to every detail to ensure you'll enjoy your stay. We highly recommend these condos.

Balsam's Resort
St. Ignace, Michigan

Telephone: 906-643-9121 • 313-791-8026
Email: balsams@sbcglobal.net
Website: www.balsamsresort.com

Owners:	Steve and Sara Makowski
Accommodations:	9 cottages, a six unit motel on Lake Michigan.
Extras:	Cottages: fully equipped kitchens, microwave, CATV, linens provided, fireplace in most, BBQ grill, fire pit, lawn furniture, play area, 200 ft. of sandy beach. Motel: microwave, CATV, refrigerator, coffeemaker.
Rates/Payment:	Weekly $655 to $700; Nightly $45 to $110. Major credit cards, check.
Miscellaneous:	Check with owners regarding pet policy.
Open:	June through October.

We love crossing the Mackinac Bridge to the Upper Peninsula. This pristine region of Michigan is nature at its finest, with small urban pockets separated by miles of quiet roads and scenic forests. Leave the bridge and head west, out of St. Ignace on US 2 for about 15 minutes. Hug the sandy Lake Michigan shoreline until you reach the traditional log cabin resort called Balsam's Resort.

Traditional log cabins by the Hiawatha Forest.

Rustic cabin interiors set the mood for your back-to-nature vacation.

Now if you've never stayed in an authentic log cabin, this will be a unique experience. It's hard to find this type of log cabin today. Balsam's cabins are rustically designed, both inside and out. The resort is set on a 40-acre lot along the stunningly beautiful Hiawatha National Forest. It is surrounded by trees and wild flowers. There's even a babbling brook running through the grounds. If you're looking for tranquility, this is it.

The forest separates each cottage from the other. Every unit has its own outdoor furniture, barbecue grill and fire pit. There's nothing better than cooking over an open fire. When was the last time you slid a hotdog on a stick and actually cooked it over an open fire? It's better than a frank at the ballpark.

The interiors of these 70-year old cottages were true to the log cabin theme. One and two bedroom units are cozy, handling four to seven guests. They

Unique, handcrafted furniture continues the rustic theme.

even have an old-fashioned, one-room cabin. Balsam's is well cared for by Steve and Sara Makowski and their groundskeeper. The main rooms have sofas, tables and chairs (some are uniquely hand crafted) with wood floors and throw rugs. Several of the units we saw had stone fireplaces, a nice touch for those cool summer evenings. Even though this is going to be a back-to-

Across the street, Balsam's wonderful beach is very private.

nature family vacation, should you want to watch TV, they have cable. Many log cabins can be drafty or leak when it rains. This is not the case at Balsam's, since the windows and roofs looked new.

You won't have to do all of your cooking over the fire pit or on the grill. Kitchens are contemporary and fully equipped with modern appliances, microwave and just about all the kitchenware you'll need. Bathrooms are small and clean with a tub/shower or just shower. The simple, cozy bedrooms have good mattresses that will feel great at the end of a long day. Paneled walls have been buffed to a fine shine. Linens are included.

Before exploring the region, you may want to take the family down to their uncrowded, sandy beach, just across US 2. This is the perfect spot to relax and take a dip, read a good book or just chat with the new friends you will meet at the resort. There is also a play area for children, shuffleboard and that beach is calling out for a spirited volley ball game or some fun sand castles.

Since St. Ignace is only minutes away, you can spend a day shopping and seeing the sights in the big city. St. Ignace is one of the UP's largest cities and has some great eateries, casinos, shops, museums and much more. Why not take the ferry over to Mackinaw Island, walk the historic streets and visit Fort Mackinac? This area of the UP is known for biking and hiking trails, Native American museums, lighthouses and some great golf.

Tired of congested, over priced resorts and want a really fun vacation? Well folks, one of our favorite rustic log cabin resorts has to be Balsam's. Their prices are reasonable, the grounds are beautiful and they're close to just about everything in the Eastern UP.

Island View Cottage
St. Ignace, Michigan

Telephone: 906-643-6198 • 214-850-2514
Email: mmgang@nmo.net

Owners:	Mike and Joanne McMahon
Accommodations:	Private cottage on Lake Huron, 2 bedrooms (sleeps 4-6),
Extras:	Fully equipped kitchen with microwave and dishwasher. TV, DVD player, gas grill, washer/dryer. Ceiling fans. Linens included.
Rates/Payment:	Weekly, $600. Check.
Miscellaneous:	Overlooks Mackinac Island. No pets/smoking.
Open:	Year around.

One of the very nice discoveries we made during a recent UP trip is the homey, Island View Cottage. Off South Street in St. Ignace, the cottage sits on an open lot in front of a wide expanse of lawn that takes you to water's edge and a view of Lake Huron and Mackinac Island.

Island View is nicely located, just minutes from the Mackinac Island boat docks and about 30-minues from Sault Ste. Marie and the Soo Locks. The very scenic Tahquamenon Falls is about 90-minutes away with Mackinaw City just over the bridge.

Enjoy a private view of Mackinac Island.

Living room smugly fits sofas and chairs.
Kitchen is sparkling clean and includes a dishwasher.

Entering the home through the side door, you'll pass a washer and dryer before moving into the fresh and appealing full kitchen. Its surrounding cabinets are well stocked with an assortment of dishes, glasses, pots, pans and cooking utensils. We were especially pleased to see the kitchen equipped with automatic dishwasher, a feature usually found in higher-priced rentals.

Passing through the open kitchen, we moved into the dining area with table sitting before a door wall leading to the outdoor deck and view of the grounds and lake. Just ahead is the small main living room that was snugly furnished with a rocker and two sofas. This room also included TV and DVD player ready to pop-in your favorite movie and relax after a busy day.

An expanse of lawn takes you to water's edge and Mackinac Island on the horizon.

There are also two immaculate but relatively small bedrooms. At the time of our visit, each had a set of twin beds. Joanne informs us, however, that they were planning on replacing one set of twins with a queen bed.

Island View Cottage is just minutes from historic downtown St. Ignace. Established in 1671, it is the third oldest community in the U.S. and known as the "Gateway to the Upper Peninsula". It's also home of the Mackinac Bridge. Resting along the Straits of Mackinac, St. Ignace combines scenic beauty and small town charm. Its downtown offers a variety of small gift shops and restaurants. During Labor Day weekend the town comes alive with celebrations that include the popular Mackinac Island Bridge Walk, related festivities and one of Michigan's most popular Native American Indian pow-wows.

If your next vacation includes a visit to this popular area, we'd like to recommend Island View Cottage. Its Mackinac Island view, comfy styling and affordable price will set the mood for your UP adventures.

Rustic Retreat Cottage
Munising, Michigan
Telephone (Fran or Bob): 906-387-4971

Owners:	Patty Bayless
Property Managers:	Bob & Fran Case
Accommodations:	Private lakefront cottage, 2 bedrooms/1bath.
Extras:	Equipped kitchen with microwave. Linens provided. TV (no cable)/VCR. Swimming beach. Rowboat/ paddleboat included. BBQ grill, outdoor fire pit.
Rates/Payment:	Weekly $650; Nightly $125. Checks or money orders.
Miscellaneous:	March through October. Pets OK, with approval.

It was a long and somewhat harried trip as we drove our little front-wheel drive car through one of Upper Michigan's rare, early fall snowstorms. Even though the driving was slow, we couldn't help but admire the uncommon beauty found in the contrast of swirling white flakes against the bright color of fall leaves.

As we turned onto a sheltered roadway in the Hiawatha National Forest, the snow suddenly slowed. The reaching arms of tree branches, like a protective mother, allowed only a scattering of flakes to float down creating a picturesque shaker-ball world.

Rustic Retreat is a lovely up north treasure.

An early fall snow storm diminished as we entered the wooded country road leading to Rustic Retreat.

Within minutes we were in the driveway of Patty Bayless' welcoming two-bedroom log cabin overlooking 16 Mile Lake. Stepping out of the car we stopped to admire the cottage's well maintained log exterior before turning our attention to the lake. Its usual calmness was now alive with rolling whitecaps that eased a bit before breaking along the shoreline. It was awesome. We could imagine how this same shoreline, during a bright summer day, would be transformed into a relaxing, wonderful spot for the family.

To ward off the growing chill, we shook the snow from our coats and eagerly entered the protection of this darling little cottage. Bob Case, one of the cottage's amiable caretakers, happily welcomed our arrival and showed us around. We were instantly wrapped in the warmth of the home's immaculate

Country kitchen is well equipped.

Decor reflects a lovely up north ambiance.

and completely appealing north woods ambiance. Patty's love for this place is apparent in its maintenance, comfort and inviting décor.

The narrow, country-styled kitchen was fully equipped and sported tall, polished cabinets with microwave, stove and refrigerator. A dining table sat in an alcove overlooking the lake. Passing through the kitchen, we were treated to an incredibly cozy living room where folksy woodcarvings, pictures and

ALL RATES SUBJECT TO CHANGE

artifacts decorated wood paneled walls. Two abundantly comfortable sofas, chair and rocker-recliner surrounded the room that also included a TV with VCR. This very inviting room would be great for relaxing after a day on the lake or day-long adventure in the Hiawatha National Forest.

Equally inviting was the colorful, enclosed sun porch with its country-reds and blues mixing with light wood-paneled walls. Surrounding windows over-looked the shoreline. Similar to the rest of the cottage, this delightful room was clean as can be and a wonderful place to sit back and enjoy the view.

There are two bedrooms at Rustic Retreat. The master bedroom is off the main living area behind sliding doors. The country styling makes this smaller room with full bed charming. We were also pleased to find a newly renovated full bath with tub shower on the first floor. Ladder-steps take you upstairs to a second sleeping area with two twins and a double bed. The ceiling is a bit low, so the grown-ups may need to watch their head as well as their step, but children should love it.

Dining alcove has window view of lake and grounds

Rustic Retreat is tucked away in the Hiawatha National Forest. If you're unfamiliar with Hiawatha National Forest, it was the inspiration for Longfellow's "Song of Hiawatha" and covers over 880,000 acres of woodland. The western section touches both Lake Superior and Lake Michigan. Its many hiking trails will take you through dense forest passageways appearing very much as they did when the Noquet Indians traveled the area.

If you're craving a little more civilization, Munising is not far away. This friendly Yooper's town has both fast food, family style dining and gift shops. It's home to the Pictured Rocks National Shoreline, one of the areas top attractions.

We couldn't have been more pleased to discover this very accommodating U.P. cottage. Patty Bayless has created a real treasure and she's willing to share it with you. Call the cottage's friendly caretakers, Bob or Fran Case, to make your reservations.

Top O' the Lake
Gulliver, Michigan

Telephone: 906- 283-3361
Email: nancy@topofthelake.com
Web site: www.topofthelake.com

Owners:	Wally and Nancy Warner
Accommodations:	Private cottage on Lake Michigan, two bedrooms.
Extras:	Satellite TV, VCR/DVD. Equipped kitchen with dishwasher. Washer/dryer and water softener. Franklin stove, ceiling fans. Linens provided. Sandy swimming beach.
Rates/Payment:	Weekly $800 (off-season day rates available).
Miscellaneous:	No Pets/smoking.
Open:	Year around.

We were traveling along US 2 in early fall. The route is particularly quiet at this time of year, though we did manage to count two passing cars, a truck, three deer and a fuzzy little bear cub (we didn't wait for the little guy's mom to appear). There was a cool bite in the air and the trees looked as though they were on fire with brilliant reds, yellows and oranges. Once in Gulliver we turned off the highway, down quiet country roads taking us closer to Lake Michigan. Our destination was a cottage owned by Wally and Nancy Warner.

Top O' the Lake was off a little road on a tree-covered driveway. Its remote location virtually traffic free. The Warner's live at the end of the drive and have recently completed their cottage. Wally and Nancy are very proud of their new guesthouse and have every reason to be…it's great! The

Tucked in the woods, at the northern end of Lake Michigan.

appealing exterior is highlighted with gray-blue shingles trimmed in white and is tucked under a towering cluster of trees making this very spacious cottage look small by comparison.

Relaxing ambiance of the great room includes serene woodland view.

Stepping in side, we were delighted by the home's open and inviting contemporary ambiance. Its large great room combined living, kitchen and dining areas. Certainly a focal point was the Franklin stove centered along a brick wall with nearby wood stacked and ready to burn. Modern, cream colored overstuffed sofa, chair and table face the stove and large window.

The TV, setup with a satellite system, gives you quality viewing channels. Natural ceramic tile covering the floor, accented with dark floral area rug, complemented the simple yet stunning décor. To the side was a comfortably sized dining table with chairs that sat before a wall of windows offering an enchanting woodland view. Accent lighting added a warm glow with a ceiling fan helping to keep things cool on those warmer days.

The ceramic tile flooring wrapped around through the kitchen, down the hall and into the bathroom. An island separates the kitchen from the rest of the house, perfect for breakfast, lunch or light snack. Preparing your meals won't be a problem because there's plenty of room and kitchenware. It even contains our favorite vacation appliance, the dishwasher.

Kitchen is immaculate and well-equipped.

Down the hall the elegant bathroom contains a double sink, vanity and tub with shower. When we're on vacation, isn't it funny how relaxing can get our clothes so dirty? Fortunately at Top O'the Lake there is a laundry room with washer and dryer, so you can relax in your favorite shorts all week and keep them clean.

One of two bedrooms ... basic but very comfy.

At the end of the hall, two large bedrooms are waiting to welcome you after a very long day. A dark blue carpet accents the white walls and beds. One room contains a queen and the other has two twins. Ceiling fans cool the night and naturally there are the Warner's signature windows. As an interesting side note, you won't find window coverings in the home. Your window shades, instead, are the natural colors of green and brown provided by the outside woods.

After we had a chance to fully appreciate the cottage, Wally and Nancy took us down to the beach. It's a short walk through the woods, but don't be afraid of

A short walk down the trail takes you to a very private stretch of Lake Michigan.

getting lost. They have marked the trail in their own special way using bunny markers, so you won't have a problem. Before jumping into Lake Michigan be sure to notice the kaleidoscope of colors from the sky, water, sand and woods. You need to sit back and enjoy it for just a moment, then jump in. Chances are very good you will have Lake Michigan all to yourself, so enjoy.

If you want to leave the beach, the area offers plenty to do. Vacationing in the UP means that you love the outdoors, so a trip here wouldn't be complete without a visit to the Seney National Wildlife Refuge, Beaver Island, or a visit to the Seul Choix or White Fish Point Lighthouses. In winter the UP is a paradise for sports enthusiasts with plenty of snowmobile trails and skiing.

Top O'the Lake is a jewel in the rough of the UP. It's a real treat for naturalists after spending the day in the great outdoors and … it's a very good value.

Sand Hills Lighthouse Inn
Ahmeek, Michigan

(Keweenaw Peninsula)
Telephone: 906-337-1744
Website: www.sandhillslighthouseinn.com

Innkeepers:	Bill Frabotta, Mary Matthews
Accommodations:	Bed and Breakfast. 8 rooms with private baths overlooking Lake Superior.
Extras:	Gourmet breakfast. Fireplace and whirlpool tub in some rooms.
Rates/Payment:	Nightly $133-$196 (includes tax). Checks.
Miscellaneous:	On the National Registry of Historic Places. Noted for being the Great Lakes' largest and last-manned lighthouse. No pets/smoking. Make reservations early.
Open:	Year around.

There's a certain mystique that surrounds the lighthouse. Perhaps it's our sense of romantic adventure that leads us to imagine the isolated life of the stoic light keeper who stood watch through nature's harshest weather to ensure safe passage of vessels and crew.

Known as "Castle of the Keweenaw", this 1919 lighthouse rests along 3,000 ft. of Lake Superior shoreline.

The lighthouse has been renovated with a dramatic Victorian theme.

Over the decades a growing number of travelers seek to experience the same isolation as they surround themselves with scenic landscapes and remote beauty that make the lighthouse experience so unique.

Visitors to Upper Michigan's Keweenaw Peninsula have the opportunity of spending one or several nights as the welcomed guests of Bill Frabotta and Mary Matthews, innkeepers of Sand Hills Lighthouse Inn. Known as the "Castle of the Keweenaw", this light-bricked lighthouse rests along 3,000 ft. of private Lake Superior shoreline.

Built in 1919, Sand Hills was the Great Lakes' largest lighthouse and was finally decommissioned in 1954. Thereafter, the once impressive lighthouse fell into disrepair until Bill Frabotta, a Detroit photographer and artist, purchased the station in 1961.

About 30 years passed before renovations began. Because the interior was so badly deteriorated, much of it was torn

Antiques and historical detail fill the hallways.

Deep wine-colored velvet with gold threads highlight the Olivier Room.

down. Wanting the redesign to reflect a Victorian theme, Bill worked with builders to recreate the period. In 1995, Sand Hills opened as one of Michigan's rare lighthouse bed and breakfasts.

There are eight guest rooms that Mary and Bill like to describe as "theatrically-styled Victorian" with plenty of "drama". One such room is their Olivier Room, named for well-known British thespian, Sir Lawrence Olivier. Deep wine-colored velvet detailed with gold thread drape the massive four-poster bed crowned with an ornamental, carved wood canopy. Window treatments reflect similar drama. Adding to this are antiques and photographs reflecting the 1920's theatrical era, reminiscent of Olivier's early stage years.

Certainly all of Sand Hills' guest rooms are distinctively styled with high Victorian drama. Though not large, each is comfortably sized. Also, like many historical lodgings, closets have been converted to private baths, so bathrooms may not be as spacious as you're accustom.

Walking through the lighthouse's several floors is like experiencing a bit of history with beautifully restored antiques and period pieces seen throughout. Sprinkled among the many early century wall hangings are some of Bill's skillfully painted portraits completed during his earlier career as artist/photographer.

After speaking with a few of the inn's former guests, there's little doubt that innkeepers Bill and Mary are as colorful as their home and are part of the unique ambiance of Sand Hills. They pride themselves on being gourmet cooks and enjoy presenting guests with, as Mary proudly explains, "wonderful

Guest room decor continues the Victorian theme.

breakfasts". When asked if they have any particular specialties, Mary smiled and said, "Everything."

Guests at the inn enjoy leisurely strolls along the craggy shoreline or exploring the rugged beauty of the Porcupine Mountains. Copper Harbor is just minutes away with a variety of shops and historic Fort Wilkins State Park, located almost at the tip of the Keweenaw Peninsula. After an adventurous day, you'll look forward to returning to Sand Hills for evening dessert, which is an elegant treat for the palette. During this time Mary will frequently sit at the grand piano in the small drawing room, stacked with books, magazines and memorabilia, and play some of her favorite pieces. It's an intimate evening Mary and Bill enjoy sharing with guests.

If a Michigan lighthouse adventure is on your agenda of vacation experiences, we suggest you plan your trip early. Sand Hills Lighthouse Inn in Ahmeek books many months in advance.

Crystal Mountain Resort
Thompsonville, Michigan

Telephone: 800-968-7686 • 231-378-2000
Email: info@crystalmountain.com
Website: www.crystalmountain.com

Accommodations:	Hotel/homes, condo resort.
Extras:	Downhill, cross-country skiing and golfing community. Ice skating rink. Standard hotel rooms plus luxury homes and condominiums with well-equipped kitchens. Lodgings feature: A/C, fireplaces, CATV, DVD/VCRs, whirlpool tubs. Restaurants on premises. Indoor and outdoor swimming pools, hot tub, fitness center and massage. Planned activities include canoeing, horseback riding, day camps.
Rates/Payment:	Numerous price packages. Check, credit cards.
Miscellaneous:	Handicap accessible. No pets. Noted for skiing, snowboarding, racing and telemarking schools. Golf instruction. Special attention to children's programs.
Open:	Year around.

Set on 1500 acres with access to thousands of additional acres of state land, it's easy to understand why Crystal Mountain Resort is one of Northwestern Lower Michigan's premier skiing, golfing and family retreats. This beautifully

Premier ski, golf and year around family retreat.

landscaped, expansive resort also offers some of the finest lodgings in the area making it a wonderful getaway throughout the seasons. Before we get into their fabulous lodgings, however, let us tell you about some of the things that make Crystal so unique.

Crystal has programs and activities for all to enjoy, whether it's a romantic getaway, a family fun trip or an active adventure experience. Even if you're not a snow or golf enthusiast,

Snowboarding, downhill & cross-country skiing highlight wintertime activities.

there's still plenty to keep you busy. Take advantage of their outdoor and indoor pools, hot tubs and tennis courts, hiking trails, shops and restaurants. There are even planned canoeing, tubing and horseback riding trips, as well as day camps for toddlers.

The resort is proud of its award-winning schools for skiing, snowboarding, racing and golfing that are run by some of the state's best instructors. In fact, Crystal was recognition by Golf Magazine as offering one of the nation's "Top 15 Golf Schools". Crystal has also been ranked as #1 in Services, #1 in Family Programs and #1 in Lodgings by SKI Magazine.

Crystal's two courses will challenge golfers at all levels of skill.

Cross-country skiers enjoy 40 kms of lighted trails.

In the winter, snow is what Crystal is all about. Their 45 downhill runs attract skiers and snowboarders throughout the Midwest. Their variety of runs includes challenging Black Diamonds for the experienced to gentler slopes for beginners. Crystal even schedules racing and telemarker events throughout the winter season. Are you a cross-country ski buff? Crystal has 40 kms. of well-groomed, lighted ski trails that wind through the quiet north woods.

Kinlochen Lodge has an "Old World Celtic" theme.

Luxury suites, condos and townhouses offer the ultimate in comfort.

The rest of the seasons, golf enthusiasts get into full swing on Crystal's two courses. Their championship 18-hole Mountain Ridge offers panoramic views, tree-lined fairways and impressive waste bunkers while the more relaxed Betsie Valley offers open

Crystal's standard rooms will guarantee a good night's sleep.

meadows and gentle streams. Don't be surprised to see an occasional woodland friend peak through the trees or meadowland clearings.

Their condos and townhouses are diverse in style and size. Some offer a spacious 3,000 sq. ft. of living space with 4 bedrooms. The selections we visited were warm and inviting and packed with features. Some of their amenities, besides those previously mentioned, include full kitchens with dishwashers, chalet ceiling great rooms with rich wood floors, deep leather sofas, fireplaces, VCR and DVD systems. Master bedrooms have their own private baths and whirlpool tubs. Much of the décor reflect a northern Michigan ambiance. The Mountain Top townhouses, with three floors, are upscale with some of Crystal Mountain's best views.

Other distinctive lodgings at Crystal can be found at the Celtic-themed Kinlochen home. Built to specifications reflecting Old World Celtic architecture, and home of the sumptuous Thistle Pub and Grille, Kinlochen offers one to three bedroom units. Each of the lodgings in Kinlochen reflect a style reminiscent of Scotland's great castles. They were our personal favorites of the resort's many accommodations.

Without a doubt, Crystal Mountain Resort will make the perfect escape for you and those you love. We highly recommend the resort throughout the seasons but be warned ... once you come here you may never want to leave.

Ellis Lake Resort
Interlochen, Michigan

Telephone: 231-276-9502
Email: ellislakeresort@chartermi.net
Website: www.ellislakeresort.com

Owner:	Keith and Joan Attwood
Accommodations:	Resort on Ellis Lake, 7 cabins, 1 chalet, 3 log rooms.
Extras:	20 wooded acres. Hiking trails link to Michigan Shore-to-Shore. Double beds, some queen or king. Private baths. Linens included. Cabins/chalet with kitchen area, picnic table, grill and campfire pit (wood included). Many with Franklin firestove. Lodge rooms with mini-refrigerators. Includes rowboat and canoe. Paddleboat rentals. Outdoor hot tub. Dock and swimming raft.
Rates/Payment:	Cabins/Chalet Weekly $590-$1,160; Rooms, Daily $58-$225.
Miscellaneous:	Pets OK with fee. Most lodgings rustic-style.
Open:	Year around.

We first heard about Ellis Lake Resort from our cousin who, during a family get together, elaborated on their annual winter trips to Interlochen and their favorite rustic northern getaway. As cousin Doug said, "It's nothing fancy, but it's clean and great for a winter escape." He and his wife just loved the resort's scenic grounds where they could get out their cross-country skis and

Resort's 20-acres of wooded grounds is found just off US-31.

Lakefront at Ellis.

explore the trails starting just outside their door. They also liked the fact that they could schedule private time for the hot tub, hidden in the wooded grounds, without having to enjoy its invigorating bubbles with strangers. Well, of course, that sent us out to Ellis Lake for a little look-see.

Approaching the resort, about 100 ft. off US-31, we immediately noted its wooded setting, similar to a park campground. Three of the seven wood-framed cabins were nestled amongst the trees just off the highway with the remaining cabins, motel rooms and larger chalet down the resort's road. We thought it was a nice touch that each cabin's front yard had its own picnic table, charcoal grill, chairs and private campfire pit.

Wintertime at Ellis is serene. You can cross-country ski from your door.

Built in 1939, Ellis Lake is one of the area's older vacation resorts. Current owners, Keith and Joan Atwood, have focused on maintaining the cabins with the same rustic feel of its earlier days. Most of the cabins are one room

Cabins have private fire pit, picnic table and charcoal grill.

with one or two beds (sleep 2-4), a small equipped kitchen, sofa and chair. Walls are either log or hand-trowel cement. Throw rugs cover cement floors and simple bathrooms have stall showers. One cabin sleeps 6 to 8 as does their newest chalet. All lodgings have gas wall furnaces, some with

Rustic themes provide clean and simple comforts.

The Chalet breaks from the rustic theme, with a more contemporary style.

woodstoves. To keep the rustic feel, there are no TVs or phones. Though certainly not luxurious, we found the cabins to be clean and with basic comforts.

The newest addition to the resort, and a break from the rustic theme, is their more contemporary chalet. We didn't have the opportunity of visiting the chalet, but were told it was built in 1991, has three-bedrooms that include a master bedroom loft with king and two twins. We also weren't able to visit their three log, motel-style rooms with private bath and entrance.

Strolling through the grounds, we found ourselves at the edge of the resort's spacious (almost 900 ft.) beach. Its primary base was sand with a small bit of natural grass and reeds. Ellis is a 60-acre no-wake inland lake, which keeps it free of ski-doos, powerboats and other noisy distractions. It's a quiet area known for good fishing and abundant wildlife.

The lake on this sunny day was absolutely brilliant with its sparkling waters catching the sky and trees like a giant crystal ball. A small dock reached out into the lake and, beyond that, a diving raft. Back at water's edge canoes, rowboats and paddleboat were waiting guests' use. A large, furnished deck overlooked the lake and was a great spot for folks to chat or simply kickback and enjoy the sun after a little fun in the lake's calm, cool waters.

One of the resort's nicest features is its 22 acres of woodland that include hiking, cross-country and snowshoe trails. Its property links into the Michigan Shore-to-Shore Trail that runs the width of our state, from Lake Michigan to Lake Huron. This historic, 3,000 year-old trail system was originally an Indian trading trail and has been left relatively unaltered. Ellis' grounds and linking trail system offers nature's diversity including natural wetlands and dense woodlands… a true outdoors experience.

After an active day, schedule some time to relax in the private hot tub.

After your active day on the lake or trails, the resort's relaxing 6-person hot tub awaits. This area is surrounded by pines, giving it a sense of being hidden in the woods. Guests book specific times for the hot tub so they can enjoy a little privacy. In fact, the Ellis Lake hot tub has gained recognition … rated #2 in Northern Michigan and #5 in the state by AAA members.

We certainly can see how some couples and families would be drawn to the rustic ambiance of Ellis Lake Resort. If this sounds like your type of getaway, give Joan or Keith a call and let the outdoor adventure begin.

Hanmer's Riverside Resort
Benzonia, Michigan

Telephone: 231- 882-7783 • 800-252-4286
Email: gostay@hanmers.com
Web site: www.hanmers.com

Owners:	Joe and Joyce Wittbrodt
Accommodations:	11 cabins (sleep 2-12) on the Betsie River.
Extras:	Full kitchens with microwave, A/C, telephone, CATV/ VCR, linens/towels included. BBQ grill, picnic table, lawn furniture, fire pit with wood, enclosed and heated four seasons pool/with whirlpool. Fish cleaning station and freezer. Cabin features vary and include: covered and screened porches, fireplace.
Rates/Payment:	Weekly $500 to $910; Nightly $75 to $135. Major credit cards.
Miscellaneous:	Handicap access. No pets. Campsite available. Canoe rentals with special guest rates. Numerous year around specials and activities.
Open:	Year around.

Northwest Lower Michigan is a very popular region for Michigan vacationers, well known for its natural beauty and diverse activities. The area is populated with plenty of luxury resorts and hotels, private homes and glorious bed and breakfasts. Yet there is still a warm spot in our hearts for the friendly,

Hanmer's is located along the serene Betsie River.

Clean and comfy, cottages offer some nice features, such as A/C.

Cabins include full kitchens, living and dining areas with one or two bedrooms.

relaxed, homey atmosphere of a traditional cabin resort. Resting along the lazy Betsie River, Hanmer's Riverside Resort is just that type of place.

Family owned and operated for nearly 30 years, its current owners, Joe and Joyce Wittbrodt, seem to enjoy their resort as much as their guests. Your exuberant and gracious hosts keep their traditional cabins and grounds clean and comfortable. The units range from one-room cabins to two-bedroom cottages and a duplex. Each is space-efficient and even the smaller lodgings have enough room to be comfortable.

Cabin interiors are cheerful with light paneled or white walls accented with a mix of sofas, tables and chairs. Kitchens are fully

Hanmer's smallest, one-room cabin had been completely renovated and was our favorite.

equipped. One and two bedroom cottages can easily handle six with sufficient living and kitchen space. Joe and Joyce are continually working to keep these units updated, which isn't easy when you operate a four-season resort. In some of the recently renovated kitchens and bathrooms, we noted attractive cream or light gray ceramic tile and new countertops. Bedrooms are simply furnished with double and twin beds.

For larger families, we really liked the duplex (cabins 10 and 11). Each holds six people and, by opening the door that separates the units, you have a place to accommodate 12.

Our personal favorite was actually their smallest cabin. This one-room hideaway is charmingly decorated and rather romantic with gas-log fireplace and a real cozy ambiance.

Another nice feature at Hanmer's is the cottages overall proximity to the Betsie River. Imagine opening your windows in the evening and hearing the water and night sounds. In the morning you might wake-up

Snow time is 'fun time' at Hanmer's.

to find a deer sipping from the Betsie. We bet you'll feel your blood pressure drop a notch or two. Most have porches where you can kickback and enjoy a morning cup of coffee. As the day heats up, why not take your lawn chair right down to the Betsie River and let the water cool your feet and soothe your body.

When it's rainy or cold at most traditional resorts, you spend the day inside playing table games and trying to keep your children from going crazy (or making you crazy). At Hanmers, in bad weather, you can spend the day at their enclosed, heated pool. Or, after an exhausting day of snowmobiling or skiing, just imagine yourself soothing tired muscles in the invigorating bubbles of the whirlpool. Many of the major summer/winter resorts also have indoor swimming pools. You need to make a choice. Do you want to swim with a few other families you've built a friendship with, or with 300 families you probably have never met ... or will meet again?

A really nice feature at Hanmer's is the special packages Joe and Joyce have creatively put together to accommodate all four seasons. One of our favorites is the Grand Traverse City Dinner Train package. Most people think of taking the train in the summer months, but you may want to try the fall, winter or spring when it gets dark early. The train's large, outside halogen floods reflect over the passing rivers and woodlands creating a mystical and romantic mood as you enjoy a five-course meal.

After nearly 30 years, the Wittbroth's still love caring for their family resort and guests. With all the area activities and variety of cost saving packages Joe and Joyce have put together, think Hanmers winter, spring, summer and fall.

King Lakefront Home
Lake Skegemog, Michigan
Telephone: 248-349-4716
Email: jking1@peoplepc.com

Owner:	John King
Accommodations:	Private home on Skegemog Lake. 4 bedrooms/2 bath.
Extras:	Equipped kitchen with dishwasher, microwave. Fireplace, skylights, cathedral ceiling. Satellite TV and DVD player. Gas grill. Large beachfront deck. Sandy swimming beach. Rowboats and paddleboat included. Private boat mooring. Swing set, basketball, tetherball and horseshoes. Includes linens.
Rates/Payment:	Weekly $1,500 to $2,500 (seasonal).
Miscellaneous:	No pets/smoking.
Open:	Year around.

Are you among the many who seek a very private beachfront home … with emphasis on beach? Well just sit back, relax and let us tell you about John King's spacious lakefront home. Tucked along the sandy shores of Skegemog Lake, this truly is a home-away-from-home. And it not only has a very nice beach, but enough outdoor room to enjoy a rousing game of badminton, volleyball or for tossing a Frisbee. John has even setup a basketball pad in

John King's spacious home on Skegemog Lake.

The home's sandy beach and waterfront deck are very appealing.

the back and a swing set for the kids. Areas for Tetherball and horseshoes are found in the front yard.

Tall pines and trees surround the home, creating a very private setting. Of course, what makes all this even better are the scenic views and a wonderful little sandy beach with well-maintained deck overlooking the lake. To make your lake experience even more enjoyable, John has a couple of rowboats and a paddleboat waiting for your water exploration. Of course, if you'd prefer, bring your own powerboat or rent one nearby and dock it at the home's private mooring.

As one might expect from the home's expansive exterior, the multilevel interior has plenty of room. Entering through the short hallway, a stairway takes you to the upstairs bedrooms. Straight ahead is the step-down great room with cathedral ceiling. The home's immaculate, fully equipped kitchen also

includes a dishwasher. A cozy dining area offers a picture perfect view of the grounds and lake beyond.

The hub of in-door activities will certainly be in the great room. It's a relaxing spot with wood burning fireplace (not available for summer use) along with a 32-inch satellite TV offering over 100 channels. There's even a DVD player. The room is furnished with a simple assortment of sofa, chairs and tables. It's apparent this area is a hub of activity for many guests with walls

The great room is a hub of activity.

This master bedroom is one of four.

and furnishings showing some wear. In fact, touching-up the walls and re-placing floor coverings are on John's 'to do' list for 2005.

The master bedroom, one of four, is spacious. If you like a really firm mat-tress, you'll love the queen bed here. There's also a good size walk-in closet. Don't be surprised to see the windows without coverings. None are needed. The surrounding trees provide a lovely, natural protection. Additional bed-rooms, though not as large as the master bedroom, are comfy and include double and twin beds.

For those unfamiliar with Lake Skegemog, it's part of the Chain O'Lakes that connects into Elk Lake and Torch Lake (according to National Geo-graphic magazine, Torch Lake is considered the second most beautiful lake in the world). Lake Skegemog is relatively shallow (up to 20' deep) and spans more than 2,560 acres. In addition to safe swimming and scenic boat-ing, it's also considered one of Michigan's best fishing lakes, known for its small and largemouth bass, pike, crappie and panfish. Michigan Sportsman Magazine ranks the lake as "…the muskie hunter's favorite" in the Chain O' Lakes with some musky catches ranging upwards of 30 pounds.

We certainly enjoyed our brief time at King's Lake Skegemog rental. In fact, it was difficult pulling ourselves away from the water and view. It's easy to get spoiled here … great views, nice little beach, quite setting with lots of room. Oh well, enough day-dreaming. We suggest you book early.

Serenity Bay Acres & Bass Cove Cottage Traverse City, Michigan

Telephone: 231-946-5219
Email: info@haroldsresort.com
Website: www.haroldsresort.com

Managers:	Rolf and Kathy Schliess
Accommodations:	Two homes (3 to 4 bedroom) on Spider Lake.
Extras:	Fully equipped kitchens, wood burning stoves, BBQ, pontoon boats, docks, private decks, ceiling fans, CATV, VCR, fire pits. Linens not provided. *Serenity Bay Acres* also includes: swing, on 2 acres with 550 ft. water frontage. *Bass Cove Cottage* also includes: washer/dryer, 2 baths, pool table, hot tub (not available in the summer). 150 ft. sandy swimming beach.
Rates/Payment:	*Serenity Bay*: Weekly: $1500, Nightly: $160 to $300, *Bass Cove Cottage*: Weekly $2600, Nightly $200-$400. Check.
Miscellaneous:	No pets/no smoking.
Open:	Year around.

On a recent trip to the Traverse City area, we took some time to stop by and visit our friends Rolf and Kathy Schliess, owners of Harold's Resort. Besides operating their very successful resort, Rolf and Kathy also manage several

Serenity Bay, one of two Spider Lake homes.

Serenity has spacious living and sleeping areas.

private homes in the area. We had the opportunity to see two of their newest properties, Serenity Bay Acres and Bass Cove, both on Spider Lake. 100 miles from the nearest neighbor. While that's not literally true, the view from Serenity's deck is very private with the homes next door not visible. The wooden deck is large with picnic table and swing. To keep the natural setting undisturbed, the deck has been built around several mature white birch trees that act as your umbrella.

A stairway leads to the water's edge where a pontoon is waiting for you. Cruise the lake or head on over to a nearby beach (Serenity does not have a beach). Kathy tells us that many of the guests take the boat out a little way and use it as a raft, diving right off into the lake's cool water. Serenity is located on a "no wake" bay of Spider Lake that is shallow, warm and good for swimming.

Bass Cove can easily accommodate two families.

Inside, the home is warm and cozy with just the right ambiance for its up north setting. The interior is paneled with a black Franklin stove resting dramatically against a massive stone wall. Opposite is a door wall looking out to the woods and water. The carpeted room includes a TV, cushy sleeper-sofa and chair. Off to the side is a dining table sitting in front of another door wall. We can only imagine sipping coffee in the morning and watching the

Bass Cove also features a pool table on the lower floor.

mist skimming the lake's surface. The fully equipped kitchen includes a microwave and plenty of open cupboards. Located between the two bedrooms is a spacious full bath.

Downstairs, bedrooms are moderately sized. The larger one has a queen bed and the second room a full bed. A third bedroom is on the second floor and features a high ceiling, four twin beds and plenty of room to move around. Serenity Bay Acres is a lovely home that could comfortably accommodate six adults or a family of eight.

Our next stop was Bass Cove Cottage, a 2,000 sq. ft., two-story home surrounded by pines and oak trees. What's nice about Bass Cove is that it has two completely separate living areas with kitchens and can comfortably sleep up to 12, making it ideal for two or three families.

The styling of Bass Cove is a rather fun, 60's retro. The first thing we noted was the orange shag carpet, yellow counter tops and dining set right out of the old TV show, "Happy Days". The only thing missing was "The Fonz". More than being fun, however, it is really a very functional cottage. The upstairs living area has ample space and lots of windows to enjoy scenic views of the lake. Sofa, love seat and chair are positioned around the brick wall with fireplace and TV. Paneling gives the room a warm feeling while the ceiling fan will help cool you on those warmer days. The kitchen is great with a full size refrigerator, cupboard space and an eating area for light meals. The dining area features two door walls that reveal a view of woodlands and lake.

Bass Cove's lower level can be used as a rec room or completely separate living quarters. The living area is highlighted with a Franklin stove, sofa, chair and TV. Off the living room is a compact kitchen. There's even a pool table that will provide hours of fun in the evening. Bedrooms are comfortably sized with a queen and two full beds. The door wall at this level leads

Both homes offers a picturesque view of Spider Lake.

you out to the patio and grounds.

Bass Cove has a beautiful 150 ft. beach with shallow, warm water. There is a dock and a 12-passenger pontoon boat to help you explore the lake. Outside you have the very necessary fire pit, BBQ grill and picnic table.

All in all, Serenity Bay and Bass Cove are two wonderful choices in this prime vacation area. Both offer reasonable rates and a terrific view of the lake.

The Veranda B&B
Harbor Springs, Michigan

Telephone: 231-526-0202
Web site: www.harborspringsveranda.com

Owners:	Marty and Lisa Sutter
Accommodations:	Bed and Breakfast. 7 rooms with private baths.
Extras:	Full breakfast, afternoon tea, fresh cookies, evening wine and appetizers, private baths, telephone, TV, A/C, CD, fine linens. Some rooms with: Jacuzzi, King or queen beds, fireplace, refrigerator, patio or balcony.
Rates/Payment:	Nightly $125 to $350, some rooms with seasonal rates, most major credit cards.
Miscellaneous:	Museum quality antiques and original area artwork in rooms. No smoking/pets.
Open:	Year around.

This was the fifth long day of our road trip. It was late afternoon and exhaustion was settling in as we approached The Veranda at Harbor Springs. As it came into view, however, we couldn't believe our eyes and suddenly came alive. The lush grounds surrounding this majestic 100 year old home exceeded the beauty in a Norman Rockwell painting.

Beautiful B&B sets the mood for a romantic getaway.

The story behind how the house arrived on this quiet residential street in Harbor Springs is as remarkable as the home itself. In 1870, the original owners Edwin and Anna Ferguson, moved to Petoskey and built the home. A few years later they had the home dragged across the frozen waters, by horse, to its present location, a quite street in the quaint resort community of Harbor Springs.

Captain's is one of their most requested guest rooms. It was our favorite as well.

Inside, the elegant guest rooms vary in size with distinctive decor. One of our favorites was the Captain's Quarters designed to represent the interior of a ship. Heavy, deep mahogany furnishings and rich colors fill the room with an early 1900's nautical theme. Much of the wood and artifacts actually came from luxury ships of the late 1800's and early 1900's. The Captain's Quarters

Intricate wood carved headboards are a distinctive touch.

also includes a sitting area with fireplace. This truly unique room offers no off-season discounts.

In many of the rooms you'll find the intricately carved woods that build upon a luxurious 1900's theme. In striking contrast is The Harbor Suite with its light woods, spacious feel and bright appointments. Its private balcony filled with white wicker, overlooks the gardens and offers a magnificent view of downtown Harbor Springs and the harbor. A perfect spot for that romantic weekend, it provides a Jacuzzi tub/shower surrounded by windows and flowerboxes spilling over with blooms. The king bed is covered with a floral print cover and brimming with pillows.

Regardless of which you choose, each of the seven rooms has its own special appeal. Original artwork, lovely antiques and amenities not always found in a bed and breakfast will appeal to the most discerning guest. Sooner or later however, you have to leave the room and one way to get you up and out in the morning is the aroma from their sumptuous breakfasts. Specially prepared egg dishes exquisitely displayed on your plate with fresh fruit, pastries and plenty of coffee will start your day. In the afternoon enjoy homemade cookies and refreshments then end your day with dessert and a fine wine.

First floor common rooms are truly welcoming to guests. The glass-enclosed veranda is furnished in white wicker and offers a window to the city while you enjoy your breakfast. During the day, it's the perfect spot to relax and

Sitting rooms offer both formal and informal atmosphere ... depending on your mood.

socialize. On cooler days, breakfast is served in the formal dining room with dark woods, lace tablecloth and crystal chandelier. Small, intimate sitting areas are appealing in either a contemporary or turn-of-the-century style.

The area offers a variety of activities for visitors from boating and cruises to art galleries and antique shops. Naturally, there are some fabulous restaurants from casual to fine dining along the waterfront. You may want to stop at Petoskey's Gas Light district for shopping. This is a resort community for boaters. Many people with permanent summer homes spend long days out on the lake enjoying their boat. So, for visitors to the area, a day lounging at the beach will also include watching the diversity of boats cruise along the waterfront.

For those who enjoy Michigan's bed and breakfast experience, The Veranda is a must. Its unique rooms, antiques and the amiable innkeepers' attention to guest comforts will make you feel welcome.

Historic Nickerson Inn
Pentwater, Michigan

Telephone: 231-869-6731
Email: Nickerson@voyager.net
Website: www.nickersoninn.com

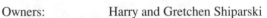

Owners:	Harry and Gretchen Shiparski
Accommodations:	Bed and Breakfast. 13 guest rooms with private baths.
Extras:	Full breakfast. Individual room heating and A/C. Queen or twin beds. Three rooms with gas-log fireplace, Jacuzzi, private balcony.
Rates/Payment:	Nightly $100-$250. Check, credit cards.
Miscellaneous:	Restaurant on premises (noted for exceptional cuisine). No smoking/pets. Ambiance appropriate for children 12 and over. No TVs.
Open:	April to October.

During a recent trip to the cozy village of Pentwater, we took some time to stop by the town's Historic Nickerson Inn. Sitting atop a sandy hill with Lake Michigan peeking between tree tops, the inn has served guests for over 90 years. Charles and Medora Nickerson began operation of the inn on July 1, 1914. In fact, Charles laid the first handmade block using sand from the dune

Historic Nickerson Inn, built in 1914.

upon which the inn now sits. Together, with their family, they ran the inn for many years building a reputation for gracious and caring hospitality.

Since then, the inn has changed hands several times with each new owner proudly carrying on the fine tradition of Charles and Medora. Owners since 1992, Harry and Gretchen Shiparski, are part of the inn's rich history. Now joined by their son, Christopher, and daughter-in-law, Betsie, they feel privileged to offer guests the spirit and genuine hospitality that has been its trademark for so many years.

The grand front veranda is reminiscent of an earlier time.

There is indeed a unique historical charm to this spacious 13-room inn. In fact, as you pull your car into the driveway you'll begin the transformation. The grand front veranda with its wicker-filled furniture is very reminiscent of a day when guests would leisurely sip lemonade as they watched the horse-drawn stagecoach pass by.

The experience continues as you enter the main lobby where a stone fireplace, lace curtains,

Stone fireplace and antiques set the mood.

Nickerson's suites offer more contemporary luxuries and scenic views.

antiques and rich colors of wine and hunter green wrap you in the warmth of an earlier time. Just beyond the main lobby is a spacious, candle-lit dining room that is well-known in the community for its fine cuisine (more on this later).

The inn's 13 guest rooms, found on the upper floors, offer a uniquely diverse blend of styles and amenities. Certainly all have important updates, such as individual room heating, air conditioning and private baths. Loggers Run reflects a rustic woodsman's theme with log walls, hand-hewn log bed, chairs and table. Jennifer's Room is sweetly romantic with light florals, natural wicker bed and a view of Lake Michigan and the dunes. Seascape is a wonderful reflection

Sitting areas throughout the inn invite quiet conversation.

of a seafarer's room with its ship's wheel bed. Their newest additions are Lakeview, Sunrise and Sunset. Very spacious, these upscale rooms feature gas log fireplace,

spacious Jacuzzi tubs and private or semi-private balconies. Lakeview Suite is their most popular room, and we could definitely see why. This bright and cheerful room creates a wonderfully romantic atmosphere with its wall of surrounding windows and balcony offering an enchanting view of woodlands, dunes and Lake Michigan beyond.

Breakfasts are served in the bright sunroom.

Certainly part of the Nickerson Inn experience is their wonderfully prepared full breakfasts (included with your stay) or dinner specialties (additional charge). Most times breakfasts are served in their airy sunroom with relaxing view of the grounds and a bit of Lake Michigan. Their charming main room is generally reserved for their romantic, candlelight dinners.

Nickerson's restaurant proudly maintains its reputation as one of the area's finest dining establishments. They use only the freshest ingredients and have arrangements with local farmers to ensure 'just picked' quality. Certainly a primary contributor to the restaurant's success is the inn's dedicated head chef, who just happens to be the incredibly talented Christopher Shiparski. With his culinary expertise, Christopher has brought a distinctive European influence to the inn's menu.

Pentwater, the little community surrounding Nickerson, was founded back in 1853. At that time the area's primary residents were Ottawa, Chippewa and Pottawatamie Native Americans. In fact, the name "Pentwater" is an American Indian term meaning 'penned-up waters'. Today, Pentwater retains its small-town ambiance with its main streets offering several homey shops and restaurants. Perhaps one of the area's most popular attractions is the Silver Lake Sand Dunes, located in nearby Hart. The dunes, tucked between Lake Michigan and Silver Lake, offers a diverse collection of recreational activities including adventurous dune buggy rides, jeep tours, awe-inspiring beaches and excellent fishing and boating. For hikers, cross-country skiers or bicycling enthusiasts, the Hart to Montague rail trail offers 22 miles of paved pathways.

The Historic Nickerson Inn is a lovely retreat that harmonizes perfectly with its surrounding community. The next time you're planning a southwestern Lower Peninsula trip, give them a call. You won't be disappointed.

Inn at Ludington
Ludington, Michigan

Telephone: 800-845-9170
Email: info@inn-ludington.com
Website: www.inn-ludington.com

Owner:	Kathy & Ola Kvalvaag
Accommodations:	Bed and Breakfast, 6 rooms with private baths.
Extras:	Full buffet breakfast. All rooms with A/C, CATV, some with wood-burning fireplace.
Rates/Payment:	Nightly $100-$125.
Miscellaneous:	No pets. Seasonal getaway packages.
Open:	Year around.

When many think of a bed and breakfast, it often takes the form of a classic, Victorian-styled home complete with fanciful, ornate designs and tall peaked roofs. For those fascinated by the elegantly romantic ambiance of the classic Victorian, you'll enjoy the charming Inn at Ludington. Built in 1890 and located close to Ludington's historic Old Town, the home is recipient of the Haskell Award for Historic Preservation by the Mason County Historical Society and listed on the Michigan Historic Register.

Built in 1890, the inn features distinctive Victorian architecture.

Current owners, Kathy and Ola Kvalvaag, are proud of their home's historical background and continue renovation projects to maintain its appeal. The Kvalvaag's have designed six inviting guest rooms with European, Scandinavian, Mediter-

The spacious Great Lakes Victorian Suite is bright and appealing.

ranean, Victorian and American Country themes. Each room is fully air conditioned with cable TV. One of our favorites was their spacious second floor Great Lakes Victorian Suite with welcoming wood-burning fireplace and sitting area. A Victorian floral theme is seen throughout, including wallpaper and lovely spread covering its plantation-style king bed. Their Little Europe room is another of our favorites. This enchanting room also features a wood-burning fireplace and queen size bed. Its cheerful blues and sunny yellows are inspired by Provance. This spacious room has a reading area by the fireplace and plenty of what Kathy terms "waltzing room".

Of course we can't overlook their special breakfasts, served in the elegantly casual dining room with crystal chandelier and formal dining table. Its lovely fireplace, on cooler days, adds an inviting glow to the dining experience.

Southwestern room reflects Americana.

Beginning at 7:00 a.m., freshly brewed coffee, yogurt, cereal and pastry are available. Main courses vary with Kathy happy to tailor breakfast to your particular request. Serving times are also pre-determined by guests. Early risers or those seeking a more leisurely start

The bright colors of Little Europe are inspired by Provance.

to the morning can be accommodated (8:00 a.m. to 10:00 a.m.). On full house days Kathy likes to offer what she calls her "buffet extravaganza" that includes a wonderful assortment of hot and cold dishes and other delectable edibles.

After breakfast, it's time to begin your Ludington adventure. Once again, Kathy and Ola are happy to accommodate by offering a variety of adventure packages. Some of these include horseback riding, jeep or dune buggy rides, canoe trips, plus fabulous air and land scenic tours. Murder Mystery Week-ends continue to be very popular.

If you'd like to find your own special adventure or spend the day at the beach, no problem. The inn isn't far from beautiful Lake Michigan beaches. For nature enthusiasts, head out to Ludington State Park, frequently called the "Queen of Michigan's Parks". This picturesque park features 14 miles of hiking and biking trails winding through virgin forests and dunes with miles of fabulous sandy beaches. Of course, one of the most awesome dune expe-riences can be had at Silver Lake Sand Dunes (20 miles south of Ludington).

White Pine Village is another enjoyable stop. This charming, nostalgic vil-lage preserves the small-town atmosphere of the late 1800's and features 21 historical buildings. Events are planned throughout their season. The village is open from mid-April to mid-October.

For good times and relaxing nights, give Kathy and Ola a call. They're happy to accommodate.

Khardomah Lodge
Grand Haven, Michigan

Telephone: 616-842-2990
Email: khardomahlodge@chartermi.net
Website: www.khardomahlodge.com

Owners:	Mo and Patty Rasmussen
Accomodations:	Lodge with 16 bedrooms/5 baths, 2 suites, 1 cottage.
Extras:	Varies with units and include: fireplace, CATV, AC, telephone, full kitchens, garbage disposal, dishwasher, washer/dryer, hot tub, Jacuzzi.
Rates/Payment:	*Lodge* weekly $4,190 and up; Nightly $625 and up. *Suites* weekly $975 and up. Nightly $125 and up; *Cottage* weekly $1,100. Credit card, check.
Miscellaneous:	Service and meal catering for special events, event planning and some AV equipment. No pets/smoking.
Open:	Year around.

Hundreds of years before the United States became the melting pot of the world, it was home to Native American Indians. Traveling across our state we are always reminded of their culture. It can be seen like the ripples in a pond from a tossed stone. We see it in certain traditions, art work and names.

Spacious, historic home sleeping up to 32 people.

Serene views surround the lodge.

For example, many of our cities, forests, mountains and waters have Native American names. Today we are heading to a Michigan historical home, The Khardomah Lodge. It was named after an Ottawa Indian, Chief Khardomah, and means "happy home". The name does it justice.

Quiet sitting rooms for quiet conversations.

Built by James and Mary Beaton in 1873 as their private residence, it became a public lodge in 1915. Set on a quiet and historical Grand Haven street with trees as a back-drop, Khardomah is just a few hundred dred feet from Lake Michigan.

The bright white building with dark green trim and awnings has freshly painted white picket fencing that borders the street, porch and balcony, very reminiscent of the 1800's. It's large and hard to miss.

As we opened the door and stepped forward, we actually stepped back in time. We entered a turn-of-the-century home still echoing from its lavish, formal parties and extravagant meals and entertainment. Mo and Patty have been very careful to restore many of the original furnishings, artwork and antiques to keep its historical appeal. Several of the lodge's more intimate common areas are filled with grandfather clocks, tapestries, wicker lamps and period furnishings. Most of the rooms are paneled, some with the original dark woods of the time.

The main living area is great for large groups with overstuffed cloth and leather sofas, wicker chairs and tables in front of a stonewall and fireplace. New wood covers the walls and floor accented with a large circular area rug. It's been updated for guest comfort and includes air conditioning, cable TV, VCR, recessed lighting and more. A relaxing place to sit with friends, there's an expanse of windows providing a serene woodland view.

The massive dining area, surrounded by dark wood and bright windows, is filled with tables and can be set up to easily accommodate 30 to 200 people for special events. French doors take you out to the deck. The kitchen has a dishwasher along with several stoves and refrigerators (classic older models) to accommodate large groups.

Sleeping rooms are just that, rooms to sleep in with one or two beds, some have bunk beds. These 16 paneled rooms are smaller, but certainly serve their purpose and can accommodate up to 32 people.

Because of its size, Khardomah Lodge is perfect for family reunions, intimate weddings or business meetings. If you want your meals prepared, the chef is excellent and can handle all of your needs. There are easels and a projection screen for business purposes. If you're planning such events, you'll need to call well in advance for availability and rates.

The home offers 16 bedrooms and 5 full baths.

In addition to the lodge, there are also two suites. Both are spacious, with a woodsy-contemporary styling and will comfortably accommodate four to six people. Both feature microwave, full

Khardomah's luxury suites were a favorite.

kitchens, CATV, air conditioning and telephones. The first suite (called the Hot Tub Suite) offers a hot tub on its deck with the woods as a backdrop. This suite includes two large sofas, a kitchenette, two bedrooms with queen beds and offers its guests a robe and hairdryer so they can use the hot tub in comfort. The second "Master Suite" features a Jacuzzi in the bathroom. Plush queen sleeper sofa is centered opposite a fieldstone wall and fireplace. The full kitchen is nicely equipped and includes a garbage disposal and dishwasher. Both suites are wonderful.

A miniature Kardomah sits directly across the street. White with green trim, Loch Hame cottage is very much like the suites but a little larger with three bedrooms, sleeping up to seven. The modern kitchen includes garbage disposal, dishwasher, and washer/dryer. There is a gas grill on the porch and linens are provided. Two bedrooms are upstairs and the second floor also includes a balcony. This fashionable cottage is perfect for a family. It's hard to believe Loch Hame was built in 1887. If you walk down the block you will notice many of the homes have their original dates on them going back to the 1800's. It's a truly historic street with great old homes that are treasured by their owners.

Grand Haven is a quiet community on the banks of Lake Michigan with fabulous beaches, water sports, cruises and fishing attractions. When not on the water you may want to walk some of their historical districts and museums

The Loch Hame cottage sits across the street.

or spend the day at the Gillette Nature Center. Color tours, winter sports and nature tours fill all the seasons. There is plenty of shopping and art galleries filled with the work of area artisans. A must see is the

Musical Fountain show held every night in the summer. This is a spectacular display of dancing colored waters set to music and has been attracting crowds since 1963.

This historic community is bustling with activities all year long for vacationers. The Khardomah Lodge is the perfect spot for large or intimate groups. It's waiting to be your "Happy Home" away from home.

The Oakland
South Haven, Michigan

Telephone: 773-388-3121
Email: bobbruno@msn.com

Owners:	Lynn and Bob Bruno
Accommodations:	Private vacation home, across from Lake Michigan, 3 bedrooms (sleeps up to 10).
Extras:	Equipped kitchen with microwave. A/C, CATV, VCR, ceiling fans, washer/dryer. Linens provided. Deck, gas BBQ. Directly across from public beach.
Rates/Payment:	Weekly $2100, off-season rates available, Check.
Miscellaneous:	No pets/smoking.
Open:	Year around.

Traveling through South Haven we are always impressed with the intertwining of old and new. North Shore Drive runs along Lake Michigan and, in the summer, this residential street comes alive with vacationers. A popular past time in South Haven is sitting on your stoop or front lawn and chatting with friends as you people watch. As we walked the tree-lined street, it was not unusual to strike up a conversation with passerby's or residents sitting outside. Even with the summer crowds, it's a very casual and relaxed atmosphere. On this particular day we were visiting The Oakland, built in 1927 and currently owned by Lynn and Bob Bruno.

A classic 1927 hotel is now a shared private residence.

Surrounding windows and nicely appointed furnishings create a relaxing environment.

The Oakland used to be Mendelson's Oakland Hotel, but now has been divided into two separate living quarters, with Lynn and Bob owning one of them. Sitting about 100 ft. from the street, this massive white building can't be missed. A notable feature of the building is the rounded windows found throughout. In fact, there are 15 windows in the front of the home facing the street.

The living room is filled with contemporary furnishings. By the front windows, a glass top table with chairs is an inviting place for that morning coffee. Extending off the living area is a smaller TV room that offers a place to relax with your favorite shows or, more likely, your children's favorite cartoons.

In the back of the first floor you'll find the kitchen and dining area. This room is bright and cheerful, with a black and white checked floor offset by plenty of clean white cabinets. A really nice feature is ample room and plenty of counter space to

Well appointed kitchen.

prepare your favorite gourmet delights. The dining table sits in front of French doors that lead to the deck and yard. The deck is beautifully furnished with wooden chairs, picnic table and gas BBQ grill. It's a great spot for some private outdoor fun.

The perfect spot for an outdoor BBQ.

Upstairs there are three spacious bedrooms with queen, full, and twin beds, dressers and chairs. White walls are dramatically highlighted by dark wood bed frames and wood trim around the windows. Colorful spreads cover the beds and add a splash of color. There is also a large, updated bathroom with tub/shower and vanity. A smaller bathroom is located downstairs.

Just down the street, a short walk away is one of South Haven's greatest assets ... North Beach. Looking at the beach you may think you're in Hawaii but, no, that's just South Haven. This is a very large and simply fabulous

Three spacious bedrooms offer queen, full or twin beds.

The Oakland is just down the street from South Haven's popular North Beach.

public beach that you won't want to leave. We recommend lots of suntan lotion and plenty of film for your camera. You'll not only get great daytime pictures but also fabulous Michigan sunsets.

Venturing into the city, South Haven has plenty to keep you busy. It's a charming town full of great shops, eateries, art galleries, festivals and more. This is a town where you won't get bored. The Oakland is practically on the beach, yet not far from the main street. It's an ideal location with all the comforts of home. We think you'll like it, so give the Lynn and Bob a call.

Sleepy Hollow Resort
South Haven, Michigan

Telephone: 269-637-1127
Email: shr@accn.org
Website: www.sleepyhollowonlakemichigan.com

Property Manager:	Jackie Mortorff
Accommodations:	Over 40 cottage/apartment (sleep 4-8) on Lake Michigan.
Extras:	Daily housekeeping, equipped kitchens, microwave, A/C, CATV. Additional features may include: Flat screen TV, VCR, DVD, fireplace, dishwasher, washer/dryer, decks/patios/balconies. Outdoor heated swimming pool, 150 ft. beach frontage, tennis courts, badminton, volleyball, basketball, shuffleboard, playground.
Rates/Payment:	Weekly $1,550 to $3,685. Off-season and nightly rates available. Check.
Miscellaneous:	Handicap accessible. No pets/smoking. In-room baby-sitter. Morning/afternoon children's activities. Family movies twice weekly. Pool lifeguard. Instructional tennis pro. Deli/cocktails.
Open:	Late May through mid October.

There's nothing quite like traveling along the Lake Michigan shoreline. No matter how many times you take the trip, the scenery is always changing, always beautiful. The vision of Lake Michigan's deep blue waters broken by

Luxury resort overlooking a beautiful Lake Michigan beach.

AFTER: Recent renovations (above) have resulted in a totally fresh look.

BEFORE: At right is how Sleepy Hollow appeared in 1994.

white caps and outlined by crystal sands or rugged shorelines are always an awesome sight. Native American Indians had a name for our west coast, Ni-Ko-Nog, meaning the beautiful sunset. In the evening, the sun's deep orange glow over the water is breathtaking.

This particular Lake Michigan trip was taking us into the quaint little resort community of South Haven and one of our older west coast resorts, Sleepy Hollow. We hadn't visited the resort since 1994, and heard it had recently undergone major updates. We decided to check it out.

Opened for business in 1937, this sprawling 30-acre resort can accommodate several hundred visitors. In the summer it is a beehive of fun and activity. Quite different from what its first owner experienced. Purchased in 1888 for $2,800 by Joshua Smith, it was just a peaceful and quiet little hollow. Mr. Smith had been a very close friend of the renowned author, Washington Irving. In honor of his old friend, he named the property "Sleepy Hollow".

Driving onto the main grounds we were immediately struck by the transformation. There was no question that the Sleepy Hollow we had known

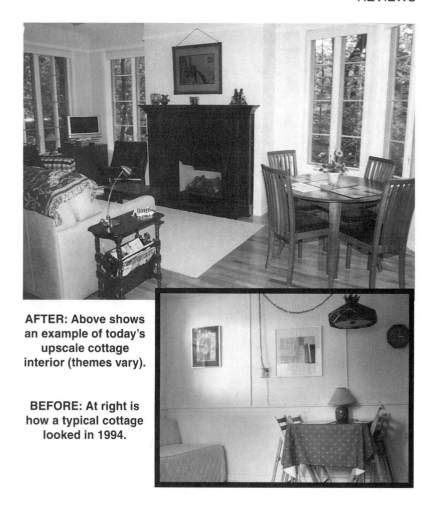

AFTER: Above shows an example of today's upscale cottage interior (themes vary).

BEFORE: At right is how a typical cottage looked in 1994.

from years back had been reborn. The property is beautifully landscaped with lighted walkways running along the cottage fronts. We were pleased to see that one of the unique features of Sleepy Hollow remained intact … the fun and interesting art deco styling of the cottages. In 1937, resort owner, Edward Gray, patterned the lodgings after the Century of Progress 1933 Chicago fair. Their geometric, simple lines continue to distinguish this resort from the other, more traditional cottages we usually see.

We first reviewed Sleepy Hollow in our 1995-96 Michigan Vacation Guide. Even then it was very impressive, but showing its age. Our comment about the cottages was "the lodgings…did not offer exceptional comfort". Well a lot has changed in 10 years. These newly refurbished units represent the ultimate in luxury. You will not be disappointed.

ALL RATES SUBJECT TO CHANGE

Interior decor varies. The cottage pictured above has a nautical theme.

The cottages and suites are stretched across the grounds in one to three bedroom units with a variety of amenities. Common characteristics include cathedral ceilings, modern furnishing, fireplaces, plush carpeting, tile floors and large windows. Most have CATV and the units we saw even included flat screen TV's. Styling is impeccable with a great deal of thought placed in

Bedrooms are nicely appointed and very inviting.

Kitchens offer quality amenities, such as dishwashers and/or stainless steel appliances.

comfort and décor. The kitchens offer every conceivable convenience including stainless steel appliances, modern refrigerators, dishwashers and tons of cupboard space. Many units also have washers and dryers for your use. There is absolutely nothing missing. Even the tastefully appointed bedrooms are spacious with twin, full or queen beds. Naturally, bathrooms are roomy and contemporary. To top it off, there is daily maid service.

What is so remarkable about Sleepy Hollow is that the grounds are just as perfect as the cottages. Children's play areas are scattered throughout and an Olympic size, heated pool sits in the center with a lifeguard present. On the outskirts are tennis courts. A tennis pro is even available to help you with your backhand. Other activities include basketball, shuffleboard, volleyball and plenty of grounds for some Frisbee or baseball. It's virtually impossible to be bored. By the lake, a long flight of stairs goes down to a sandy beach where the inviting Lake Michigan waters await.

Sleepy Hollow is a family resort that caters to both parents and children. There are daily children's group activities and team sports for their enjoyment. In the evening if mom and dad want to take in a local play or go out for a romantic dinner in the city, the resort provides in-room baby sitters. There are also family movies shown twice a week. To help you relax in the afternoon or evening, head over to the deck for some outstanding deli food and maybe a cocktail. Why not? You're on vacation. This resort is so complete with activities that many families may never have to leave the grounds.

Should you decide to venture off there are lots of things to do in the area. South Ha-

Sleepy Hollow has planned children's activities.

ven has some excellent golf courses, biking trails, wonderful shops and art galleries. Walk along the harbor boardwalk to enjoy the many private yachts, stop for an old-fashion soda at the local drug store or sample some chocolates or wine in town. This is a great resort community with planned events all year and everyone is welcomed.

Sleepy Hollow has gone through a lot of changes in the last 165 years or so with the most recent updates very appealing. It's an absolutely wonderful resort that will pamper the entire family. Though the price may be higher than the average resort, you're getting every penny's worth. If you want your next vacation to be a fabulous time to remember for years to come, you don't have to leave the country. You just have to head over to Sleepy Hollow.

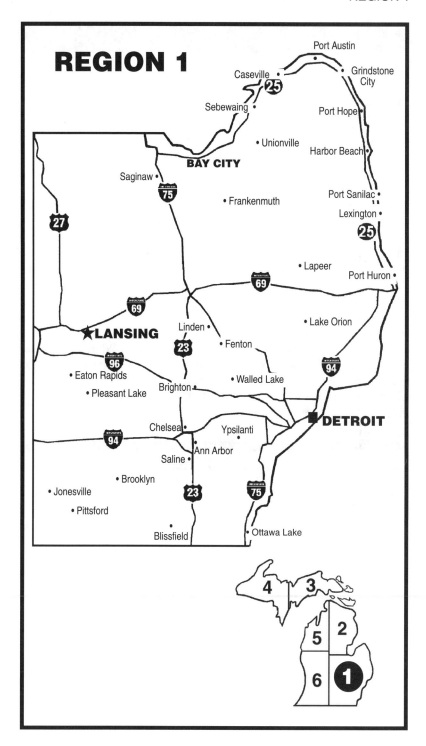

REGION 1

Port Austin

Caseville •
25

Grindstone City

Sebewaing •

Port Hope •

• Unionville

Harbor Beach •

BAY CITY

Saginaw •
75

• Frankenmuth

Port Sanilac •

Lexington •
25

• Lapeer

Port Huron •

69

69

★**LANSING**

Linden •
23

• Fenton

• Lake Orion

94

27

96

• Eaton Rapids

• Pleasant Lake

Brighton •

• Walled Lake

■**DETROIT**

94

Chelsea •

Ypsilanti

Saline •

Ann Arbor

• Brooklyn

75

• Jonesville

23

• Pittsford

•
Blissfield

• Ottawa Lake

4   3

5   2

6   1

BLISSFIELD & THE IRISH HILLS AREA

INCLUDES: ADRIAN /OTTAWA LAKE • BROOKLYN • JONESVILLE • PITTSFORD

Surround yourself with the beauty of the **Irish Hills,** a unique blend of modern and historic. Visit the Croswell Opera House, in Adrian, the oldest continuously operating theater of its kind in Michigan. It features live theater productions as well as special art exhibits. Michigan Futurity is the place to be for horse racing excitement.

Picnic by one of the Irish Hills' 50 spring-fed lakes, ride amongst its beautiful rolling hills, and take a trip to historic Walker Tavern in Cambridge State Historic Park. Enjoy a nature walk through the 670-acre Hidden Lake Gardens at Michigan State University. Of course, there's always the fun of Mystery Hill. Ready for more? Then step back in time to the 1800s and enjoy the pioneering spirit that lives on at Stagecoach Stop U.S.A. Sit back with a sarsaparilla in the saloon, pan for gold, or take a train ride ... but be careful ... we hear there's masked bandits in the area.

Join the excitement of Indy and stock car races each summer (June-August) at the Michigan International Speedway in the Irish Hills. While enjoying the beautiful fall colors, don't forget to stop in **Brooklyn** and join the fun at Oktoberfest or their arts and crafts festival. Anyone for cross-country skiing or snowmobiling? No matter what time of year, the Cambridge State Historic Park and the Irish Hills are always waiting.

BLISSFIELD

HIRAM D. ELLIS INN

(517) 486-3155
BED & BREAKFAST

All rooms in this 1880's 2-story brick Victorian inn offer CATV, private baths, spa services available with reservation. Come, relax and enjoy the many antiques and specialty shops in the area. Full breakfast served each morning. 4 rooms. Business discounts.

Nightly $90-$110 (Corporate/Business $65)

BROOKLYN (IN THE IRISH HILLS)

CHICAGO STREET INN   **(517) 592-3888 • EMAIL: chiinn@aol.com**
CARL & MARY MOORE   **BED & BREAKFAST**

Six lovely rooms with private bath, queen-bed, CATV, in-room refrigerator. Jacuzzi and fireplace suites available. Murder Mystery Dinners, Girls' Night Out, In-house massage available. A/C. Smoke-free. Evening refreshments. Rumor has it a tunnel connecting to the old railroad station was a whiskey run during prohibition. *Website: www.chicagostreetinn.com*

Nightly $79-$159

Editor's Note: Well established, reputable B&B catering to adult guests. Appealing antique styling and period pieces.

DEWEY LAKE MANOR   **(517) 467-7122 • EMAIL: info@deweylakemanor.com**
THE PHILLIPS FAMILY   **BED & BREAKFAST**

★ EDITOR'S CHOICE ★

Sitting atop a knoll overlooking Dewey Lake on 18 scenic acres, a "country retreat" awaits Manor guests! Picnic by the lake — enjoy evening bonfires. Hearty breakfast buffet served on the glass enclosed porch (weather permitting). At night, snack on popcorn or sip a cup of cider...there are always cookies! Five rooms with private baths, fireplaces and A/C. Check our Website for specials! *Website: www.deweylakemanor.com*

Nightly $75-$135

Editor's Note: Very comfy, well maintained and nicely appointed B&B. Located on spacious, rolling grounds with fabulous lake views.

DUANE LOCKE   **(734) 971-7558**
    PRIVATE COTTAGE

Lakefront cottage on Wamplers Lake, in the Irish Hills, sleeps up to 6. Features gas fireplace, TV/VCR, modern private bath with tub/shower (soft water). Excellent swimming, fishing, boat included. Near MIS. Available year around. No pets.

Weekly $900

JONESVILLE

MUNRO HOUSE & DAY SPA   **(517) 849-9292 • (800) 320-3792**
MIKE & LORI VENTURINI   **BED & BREAKFAST**

★ EDITOR'S CHOICE ★

Located at Highways 12 and 99 in South Central Michigan, we cater to romantic getaway couples and single business travelers. Queen beds, private baths, fireplaces, double Jacuzzis, CATV, full breakfast. 100% air conditioned and smoke free. Murder Mystery Dinners, Massage and Spa Packages available. *Website: www.MunroHouse.com*
Nightly $109-$199

Editor's Note: The history associated with this lovely B&B along with uniquely styled rooms make this a nice choice.

OTTAWA LAKE

ISLAND RESORT AT THE LEGACY   **866-820-5270**
CONTACT: MELISSA SHEPPARD   **EMAIL: msheppard@legacyislandresort.com**
GOLF/FAMILY RESORT

Relax at our golf and family resort in beautiful Ottawa Lake featuring our premier course, "The Legacy" by Arthur Hills. Fully-furnished, timber-framed cottages include A/C, full kitchen, sleeping arrangements for 12, two full baths, fireplace, two 25" color televisions with Satellite and VCR, outdoor patio area with charcoal grill, picnic table and four-person Catalina Spa. Recreatonal features include fishing lake, swimming lake, sand volleyball, basketball, softball field, horseshoes, two picnic pavilions, bonfire ring, children's playground, indoor pool and hot tub. No pets/smoking. *Website: www.legacyislandresort.com*

Weekly $693-$1,400   Nightly $149-$225

PITTSFORD

THE ROCKING HORSE INN	(517) 523-3826
MARY ANN & PHIL MEREDITH	EMAIL: rockingh@frontiernet.net

BED & BREAKFAST

Spend peaceful moments on the wrap around porch of this Italianate-style farmhouse while sipping lemonade and eating the dessert of the evening. Full breakfasts. Close to Hillsdale College, shopping, golf, 15 minutes to Michigan Speedway. Four rooms with AC, TV, VCR, private baths. *Website: www.bbonline.com/mi/rockinghorse*

Nightly $50-$80

Editor's Note: Homey atmosphere with charming decor. Another nice choice for the area.

ANN ARBOR/CHELSEA • BRIGHTON SALINE • WALLED LAKE • YPSILANTI

Ann Arbor, home of the University of Michigan. This cosmopolitan area offers year around activities for its visitors, from arts and crafts to live theater and entertainment. While here, be sure to stroll the many unique shops. Visit the University of Michigan planetarium. Canoe, swim or hike in Gallup Park. In late July, arts and craft enthusiasts never miss the Ann Arbor Art Fair featuring noted artisans from across the country. Only 10 miles from Ann Arbor rests **Saline.** Well known for its historic homes and antique shops, the area hosts nationally recognized antique shows from April through November. **Ypsilanti**, home of Eastern Michigan University, is also a city of diverse activities. Among its many points of interest include Wiard's Orchard which offers fresh cider, tours and hayrides. Enjoy the festivities for the yearly Heritage Festival (celebrated each August) commemorating its early French settlers.

Surrounded by lakes, the **Brighton** area offers excellent golf courses, parks, downhill and cross country skiing. In the summer, Independence, Folk Art and Farmer's Market festivals abound at Mill Pond located in the heart of the city.

ANN ARBOR AND CHELSEA

ANN ARBOR BED & BREAKFAST   **(734) 994-9100**
PAT & BOB MATERKA   Email: pat@annarborbedandbreakfast.com
     BED & BREAKFAST

Overlooks the University of Michigan central campus. Features include A/C, CATV, VCR and high-speed Internet. Some rooms with fireplace and mini-kitchens. Walk to theaters, concerts, Arboretum, Kerrytown and Ann Arbor's Main Street. Nine rooms/private baths. Full breakfasts. No pets/smoking. *Website: www.AnnArborBedandBreakfast.com*

Nightly $129-$149

THE URBAN RETREAT BED & BREAKFAST   **(734) 971-8110**
     BED & BREAKFAST

Contemporary ranch-styled home, antique furnished, set in a quiet neighborhood, minutes from downtown and UM/EMU campuses. Adjacent parkland with walking trails. Breakfast served overlooking the garden. Member National Wildlife Federation "Backyard Wildlife Habitat." Resident housecats. A/C. 2 room. Inspected and approved. By reservation only. *Website: www.theurbanretreat.com*

Nightly $60-$75

WATERLOO GARDENS BED & BREAKFAST   **(734) 433-1612**
     EMAIL: gary.offenbacher@prodigy.net
     BED & BREAKFAST

Contemporary ranch home located on the north end of Chelsea near Ann Arbor. Guest rooms offer private and shared baths. Large Jacuzzi, video library, fitness equipment and great sunsets. A/C. Full breakfasts. No smoking. We have Golden Retrievers. *Website: www.waterloogardensbb.com*

Nightly $85 (single) - $135 (2 bedroom suite)

BRIGHTON

BRIGHTON HOME   **(810) 227-3225**
     PRIVATE HOME

Built in 1990, this home sleeps 8 and is completely furnished. Located in a secluded area. The balcony overlooks the water only 10 ft. away. Features fully equipped kitchen, microwave, freezer, dishwasher, washer and dryer, use of rowboat and dock.

Weekly   (summer) $900   (off season rates available)

SALINE

THE HOMESTEAD BED & BREAKFAST   **(734) 429-9625**
SHIRLEY GROSSMAN   **EMAIL: homesteadbb@earthlink.net**
                   BED & BREAKFAST

1851 circa brick farmhouse filled with period antiques, features comfort in Victorian elegance. Cross-country ski, stroll or relax on 50 acres of farmland. Only 10 minutes from Ann Arbor. A/C. Corporate rates. 5 rooms. Full breakfast. Friendly housecats.

Nightly $40-$75

WALLED LAKE

MICHIGAN STAR CLIPPER DINNER TRAIN   **(248) 960-9440**
                   BED & BREAKFAST

The perfect mini-vacation ... a fun-filled overnight train experience! Enjoy hors d'oeuvres, cocktail hour, five-course dinner and entertainment. Eight cozy French-style rooms feature silk moire wall coverings and gold gilded paintings or a 50's berth-style with half bath. Full breakfast prior to disembarking. *Website: www.michiganstarclipper.com*

Saturday Overnight Package: $287/couple   Dinner Train only $77

YPSILANTI

PARISH HOUSE INN   **(800) 480-4866 • (734) 480-4800**
CHRIS MASON   **BED & BREAKFAST**

★ EDITOR'S CHOICE ★

1893 "Queen Anne" styled home first constructed as a parsonage. Extensively renovated in 1993. Victorian styled with period antiques. Fireplace, CATV, video library/VCR's, central A/C, telephones. Hearty breakfast. Near golfing, antiquing, biking and restaurants. No smoking. 8 rooms with private baths.

Nightly $92-$160 (Corporate Rate $85)

Editor's Note: Appealing rooms and knowledgeable innkeeper make this a nice choice for vacation or business travelers.

LANSING

INCLUDES: EATON RAPIDS • PLEASANT LAKE

Lansing has been our state's capital since 1847. Visiting the State Capitol building is an absolute must for travelers. Guides conduct free tours daily. Also take some time to visit the Michigan Historical Museum and explore our dynamic and exciting past. Relax on a riverboat cruise of the Grand River. There's also plenty of excellent golfing, shops, galleries, live theater and restaurants. The Boars Head Theater (Michigan's only resident theater) and Woldumar Nature Center are additional attractions.

If you're looking for an intimate and distinctive dining experience, you'll want to try Dusty's English Inn in Eaton Rapids — only a short drive from Lansing. For simpler yet well prepared homemade meals, you'll enjoy Ellie's Country Kitchen on East Grand River in Williamston for breakfast, lunch and dinner. Just down the street, is the Red Cedar Grill with its casually upscale atmosphere.

LANSING & EATON RAPIDS

DUSTY'S ENGLISH INN　　　　　**(517) 663-2500 • (800) 858-0598**
BED & BREAKFAST

Resting along the Grand River, amidst lovely gardens and woodland trails, this elegant English Tudor-style home is decorated throughout with antiques and reproductions. Its intimate restaurant offers fine dining and cocktails in the European tradition. Full English breakfast is served each morning.

Nightly　　　$105-$175 (dbl., plus tax)

PLEASANT LAKE

ROCKFISH INN   (517) 769-6448
HEIDI/MIKE RITCHISON   PRIVATE COTTAGE

★ EDITOR'S CHOICE ★

Vacation cottage on all sports lake with sandy bottom. 3 bedrooms, sleeps 5-7, one bath, fully carpeted, with large fully equipped kitchen. Walk to fine dining, playground and 27 hole golf course (x-country skiing in winter). Enjoy fabulous sunsets, grassy sunbathing area, private dock, boat hoist, TV with VCR. Grill provided. Open year around.

Weekly $500-$600

Editor's Note: Well maintained cottage on narrow lot. The wood deck offers a great view of lake.

LAKE ORION • PORT HURON • LAPEER

Port Huron joins Lake Huron's waters with the St. Clair River. This port town is the home of the Blue Water Bridge, arts and craft fairs, waterfront dining and wonderful views from the shoreline. While in the area, visit Fort Gratiot Lighthouse and the Knowlton Ice Museum. In July, enjoy the excitement of the Blue Water Festival and the 3-day Port Huron to Mackinac Island Yacht Races.

Approximately 35 miles west of Port Huron is the scenic countryside of **Lapeer**. Surrounded by orchards, the area is known for its blueberry farms. The many lakes and streams in this region offer good fishing. In the winter, enjoy one of Lapeer's groomed cross-country ski trails.

LAKE ORION

TIKI JOE'S PLACE   **(248) 252-0074**
JOE & MELINDA ROGERS   **EMAIL: trackerman@ameritech.net**
PRIVATE COTTAGE

An Island Escape! Two-bedroom (sleeps 8) cottage on a 5-acre island. No roads or bridges yet minutes from shopping/restaurants. Features 1.5 baths, A/C, TV (no cable), VCR, kitchen with dishwasher, fireplace, Jacuzzi. Paddleboat and fishing boat. Small pets OK. Open year round. *Website: www.tikijoesplace.com*

Nightly $125-$175

LAPEER

HART HOUSE   **(810) 667-9106**
ELLIE HAYES   **BED & BREAKFAST**

Listed on the National Historic Register, this Queen Anne B&B was home of the first Mayor, Rodney G. Hart. Full breakfasts served each morning. Private baths. 4 rooms. No smoking.

Nightly $40-$50

PORT HURON

THE VICTORIAN INN   **(810) 984-1437**
MARVIN/SUSAN BURKE   **BED & BREAKFAST**

Queen Anne styled inn, authentically restored, offers guests a timeless ambiance. Each room uniquely decorated. Enjoy the Inn's classically creative cuisine, fine wines and gracious service. Pub in cellar. One hour from Detroit. 4 rooms, private/shared baths.

Nightly $100-$150

LEXINGTON • PORT AUSTIN • CASEVILLE

INCLUDES: GRINDSTONE CITY • HARBOR BEACH • PORT HOPE
PORT SANILAC • SEBEWAING • UNIONVILLE

Known for its historic homes, **Lexington** has excellent boating, fishing and swimming. Visit the general store (dating from the 1870's) and indulge in the tasty nostalgia of their "penny candy" counter. Walk to the marina and visit the old lighthouse which was built in 1886.

Further north is **Port Hop**e, home of the Great Lakes State Bottomland Preserve. This unique underwater preserve actually covers the eastern shoreline from **Port Austin** to **Harbor Beach**. Noted for its numerous underwater shipwrecks dated to the 19th Century, it attracts many divers to its cool waters. The Lighthouse County Park off M-25, just outside town, is an ideal spot for scuba diving enthusiasts to begin their tour.

As you continue, take the turn off to **Huron City**. Established around 1861, the region and town were consumed by horrific fires in 1871 and 1881. Preserved by the town's descendants, Huron City is now listed as a historic district in the National Register of Historic Places. Visitors coming to this museum town can experience rural life as it was in the 19th Century. You can explore 10 of the fully restored building which include a Victorian mansion (Seven Gables home), the General Store and an original 1837 log cabin that survived the 19th Century fires. The Village and Seven Gables home is open July-Labor Day.

Grindstone City, with its fine harbor and marina facilities, is well-known by fishing enthusiasts as the place to catch good bass, perch, steelhead, salmon and brown trout. In its early days, Grindstone City produced most of the world's grindstones. Many of the town's namesakes may be seen along the beaches and throughout the little community.

Celebrate both outstanding sunrises and sunsets at the tip of the thumb in **Port Austin**. Discover the rolling sand dunes hidden behind the trees at Port Crescent State Park. Relax on its excellent 3-mile beach. This is also a bird watcher's haven with abundant numbers of hawk, oriole, osprey and bluebird populations. Bring your camera for some scenic shots of the Port Austin Reef Lighthouse. We also suggest keeping your camera handy as you enjoy one of Lake Huron's incredible sunsets at Bird Creek County Park.

Moving around the thumb is **Caseville.** Drive along its half-mile stretch of Saginaw Bay Beach. Here's a great area for perch fishing, boating, swimming and just plain relaxing. A favorite for both residents and vacationers is the Sleeper State Park, noted for its excellent beach and, in the winter, its well-groomed cross country ski trails. Visit some of the communities unique gift shops along Main Street.

For a unique dining experience in Port Austin, try *The Bank* on Blake Street ... a little pricey, but worth it. This historic former bank is now an excellent restaurant, noted for its sourdough bread with herb butter and freshly prepared meals. Another excellent dining treat is offered at the *Garfield Inn* on Lake Street that serves as both a B&B and elegant restaurant. *The Farm Restaurant,* off M25, is another well known, reputable eatery. For more casual, relaxed dining you'll want to stop at the *Port Hope Hotel Restaurant* (in Port Hope) where we understand they prepare some hearty and very tasty hamburgers and other basics at affordable prices. In the Port Sanilac area, fresh perch is served up daily at *The Bellaire Lodge*. Check out *Mary's Diner* for good, old-fashion family-style meals. Craving pizza? Then head over to the *Dry Dock Cafe* on S. Ridge Street. For finer dining, check out *Palermo's Stone Lodge,* just of M-25 at the south end of town.

CASEVILLE

Bella Vista Inn & Cottages   (989) 856-2650
Chalets/Cottages/Suites/Motel Resort
1 bedroom efficiencies with kitchenettes, 2 bedroom cottages with full kitchens, luxurious chalets. Motel/cottages with lake views from picture windows and screened porch, CATV. Heated outdoor pool, grills, picnic tables, sun deck, swings, 400 ft. of beach. *Website: www.bella-caseville.com*

Nightly $69 (starting at)   Weekly $725 (starting at)

Crews' Lakeside Resort   (989) 856-2786
Cottage Resort

★ EDITOR'S CHOICE ★

Seven new, spacious cottage-style condos on the shores of Lake Huron. Two upstairs bedrooms, two fireplaces (one in master bedroom), two full baths, equipped kitchen. Bring linens. CATV and ceiling fans. No pets. Open May-September. Great beach, basketball and tennis courts. $200 deposit. *Website: www.crewslakesideresort.com*

Weekly $848-$1,113

Editor's Note: Very impressive two-level cottages. Upstairs master bedroom (with fireplace) beautifully designed. Highly recommended resort for this area. See our review in this edition.

DALE'S LAKEFRONT HOMES
& COTTAGES

(989) 874-5181 • dlfc102@avci.net
HOMES AND COTTAGES

★ EDITOR'S CHOICE ★

Seven newly built and/or renovated homes/cottages on the shores of Saginaw Bay. Includes 2-4 bedroom cottages (sleeps 5-10), equipped kitchens, ceiling fans, CATV, private balcony. Bring linens, pillows, towels. Excellent swimming beach. Handicap friendly. No smoking. Ask about pets. *Website: www.daleslakefrontcottages.atfreeweb.com*

Weekly $800 (and up)

Editor's Note: The lodgings we saw ranged from very spacious to comfortably sized. All very clean and well maintained. The newer homes are an Editor's Choice. See our review in this edition.

THE LODGE AT OAK POINTE

(989) 856-3055
BED & BREAKFAST

★ EDITOR'S CHOICE ★

Secluded, romantic retreat two hours from Detroit Metro area. Beautifully styled rooms, two-person whirlpool tub, gas log fireplace, queen canopy bed, private screened porch overlooking pond. All in this 11,000 sq. ft. log lodge on 30 wooded acres with walking trails. Handicap access. Continental Plus breakfast. *Website: www.oakpointelodge.com*

Nightly $79-$110

Editor's Note: Beautifully designed, romantic rooms all with picturesque views. Up north lodge ambiance. No TVs in rooms ... a retreat atmosphere. Highly recommended for the area. See our review in this edition.

GRINDSTONE CITY

WHALEN'S GRINDSTONE SHORES   **(989) 738-7664**
CABIN/GUEST ROOM RESORT

Located in Historic Grindstone City at the top of the thumb on a scenic harbor waterfront. Five efficiency units with kitchen facilities and CATV. Five guest sleeping rooms. Air conditioning. Gift shop. Laundry room. R.V. Park. Dump station. Boat docks. Good fishing. Charters available. Call for reservations.

Nightly $45-$85

Editor's Note: Nice spot for fishing enthusiasts. Clean, small, basic cottages, closely spaced. Scenic harbor. Comfortable sleeping rooms at the main house.

HARBOR BEACH

ANGEL VIEW COTTAGE   **(810) 359-2140**
DENISE & CURT MANNINEN   **PRIVATE COTTAGE**

Clean, cozy cottage, remodeled in 2002. On Lake Huron near Harbor Beach. Two bedrooms, walk-in shower. Bed linens provided, bring towels. Complete kitchen, living room with TV-VCR, fireplace. Outside patio, BBQ, firepit. Birdwatchers' paradise. Fishing, swimming, boating nearby. Pets OK. No smoking. Open year around.

Weekly $700 (3 days/$375)

LEXINGTON

BEACHCOMBER RESORT MOTEL & APARTMENTS   **(810) 359-8859**
COTTAGE/MOTEL RESORT

Spacious grounds, sandy beach, swimming pool, tennis court, barbeques, comfortable rooms, A/C, TV, family units, efficiencies, cottages, special occasion suite with fireplace and kitchenette facing beach. No pets. 4 miles north of Lexington on M25 on Lake Huron.

Nightly $51 (and up)

COZMA'S COTTAGES   **(810) 359-8150 • (313) 881-3313**
COTTAGE RESORT

On 2 acres in a secluded, beautiful, park-like setting along 200 ft. of private, sandy beach. Sleeps 4-6 people. Newly decoated. All new beds. Ceiling or wall fans. Volleyball/badminton court, shuffleboard, horseshoes, kiddie swings. BBQ grills, picnic tables, bonfires on beach nightly. Ideal for family reunions.

Weekly $525 (and up)

LITTLE WHITE COTTAGES

(616) 669-5187
PRIVATE COTTAGES

Right on Lake Huron! Experience a real old-fashioned cottage with a comfortable blend of antique and modern furnishings. Swing serenely on our beautiful, shady bank as you contemplate the majesty of Lake Huron only steps away. Low bluff and excellent beach for swimming. Delightfully unique cottages have

Exterior of Nymph

large screened porches, fireplaces, and are completely furnished, except linens. Relax and unwind and let the Seadog or Nymph be your "place on the lake" this summer! No pets/smoking. Sleeps 4-6.

Weekly $550-$950

Editor's Note: On a small but quiet lot. Owners continue to make significant upgrades to add to the comfort and appearance of these older cottages.

LUSKY'S LAKEFRONT

TOLL FREE: (877) 327-6889 • (810) 327-6889
COTTAGE RESORT

Voted "Michigan's Best Family Resort", *The Detroit News.* Cozy and comfortable, ceiling fans, CATV, picnic tables, BBQ grills, fully equipped kitchens, private bathrooms. Screened porches great view of lake and play area. Play area features airplane swing, play boats, tire swirl, gymset and more. Also volley ball, basketball, shuffleboard, paddle-boat and rowboat. Stop at

our novelty store for candy, ice cream and trinkets galore! All this makes for a fun, relaxing and affordable family vacation place where memories are made and treasured. Pets allowed for an additional charge. *Website: www.luskys.com*

Weekly (beginning at) $325

Editor's Note: New owners in 2000. Basic, traditional cottages. Very nice beach.

THE POWELL HOUSE   **(810) 359-5533**
NANCY POWELL   **BED & BREAKFAST**

★ **EDITOR'S CHOICE** ★

Warm and gracious 1852 Victorian architecture and decor; resting on 4 acres, tree-shaded and gardened, The Powell House is a peaceful escape. Walk to the beach, relax in the gardens or wander in town. Comfortable beds and delicious breakfasts awaits all guests. Private baths. Open all year. *Website: www.powellhouselex.com*

Nightly $85-$90

Editor's Note: Historic home, relaxed ambiance, maintained in very good condition by a caring owner.

MARLENE WILSON   **(989) 635-2911 • (866) 586-7851**
PRIVATE HOME

3,000 sq. ft. home on 4 acres with stairway to 250 ft. of beach front. Four bedrooms (sleeps 8), furnished with equipped kitchen, washer and dryer, shower, full and 1/2 bath. CATV and VCR, picnic tables and grill. Enjoy spectacular sunrises or scenic night views of The Blue Water Bridge, or views of the grounds and waters of Lake Huron from the fully enclosed porch. Advance security deposit and payment required.

Weekly $1,300-$1,800 (seasonal rates May-Oct.)

Editor's Note: Older home on a scenic bluff overlooks the lake and offers plenty of room for those who crave it. Beach with mix of pebbles, rocks and sand.

PORT AUSTIN

CAPTAIN'S INN   **(989) 738-8321 • RES. (888) 277-6631**
DAVID & DEBBIE RAMEY   BED & BREAKFAST

★ EDITOR'S CHOICE ★

Impressively renovated, this spacious Pre-Civil War home offers an inviting blend of antiques, period styling and modern conveniences. CATV. 5 charming guest rooms (3 with private bath; 2 share a bath). Continental Plus breakfasts. Just blocks from restaurants/shops. Open year around. No pets/smoking.

Nightly $64-$125

Editor's Note: One of the area's newest B&B's. Beautifully restored and tastefully styled. A new favorite and highly recommended.

FORT TRANQUIL SANDS RESORT   **(989) 738-5925 • (989) 781-4811**
GARY HALL   COTTAGE RESORT

Six cottages on 150' of private Lake Huron beachfront. Newly remodeled cabins, sleep up to six, feature CATV, ceiling fans, private baths, equipped kitchens with stove, refrigerators and microwaves, decks and sunrooms. Join us during the 4th of July weekend for Pioneer Days! No pets. *Website: www.ftsresort.com*

Weekly $500-$750

Editor's Note: Basic, clean cottages. Fun fort-style atmosphere. Recent updates to wood/pine exterior/interiors very nice. Some furnishings/appliances showing wear.

KREBS BEACHSIDE COTTAGES   **(989) 856-2876**
MARV & SALLY KREBS   COTTAGE RESORT

★ EDITOR'S CHOICE ★

8 cottages (1-4 bedroom) on open, landscaped grounds with a scattering of trees. Fully furnished with living area, private baths, equipped kitchens with microwaves. Picnic tables and grills. Large wooden deck overlooks 200' of sandy beach with a great view of Saginaw Bay. Open May-Nov. 15. Heated. Hunters welcome. Pets allowed off-season.

Weekly $650 (and up) Reduced/daily rates spring/fall

Editor's Note: Simple, clean, comfortable cottages on spacious grounds, affordably priced with warm and caring owners make this a choice spot to stay — reserve early.

KREBS LANE COTTAGES
DAVE & WENDY KREBS

(313) 886-5752 • (989) 738-8548
COTTAGE RESORT

Set vertically to the water, these 5 clean, well maintained cottages sit on a 300 ft. x 50 ft. lot of sandy beach on Saginaw Bay. Includes equipped kitchens with microwaves and hook-up for cable TV. All units accommodate 6.

Some offer lake views. Bonfire pit. No pets.
Weekly $695-$795

LAKE STREET MANOR

(989) 738-7720
BED & BREAKFAST

Historic brick Victorian. Furnished with antiques and features large bays, high peaked roof and gingerbread trim. Hot tub, in-room movies, private and shared baths. Brick BBQ's and bikes for guests' enjoyment. Fenced 1/2 acre. 5 rooms/queen beds, AC. *Website: www.hometown.aol.com/ lakestreetmanor*
Nightly $65-$75 ($75-$85 Weekends)
Editor's Note: Homey accommodations close to the center of town.

LAKE VISTA MOTEL & COTTAGE RESORT
RON & MARY GOTTSCHALK

(989) 738-8612
EMAIL: lakevista168@yahoo.com
MOTEL/COTTAGE RESORT

★ Luxury Suites - EDITOR'S CHOICE ★

On the shores of Lake Huron and Saginaw Bay. All motel and cottage units with queen size beds. A/C, refrigerators, microwaves, CATV. Deluxe penthouse suites available. Heated pool, guest lau ndry and snack bar. AAA. No smoking/pets. *Website: www.lakevistaresort.com*
Weekly $615-$800
Editor's Note: Beautifully landscaped grounds. We were happy to see some needed renovations to the cottages. Motel rooms are clean and comfy. Their new 'luxury' suites are impressive. See our review in this edition.

RE/MAX SUNRISE ACC.   (866) 738-2255 • (989) 738-2255
INCLUDES: HARBOR PINES CONDOS   PRIVATE CONDO/COTTAGE

★ E D I T O R ' S   C H O I C E ★

Spacious condo and cottage located on the beautiful shores of Lake Huron and Saginaw Bay. Two bedroom condo features fireplace, A/C. Both condo and cottage have fully equipped kitchens. No pets.

Weekly $750 and $850

Editor's Note: Contemporary condominium with lake view ... very nice.

RIVER OAKS COTTAGE   (586) 322-8702
LINDA JACKSON   Email: riveroakscottage@comcast.net
PRIVATE COTTAGE

Newer cottage on 2-acre wooded lot on the river. Hot tub on screened porch. Can sleep 10+. Wood stove. Fully equipped kitchen with dishwasher. Two full baths. Linens included. Washer/dryer, TV/VCR/DVD, CD player, firepit, BBQ and more. Call for pet/smoking policy.

Weekly $850 (and up)   Weekend $268 (and up)

Editor's Note: Appealing vaction cottage tucked away in the woods. Very private setting. Not far from Oak Beach. Very good choice for the area.

THE GARFIELD INN   (800) 373-5254 • EMAIL: garfield_inn@hotmail.com
BED & BREAKFAST

Visited by President Garfield in 1860. Inn features period antiques and premier restaurant. For that special occasion ask about the "Presidential Room". Rooms feature double and queen size beds. Complimentary bottle of champagne. Breakfasts served between 9 am-10 am. Six rooms. *Website: www.garfieldinn.com*

Nightly $110-$120

PORT HOPE

STAFFORD HOUSE   **(989) 428-4554**
GREG & KATHY GEPHART   **BED & BREAKFAST**

Only one block from Lake Huron, this nicely maintained B&B sits on an attractive open treed lot with a lovely backyard wildflower garden. Open year around. Full breakfasts served each morning. 4 rooms with private baths (one suite overlooks garden), CATV and AC.

Nightly $75-$95

PORT SANILAC

RAYMOND HOUSE INN   **(800) 622-7229 • (810) 622-8800**
GARY & CRISTY BOBOFCHAK   **BED & BREAKFAST**

★ EDITOR'S CHOICE ★

500 ft. from Lake Huron and lighthouse, 1871 Victorian Home. 7 large, high-ceiling bedrooms, 5 private baths/2 shared baths, A/C. All in period furnishings. CATV-VCR, in-room phones. Old fashioned parlor/dining room adds to charm. Open year round. Harbor Light Gallery and Gift Shop attached. No smoking/pets. *Website: www.bbonline.com/MI/raymond*

Nightly $65-$115

Editor's Note: Antiques and lovely decor highlight the Raymond House. A very nice choice for the area.

SEBEWAING

RUMMEL'S TREE HAVEN B&B   **(989) 883-2450 • EMAIL: erummel@avci.net**
ERMA RUMMEL   **BED & BREAKFAST**

A 2 room bed & breakfast with full breakfast. Features private baths, cable TV, A/C, refrigerator and microwave. Fishing for perch and walleye. Very good area for hunting duck, goose, deer and pheasant. Personal checks accepted. Open all year. Pets allowed in garage area.

Nightly $40-$55

Editor's Note: Homey lodging with friendly innkeeper who enjoy nature and her guests. Erma makes wonderful breakfasts.

BAY CITY • FRANKENMUTH • SAGINAW

Bay City, well known for its water sports, features a variety of events including speedboat and offshore power boat races. Tour the city's historical sites and view the many stately homes on Center Avenue, Wenonah and Veterans Memorial parks. Come south from Bay City and explore the historic district of **Saginaw**. Take a four-mile river walk, visit a museum or the zoo and stroll among the fragrant rose gardens in downtown parks.

Traveling south from Saginaw, you'll reach the historic town of **Frankenmuth**. The classic Bavarian style of its original settlers can be seen throughout the town's homes, buildings and shops. For many it has become a traditional yearly visit. They come to the more than 100 shops and attractions, stroll the streets, tour the scenic town, sample traditional German cuisine or their famous *all you can eat* chicken dinners. The *Bavarian Inn* and *Zehnder's* still reign as the area's most popular eateries ...and beware, the bakeries are too tempting.

One of the newer shopping adventures in Frankenmuth is The Riverplace Shops. Located on Main Street, visitors can explore 30 specialty shops offering a unique range of gifts and handcrafted items. The Riverplace Shops is also the place to enjoy a nostalgic tour of the Cass River onboard the Bavarian Belle paddle wheel boat. At the close of each night, a special laser light show is given for all to enjoy.

While you're in Frankenmuth, be sure to take a horse-drawn carriage ride through the charming town. And, of course, you must visit Bronner's Christmas Wonderland where holidays are celebrated year around. Spend the night and start shopping early the next morning at the area's largest designer outlet shopping mall, Birch Run.

BAY CITY

CLEMENTS INN
(800) 442-4605
DAVID & SHIRLEY ROBERTS
BED & BREAKFAST

This 1886 Victorian mansion offers 6 comfortably elegant rooms with private bath, TV/VCR and phone. Six fireplaces, central A/C. Enjoy a romantic evening in 1 of 2 whirlpool suites with in-room fireplaces. *Website: www.clementsinn.com*

Nightly $75-$190

KESWICK MANOR   **(989) 893-6598** • EMAIL: innkeepers@keswickmanor.com
BED & BREAKFAST

Relax in the comfort of a traditional English inn. Enjoy stylish decor and unsurpassed personal amenities. Four rooms furnished with heirlooms. Includes multi-room Jacuzzi suite and luxury suite with fireplace. A/C. Full breakfasts. *Website: www.keswickmanor.com*

Nightly $89-$189

FRANKENMUTH

POINT OF VIEW
(989) 652-9845
ED AND BETTY GOYINGS
PRIVATE COTTAGE

★ EDITOR'S CHOICE ★

Completely remodeled two-room cottage includes a Florida Room on the Cass River. Features open great room with original maple floors, fireplace, bar, dinette, furnished kitchen, private bath. Includes CATV, phone, A/C, grill and picnic table. Linens included. Sleeps 6. Children under 12 FREE.

Weekly $400 (based on 1 person/$35 each add'l. person)
Nightly $65 (based on 1 person/$25 each add'l. person)

Editor's Note: Betty has a talent for interior design and it shows in this delightfully cozy cottage. Lovely location.

SAGINAW

BROCKWAY HOUSE BED & BREAKFAST
(989) 792-0746
DICK & ZOE ZUEHLKES
BED & BREAKFAST

On the National Register of Historic Homes, this 1864 B&B was built in the grand tradition of the old southern plantation. Near to excellent restaurants and antique shops. 4 rooms, private baths, A/C. Two-person Jucuzzi suite. Full gourmet breakfast served each morning.

Nightly $95-$225

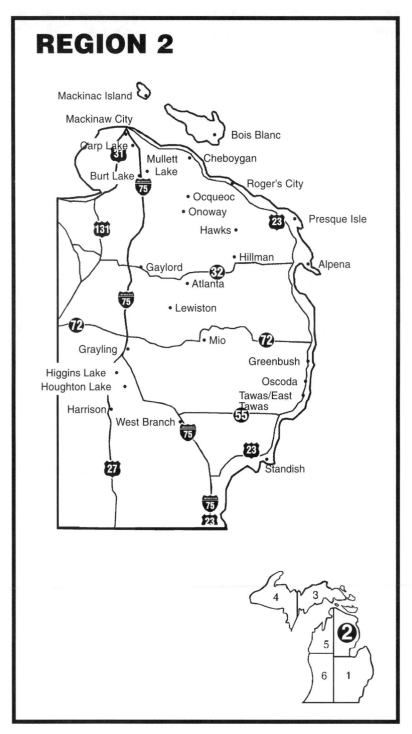

REGION 2

Mackinac Island

Mackinaw City

Carp Lake

Bois Blanc

Mullett
Lake

Cheboygan

Burt Lake

Roger's City

Ocqueoc

Onoway

Presque Isle

Hawks

Hillman

Gaylord

Alpena

Atlanta

Lewiston

Mio

Grayling

Greenbush

Higgins Lake

Houghton Lake

Oscoda

Tawas/East
Tawas

Harrison

West Branch

Standish

STANDISH, OSCODA & THE AUSABLE AREA

COVERS: TAWAS/EAST TAWAS • GREENBUSH • MIO

Settled where the AuSable River meets Lake Huron, these series of communities offer a variety of activities from canoeing and fishing to hiking, hunting, cross-country skiing, and snowmobiling. **Oscoda** is considered the gateway to the River Road National Scenic Byway that runs along the south bank of the AuSable River. **Tawas City** and nearby Huron National Forest offers lakes, beaches and great trails. In July the area features the Summerfest with events and food for the entire family. August is famous for waterfront art fairs, golf tournaments and car shows. September tees off with more golf and Labor Day arts and crafts. During winter season, cross-country ski enthusiasts can enjoy the well-groomed trails at Corseair. In February, the Perchville U.S.A. Festival takes place — be there to enjoy the festivities.

The quaint harbor town of Harrisville offers terrific trout and salmon fishing. The Sturgeon Point Lighthouse Museum, a summer concert series, art and craft fairs, festivals and the Harrisville State Park provide a variety of both summer and winter recreational fun.

Mio, the Heart of the AuSable River Valley, excels in canoeing and winter sport activities. In June they host the Championship Canoe Race and the Great Lakes Forestry Exposition in July. While there, tour the Kirtland warbler nesting area.

To sample some of the area's down home cooking, try *The Bear Track Inn* (AuGres) noted for outstanding breakfast buffets plus a diverse menu including, of course, excellent fish. *H&H Bakery* (AuGres) has developed a proud reputation for their delicious, fresh baked goods with one of their specialties being pizza. *Charbonneau* (on the AuSable in Oscoda) offers a waterfront setting with a diverse menu. Stop by *Wiltse's* (Oscoda) for great food and some of their own micro-brewed beer. Treat yourself to a meal on the water at *Pier 23* (Tawas), known for great fish at moderate rates. Also, in the Tawas/East Tawas area, *Falco Rosso* is known for excellent Italian cuisine. Treat the children (under 12) to free dessert at the *Red Hawk Golf Club*. If your craving a big, juicy hamburger, steak or prime rib, try out *Chums*.

GREENBUSH

SID'S RESORT **(989) 739-7638**
COTTAGE RESORT

★ EDITOR'S CHOICE ★

OFF-SEASON DIS-COUNTED RATES. Also, Discount Coupons available for golf, restaurants, fishing, canoes, tube, kayak, boat rental and Dinosaur Zoo (see our website). Property reviewed and featured in the

1997/98 *Michigan Vacation Guide* as a *"highly recommended Premiere Resort"*. 11 cottages set along a sandy stretch of Lake Huron. 1, 2 or 3 bedroom cottages sleep 2-8. Renovations include cathedral ceilings, knotty pine  walls, lofts, color coordinated furnishings and remodeled kitchens. Amenities include CATV, gameroom, shuffle-board, badminton, playgrounds , picnic areas; watercraft rentals. Open May-Oct. No pets. *Website: www.sidsresort.com*

Weekly $550-$1,325 (Call for nightly/off-season rates, spring and fall specials/packages)

Editor's Note: Sid's continues to be a favorite of ours on Michigan's sunrise side. Excellent beach! Highly recommended. Make reservations early.

STADLER'S SPACIOUS SANDS

(989) 739-9440
COTTAGE RESORT

Lake Huron beach resort features five, two-bedroom (sleeps 6) cottages with private baths, equipped kitchens, ceiling fans, CATV, VCR, private deck, picnic table and BBQ grill. Enjoy the children's playground, game room, shuffleboard court. No pets. Open May 1 - Oct. 31. *Website: www.stadlersspacious sands.com*

Weekly beginning at $550

Editor's Note: Clean, traditionally styled cottage resort with an excellent swimming beach.

SUNNYSIDE COTTAGES
JOHN & DONNA WITTLA

(989) 739-5289
COTTAGE RESORT

★ EDITOR'S CHOICE ★

On the sunny side of Michigan these charming, knotty pine cottages offer equipped, tiled kitchens, microwaves, stove, refrigerator, coffeemaker and utensils. Large living room (some with sofabed), 2 bedrooms or 2 bedrooms and loft. Gas heat. CATV, VCR, BBQ, picnic table and lawn furniture. Close to area activities.

Weekly $500-$1,250

Editor's Note: Comfortably updated resort with a fabulous beach. Another of our 'favorites'. Make reservations early.

MIO

HINCHMAN ACRES RESORT
 (800) 438-0203 (MI) • (989) 826-3267
COTTAGE RESORT

★ EDITOR'S CHOICE ★

AAA Rated Family Resort. Open Aprl-November. There's something for everyone. Summer—weekly family vacations. Rest of year—secluded getaway weekends. 11 cottages (1-2-3 bedrooms), CATV, A/C, fireplaces, phones, kitchens, cribs, swimming, beach, fishing. Enjoy campfires, playground, gameroom, hiking and mountain bike trails. Canoe trips on AuSable River, canoe, tube, raft and kayak rentals. Golf, horseback riding, antique shops and Amish  community nearby. 3 hours from Detroit. No Pets. Brochure. Website: www. hinchman.com

Weekly $550-$675   Nightly $50-$150

Editor's Note: Spacious grounds in a natural setting. The resort offers diverse activities with very clean and well maintained lodgings. Good location for a very good price.

OSCODA

AUSABLE RIVER RESORT
 (989) 739-5246
COTTAGE RESORT

Three clean, fully furnished, two bedroom cottages on the AuSable River. Boat dockage, grills, fire pits, picnic tables. A half mile west of downtown Oscoda. Open May-Nov. Smoking allowed.

Weekly $490   Nightly $70

ANCHORAGE COTTAGES
JIM & SUE MURTON

(989) 739-7843
COTTAGE RESORT

Unpack and relax on our sugar sand beach on Lake Huron. One full house (The Captain's Quarters) and 6 clean and cozy, fully furnished cottages (1-3 bedrooms), with fully equipped kitchens. Grills, picnic tables, bonfire pits, volleyball, tetherball., Open May-Octob er. No pets.

Weekly $500-$1,350

EAST COAST SHORES RESORT
ROY WENNER

(989) 739-0123
COTTAGE RESORT

★ EDITOR'S CHOICE ★

Major renovations completed in 1993-94. Resort rests on 200 ft. of sandy beach, fully furnished, 2-3 bedroom beach front cabins with equipped kitchens (includes microwave, automatic coffeemaker), CATV with HBO, ceiling fans and screened porch. Enjoy volleyball, badminton, bonfires and swimming. No pets.

Weekly $525-$742   Nightly $75-$115

Editor's Note: Owners have done a very nice job renovating this traditional resort.

EL CORTEZ BEACH RESORT

(989) 739-7884
COTTAGE RESORT

On Lake Huron, these 1-2 bedroom cottages and 3 bedroom beach houses offer equipped kitchens, gas heat, linens and CATV. Also availale are BBQ's, picnic tables, shuffleboard, nighly bonfires, and large sandy beach with Tiki Hut. Fish cleaning station. No pets.

Weekly $500-$1,130 (Call for off-season rates)

Editor's Note: Owners have put major effort into updating this resort with good results. The new beach homes are a favorite of ours. Great beach.

HURON SANDS LAKEFRONT CONDO   **(888) 304-7860**
MELANIE BARNARD   EMAIL: **melanie@vacationcondocafe.com**
     VACATION CONDOS

For a memorable getaway, select from several immaculate apealing vacation rentals with many amenities. Unique AuSable River cottage, private two bedroom Lake Huron condo, and Jose Lake cabin with paddleboat offer outstanding accommodations. Year round. Inquire about dogs. *Website: www.vacationcondocafe.com*

Weekly $400-$1,000   Nightly: $99 (and up)

MAI TIKI RESORT   **(800) 231-1875 • (989) 739-9971**
MARINA & ROBERT STOCK   CONDO/COTTAGE RESORT

Unique *tropical setting* on Lake Huron. 1-4 bedroom cottages, 2-bedroom condos. Equipped kitchens, CATV, some cottages with fireplace. All units face the beach and lake. Condos have A/C. Enjoy miles of sugar sand beach, panoramic sunrises/moonrises. Picnic tables, grills, firepit, horseshoes, swingset, game/snack room. Kayak rentals. Handicap access. No pets.

Weekly $800 (Condos)'$475-$1,200 (Cottages)
Editor's Note: New owners are working hard to renovate this long-time resort. Updates still in the process. We'll look forward to seeing what transpires. Great beach area.

SHENANDOAH ON THE   **(989) 739-3997 • (941) 352-4639 (WINTER)**
LAKE BEACH RESORT   COTTAGE RESORT

Six cottages, 2 miles south of Oscoda on Lake Huron w/300' sandy beach. Features 1 and 2 bedroom cottages and 3 bedroom beachhouses. Each has fully equipped kitchen (some w/fireplaces), decks, CATV, recreation area, campfires. Open May-October.

Nightly $55-$175 (call for weekly rates)

THE HURON HOUSE   **(989) 739-9255**
     BED & BREAKFAST

★ EDITOR'S CHOICE ★

Located between Tawas and Oscoda on a beautiful stretch of sandy Lake Huron beach. Accommodations feature panoramic views of Lake Huron, fireplaces, private hot tubs, in-room Jacuzzis and continental breakfast at your door. Glorious sunrises, romantic moonrises. Perfect romantic getaway! *Website: www.huronhouse.com*

Nightly $150-$195
Editor's Note: Beautifully designed rooms, most with exceptional lake views. Charmingly landscaped courtyard. Treat yourself! Highly recommended.

Thomas' Parkside Cottages

(989) 739-5607
Cottage Resort

On Lake Huron with 333 ft. of private beach, the cottages are near the AuSable River. Includes 2, 1 bedroom and 11, 2 bedroom cottages facing the lake with enclosed porches, kitchen with stove and refrigerator, CATV. $100 deposit. No pets. *Website: www.thomasparkside.com*

Weekly $675-$800

STANDISH

Saginaw Bay White's Beach Resort
Floyd & Mary Jo Bender

(989) 846-9684
Email: beachboy3960@yahoo.com
Private Cottage

Year around, completely remodeled, cabin has 3 bedrooms/4 double cedar log beds. On a private lot with Saginaw Bay swimming, fishing, boating right out the door. CATV, full kitchen with microwave, picnic table, firepit, hot tub included. Near golfing and Marina. No smoking. Pets OK outside.

Weekly $500   Daily $85

TAWAS/EAST TAWAS

CHICKADEE GUEST HOUSE
DON & LEIGH MOTT
(989) 362-8006
PRIVATE COTTAGE

★ EDITOR'S CHOICE ★

A few steps from Tawas Bay, the park, playground and beach, and a short walk to lovely shops, restaurants, theatre and pier. A master bedroom (queen bed, chair bed, CATV), a second bedroom (twins, convertible-to-king), a glassed in front porch (trundle daybed) accommodates 7. Open plan includes fully equipped kitchen, breakfast bar, dining area, living room telephone,

CATV and fireplace. Central A/C. Outdoor umbrella table, chairs, gas grill, firepot. Linens, basics provided. Open year round. Website: *www.east-tawas.com*

Weekly $1,050 (and up)   Nightly $165 (and up)

Editor's Note: Leigh has done a lovely job in rejuvenating this cute, old-fashion cottage. Very nice choice for the area. See our review in this edition.

EAST TAWAS JUNCTION B&B
DON & LEIGH MOTT
(989) 362-8006
BED & BREAKFAST

Lovely late 1800's country Victorian home overlooking Tawas Bay on an acre of well-groomed grounds. Five tastefully decorated guest rooms feature Central A/C, private baths, CATV, electric fireplaces. Enjoy freshly prepared, elegantly presented breakfasts in the dining rooms or on the bay view decks. Charming parlor with fireplace and piano. Library, game room with fire-

place. Glassed-in wraparound porch and garden seating encourage relaxation. A hop and a skip to the beach, a few blocks to shops, restaurants, theatre and pier. Seasonal activities, festivals, concerts, scenic tours. *Website: www.east-tawas.com*

Nightly $99-$159

Editor's Note: Invitingly styled home on scenic, park-like setting. Train buffs will enjoy the operating railroad that passes through their front grounds.

RIPTIDE MOTEL & CABINS   **(989) 362-6562**
EMMA & LARRY, MANAGERS   **MOTEL/CABIN RESORT**

On Tawas Bay, this year around motel/cabin resort features large sandy beach, picnic tables, play area, CATV and BBQ grills. In addition to motel rooms, Riptide offers 4, 2-bedroom cabins with equipped kitchens, private baths, linens provided. No pets in summer.

Weekly $270-$540 (cabins assume 6 days)   Nightly $45-$90

SAND LAKE INN WATERFRONT MOTEL & STONE CABINS   **(989) 469-3553**
DON & KELLY KAMMER   **MOTEL/CABIN RESORT**

On Sand Lake ... great beach...great fishing! All units have fully equipped kitchens, CATV, BBQ grills and picnic tables. Row and paddle boats included. Nearby golfing, hiking, bicycling, canoeing, snowmobile and ORV trail. 3 Mile North of M55 and 9 miles west of Lake Huron. *Website: www.sandlakeinn.com*

Weekly $350-$650

Editor's Note: Friendly owners at this quiet, cozy little waterfront lodging. Nothing fancy but clean with panoramic view of Sand Lake. A few steps takes you down to the sandy beach area.

TIMBERLANE RESORT   **(248) 647-9634 • (248) 797-0208**
     COTTAGE RESORT

★ EDITOR'S CHOICE ★

Eight renovated cabins on Tawas Bay, 2-4 bedrooms, 1-2 baths, knotty pine interiors. Sleeps 6 - 14. Some with dishwashers, gas or woodburning fireplaces, whirlpool tub. Equipped kitchens with new appliances. Picnic tables, gas grills. Open all year. Pets extra. *Website: www.timberlaneresorts.com*

Weekly $915-$1,750   Nightly $95-$330

Editor's Note: Impressively renovated cabins. A diverse selection. From luxurious to simple, all are fresh ... even their smallest is cute and welcoming.

WEST BRANCH

CLEAR LAKE RESORT
GREG SCHWARTZ

(989) 345-2459
EMAIL: **Reservations@clearlakeresort.info**
COTTAGE RESORT

Lakefront resort on Clear Lake, an all sports, crystal clear lake that covers over 200 acres. Sandy shoreline and great fishing. Amenities include A/C, CATV, fully equipped kitchen with microwave. Larger home includes dishwasher, VCR, hot tub, fire-

place. Linens included. Open year round. No pets/smoking. *Website: www.mivg.com/clearlakeresort*

Weekly $649-$999   Nighlty $79-$119

ALPENA & THUNDERBAY

INCLUDES: ATLANTA • BLACK LAKE • HAWKS • HILLMAN • OCQUEOC • PRESQUE ISLE • ROGERS CITY

Located on the beautiful sunrise side of Michigan, visitors can enjoy a variety of activities in the **Thunder Bay** area. It's know for underwater ruins of sunken ships from another era. Or, for something a little less exerting, enjoy **Alpena's** "live" theater which presents year around plays and musicals. The area also offers a wildfowl sanctuary, lighthouses, and excellent hunting, fishing, cross-country skiing, and golf. Don't miss July's Brown Trout Festival which lures (excuse the pun...) over 800 fishing contestants to this nine-day event featuring art, food concessions and nightly entertainment.

While in the area, don't forget to visit one of the Lower Peninsula's largest waterfalls, Ocqueoc Falls, in **Rogers City**.

ALPENA

HASSIE COTTAGE (989) 734-2066 (AFTER 4 P.M.)
PRIVATE COTTAGE

One, two-bedroom cottage located on US 23 South. It is midway between Alpena and Rogers City on Grand lake.

Weekly $300

TRELAWNY RESORT (989) 471-2347
COTTAGE RESORT

Resort features 9 attractive, clean and comfortable cottages. They have 200 ft. of white sugar sand beach on Lake Huron's beautiful Thunder Bay with 3 acres of restful grounds and tall pines. On-site laundromat and game room. Cottages have full kitchens and shower-bath. No pets. *Website: www.trelawny-resort.com*

Weekly $450-$550

ATLANTA

BRILEY INN (989) 785-4784
CARLA & BILL GARDNER INN

Redwood inn with impressive windows overlooking Thunder Bay River. Rooms are decorated in Victorian Antique. Great Room, cozy den with fireplace, Jacuzzi, full country breakfast. Canoes and paddleboat available. Central A/C, CATV. Minutes from Thunder Bay Golf Course, Elk Ridge, Garland. Golf packages available. Private baths. 5 rooms. *Website: www.yesmichigan.com/brileyinn/*

Nightly $65-$75

HAWKS

NETTIEBAY LODGE (989) 734-4688
MARK & JACKIE SCHULER COTTAGE/LODGE RESORT

★ EDITOR'S CHOICE ★

Year around on beautiful Lake Nettie. One to 4 bedrooms with full kitchens, living room, private baths (linens available) and lake views. Into bird watching? NettieBay is where you want to go. Join them in classes, seminars and their birding walks. Also enjoy excellent fishing and x-country skiing. No pets.

Weekly $400-$675

Editor's Note: Excellent programs on birding and other outdoor activities. Natural and picturesque setting. Accommodations basic, clean and comfy.

HILLMAN

THUNDER BAY RESORT
(800) 729-9375
CHALET/VILLA & SUITES RESORT

Resort lodging sleeps 4-10 people with kitchens, living rooms, and decks overlooking the golf course. During summer, fall, and winter, the resort features Elk Viewing, Carriage/Sleigh Ride and Gourmet Dinners. Unique event draws rave reviews and can be combined with

the Murder Mystery Weekends, Comedy Weekends, Destination Weddings, Reunions and Corporate Meetings. Superb golf, friendly staff and moderate rates make the resort a great destination for couples, families and golf groups. New full service RV park offers paved, pull-through sites, wireless Internet and CATV. Restaurant/lounge on premises. *Website: www.thunderbayresort.com*

Nightly Package from $48 pp/day

Editor's Note: Premiere golf resort with interesting year around package programs. Wintertime Elk viewing/gourmet dinner program is highly recommended.

OCQUEOC

SILVER ROCK RESORT ON OCQUEOC LAKE
STEVE & VICKI KELLAR
(810) 694-3061
PRIVATE COTTAGE

Ocqueoc Lake is a 132 acre lake twenty miles north of Rogers City and three miles west of Lake Huron. Secluded 2 bedroom cottage with boat, color TV. ORV and snowmobile trails nearby. Great fishing for bass, walleye, pike, trout and salmon. Open all year. No pets.

Call for Rates

ONAWAY

KNOTTY PINE COTTAGES ON BLACK LAKE   **(517) 546-1586**
DON KADE   EMAIL: **Coldonkade@aol.com**
    PRIVATE COTTAGES

Two cottages containing two bedrooms, living room, bathroom and kitchen. Western shore of beautiful Black Lake. Black Lake is 10,000 acres of clea, spring-fed waers. Cottages have 50' lakefront with seawall and 80' dock for swimming, boating, water-sking and fishing. No smoking/pets. Open May-September.

Weekly $650

PRESQUE ISLE

FIRESIDE INN   **(989) 595-6369**
    COTTAGE/LODGE RESORT

Built in 1908, 17 cottages/cabins with private baths, some with kitchen/ fireplace. 7 lodge rooms with private/shared baths. Tennis, volleyball, ping-pong, horseshoes, shuffleboard. Price includes 2 meals daily, in-season. Open spring to fall. Pets OK.

	Rooms	Cottages/Cabins
Weekly	$242*	$286*

* Per adult/children less. Daily Off-season rates available.

Editor's Note: Historic resort located in a quiet, wooded setting. Cottages range in size with several maintained in rustic condition - sparse/basic furnishings.

ROGERS CITY

MANITOU SHORES RESORT   **(989) 734-7233**
BRUCE & COLLEEN GRANT   COTTAGE/MOTEL RESORT

12 acre resort on 600 ft. of Lake Huron. 4 cottages, 4 motel units, 3 log cabins with wood decks. Cottages/cabins include fully equipped kitchens. Log cabins with microwave, dishwasher, fireplace with glass sliding doors. A/C and TV/VCR. Limited handicap access. No pets.

Weekly $450-$900   Nightly $85-$200

MACKINAW CITY • MACKINAC ISLAND

Near the tip of the mitt, **Mackinaw City** is located at the southern end of the Mackinac Bridge and offers ferry service (May-October) to **Mackinac Island**. Known for its sparkling waters and natural beauty, it is visited by thousands of vacationers each year. While in the City, be sure to visit Fort Michilimackinaw. Built in 1715, the Fort was initially used as a trading post by early French settlers before becoming a British military outpost and fur-trading village. Today its costumed staff provide demonstrations and special programs. You'll also want to stop by Mill Creek Park (just east of town). Visit the historic water-powered sawmill and gristmill that recreate one of the first industrial sites. You'll also find ongoing archeological digs and reconstructed buildings here.

One of **Mackinaw City's** most popular attractions is Mackinaw Crossings and the Center Stage Theatre. It's northern Michigan's largest entertainment complex. This brightly painted, Victorian-themed outdoor complex boasts over 50 retail shops, six restaurants, a five-plex theatre, unique butterfly house and an arcade. Every hour (during the season) the outdoor amphitheater offers live entertainment plus a free laser light show every night. To add to this is the 850-seat Center Stage Theatre which features live, Broadway-style shows (tickets: 231-436-4053). If you enjoy miniature golf, check out the one right next to the Crossings. The whole family will love it. Then, for another unique treat, try the century-old *Detroit-to-Mackinac Depot Pub & Grill* which has been charmingly restored to reflect the railroad era of yesteryear.

If you're a walker, don't forget the famous Mackinac Bridge Walk on Labor Day. Join in the joy and celebrations with Michigan's Governor and thousands of others who walk the world's longest total suspension bridge.

Visit **Mackinac Island** and step back in time. This vacation land is a haven for those seeking a unique experience. Accessible by ferry, the Island allows only horse-drawn carriages and bicycles to be used as transportation. Historical and scenic, the Island is filled with natural beauty and boasts a colorful past. Explore Old Fort Mackinac where costumed staff perform period military reenactments and demonstrations. In addition, the Fort has an interpretive center that traces military life on the island during the 1800's. Stop for a refreshment or lunch at the fort's *Tea Room* which offers a wonderful, panoramic view of the straits.

Take a carriage tour, visit nearby historic buildings and homes, browse the many shops, and dine at the many restaurants. Enjoy nightly entertainment, golfing, swimming, hiking, horseback riding, and just relaxing on this Michigan resort island. There are also several fine restaurants on the island.

For an elegant dining experience, try the 107 year old Grand Hotel's formal dining room. Or, on the northwest side of the island, *Woods* is the spot for a romantic, candlelight dinner (located in Stonecliffe mansion built in 1905). For more casual dining with very good food, try the *Point Dining Room* at the Mission Point Resort. *The French Outpost*, near the Grand Hotel, is known for delicious Trapperburgers, there's also evening entertainment. Enjoy your trip to the island ...oh, by the way, don't forget to bring home some fudge.

MACKINAW CITY

THE BEACH HOUSE
(800) 262-5353 • (231) 436- 5353
COTTAGE RESORT

Situateed on 250 ft. of Lake Huron frontage, view the Bridge and Island from these 1-3 bed cottages in Mackinaw City. Units include kitchenettes (no utensils), electric heat, A/C, CATV w/HBO. Coffee and homemade muffics available each morning. Playground, beach, indoor pool and spa on the premises. Small pets OK.

Nightly $44-$160

CEDARS RESORT
(231) 537-4748
EMAIL: **alwaysdreamin@thecedarsresort.com**
COTTAGE RESORT

Four, 2 bedroom cottages on Paradise Lake, just 7 miles south of Mackinaw City. Each unit includes: equipped kitchen, bathroom, gas heat and CATV. Sandy beach - great for swimming. Dock and row boats available for your use. Open all year. Deposit required. *Website: www.thecedardsresort.com*

Weekly $450 (and up)

CHIPPEWA MOTOR LODGE - ON THE LAKE   (800) 748-0124 • (231) 436-8661
COTTAGE/MOTEL RESORT

Motel and 2 bedroom cottage units (double/queen size beds) offered. Features sandy beach, CATV, direct dial phones, indoor pool/spa, sun deck, shuffleboard, picnic area. 1 block from ferry docks.

Nightly $29-$99 (Based on dbl. occ.) Seasonal rates

Editor's Note: Clean and very nicely maintained.

NORTHERN LAKES PROPERTY MGMT.
(800) 641-8944
PRIVATE COTTAGES/CONDOS

Several waterfront condominiums, cottages and houses in Mackinaw City, Burt Lake, Mullett Lake, Black Lake, Long Lake, Lake Huron and Lake Michigan. From 1-5 bedrooms, fireplaces, king/queen/full beds. No pets/smoking. Availability year around.

Weekly $400-$3,800

WATERFRONT INN (800) 962-9832 • (231) 436-5527
COTTAGE/MOTEL RESORT

Sitting on 300 ft. of sandy beach, this facility offers full housekeeping cottages along with its motel units. Amenities included CATV w/HBO, A/C and indoor pool. Picnic and playground area on premises. Bridge and Island view.

Weekly $250-$750* Nightly $29-$99*
Based on double occupancy. Rates will vary depending on season.

MACKINAC ISLAND

BAY VIEW AT MACKINAC (906) 847-3295 • EMAIL: bayviewbnb@aol.com
DOUG YODER BED & BREAKFAST

★ EDITOR'S CHOICE ★

Victorian home offers grace and charm in romantic turn-of-the century tradition. The only facility of its type and style sitting at water's edge. Deluxe continental breakfast served from harbor-view veranda. Private baths. Open May 1-Oct. 25. 20 rooms. Major credit cards. *Website: www.mackinacbayview.com*

Nightly $95-$375

Editor Note: Located in a quiet section on the Island's main road. All rooms have water views. Historic lodging, still owned by decendant's of Fort Mackinac's doctor. Located near the marina. See our review in this edition.

CLOGHAUN (906) 847-3885 • (888) 442-5929
JAMES BOND BED & BREAKFAST

This large Victorian home is convenient to shops, restaurants and ferry lines. Built in 1884, it was the home of Thomas and Bridgett Donnelly's large Irish family. Today guests enjoy the many fine antiques, ambiance and elegance of a bygone era. Open May-Nov. 11 rooms.

Nightly $100-$165 (plus tax)

GREAT TURTLE LODGE

TOLL FREE: (877) 650-4600
BED & BREAKFAST/SUITES

Nestled among tall cedars, the lodge is located on one of the most peaceful spots on the island, near the Grand Hotel and moments from downtown activities. Just a short stroll from magnificent West Bluff sunsets. Rooms/suites

amenities vary to include: Private entrances, 1 or 2 bedrooms, king or queen beds, kitchenettes, CATV/VCR, AC, Jacuzzi. We offer one-of-a-kind Mackinac lilac trees, cloned from centuries-old island lilacs. Open year around. Smoking outside. Call about pet policy.

Website: www.greatturtlelodge.com
Nightly $59-$459

GRAND HOTEL   1- 800-33-GRAND • EMAIL: email@grandhotel.com
HISTORIC RESORT/COTTAGE

★ EDITOR'S CHOICE ★

Historic, luxury resort opened in 1887. Setting for the motion picture, "Somewhere in Time". Rooms designed and decorated with distinction with numerous amenities including mini-bar, in-room safe, CATV, coffeemaker. Masco Cottage features 4-bedroom, private baths, kitchen, living and dining area, media parlor. Full American Plan. *Website: www.grandhotel.com*

Nightly   Beginning at $205 (dbl./pp)

Editor's Note: This is the Island's premier resort. Open up the pocketbook, the Grand is not cheap ... but you'll leave with wonderful memories from an incredible experience.

Haan's 1830 Inn   Summer (906) 847-6244 • Winter (847) 526-2662
Nicholas & Nancy Haan   Bed & Breakfast

Historic home, built in Greek Revival style, furnished in period antiques. The earliest building was used as an inn for Michigan and Wisconsin. Continental breakfast on the wicker filled porch. Featured in Detroit Free Press, Chicago Tribune, Chicago Sun Times and Sears Discovery Magazine. Open May 21-Oct. 18. 7 rooms (5/private baths, 2/shared baths).

Nightly $90-$180

Joe's Island Getaway   (800) 631-5767
Joe Dressler   Private Condo

Enjoy your romantic Mackinac Island stay in our luxurious condo. Old World charm with all of today's amenities. Breathtaking view, Jacuzzi, fireplace, balcony. Hiking, biking, tennis and Grand golf course nearby.

Call for Rates

The Cottage Inn   (906) 847-4000
Email: info@cottageinnofmackinac.com
Bed & Breakfast

Located on Historic Market Street, charming turn-of-the-century inn offers guests an uncompromised standard of hospitality. 11 rooms and suite features pillow-top mattresses, private baths, in-room cable TV/VCR, telephone. Deluxe continental breakfast. Handicap access available. *Website: www.cottageinnofmakinac.com*

Nightly   (beginning at) $100

The Island House Hotel &   (906) 847-3347 • Res. (800) 626-6304
Harbor Place Apartments   Hotel & Apartments

Historic hotel perched on a hilltop overlooking Mackinac harbor. Accommodations feature indoor pool, spa, bar and fine dining. Harbor Place Apartments located separately on Main Street, sleep 4, and feature queen bed, equipped kitchen, washer/dryer, TV and full bath.

Nightly $145 & up (Hotel)*; $200-$250 (Apartments)*

*Reduced rates off-season Metivier Inn   Summer (906) 847-6234

Meitvier Inn   Summer (906) 847-6234 Email: metinn@light-house.net
Ken & Diane Neyer   Bed & Breakfast

Originally built in 1877 and recently renovated, the Inn offers bedrooms with queen size beds, private baths, and one efficiency unit. Relax on the large wicker filled front porch and cozy living room with a wood burner. Breakfast served. Open May-October. 22 rooms. *Website: www.mackinac.com/metivier*

Nightly $115-$285

LAKEBLUFF CONDOS AT STONECLIFFE (800) 699-6927 • (888) 847-0487
MARIANNE O'NEILL/PATRICIA HELD EMAIL: **marianneoneill@mindspring.com**
PRIVATE CONDO

★ EDITOR'S CHOICE ★

*Editor's Note: Lakebluff Condos (**Penthouse Studio, Gardenview, and the 1-2-3 Bedroom Suite**) are beautifully designed in a quiet, scenic setting. Highly recommended. See our review in this edition.*

PENTHOUSE STUDIO SUITE:
Located high atop the West Bluff of Mackinac Island. Beautiful one room suite sleeps two with a solarium overlooking a breathtaking view of the Straits of Lake Huron and the Mackinac Bridge. Cathedral ceiling with skylights, Jacuzzi next to fireplace, private balconies, queen size bed. Small dining area. Kitchen with microwave, bar refrigerator, CATV, TV/VCR. Golf course. Daily maid service. No smoking. *Website: www.yesmichigan.com/lakebluff*

Nightly $225 (In Season); $205 (Off Season) Mid-week, 2 Night Minimum

GARDENVIEW STUDIO SUITE (OAKWOOD BLDG.)
Located high atop the West Bluff of Mackinac Island. Charming one room

suite, sleeps two, features small kitchenette, wet bar, microwave and small refrigerator. Queen size bed, sofa, Jacuzzi with separate shower. Bayed sliding patio doors take you to balcony and overlook of Stonecliffe's gardens and grounds. CATV, TV/VCR. Golf course. Daily maid service. No smoking. *Website: www.yesmichigan.com/lakebluff*

Nightly $165 (In Season); $135 (Off Season) Mid-week, 2 Night Minimum

LAKEBLUFF Continued on next page ...

LAKEBLUFF CONDOS AT STONECLIFFE **(800) 699-6927 • (888) 847-0487**
MARIANNE O'NEILL/PATRICIA HELD EMAIL: **marianneoneill@mindspring.com**
PRIVATE CONDO

★ EDITOR'S CHOICE ★

1, 2 & 3 BEDROOM SUITE
Enjoy panoramic views of the Lake or Bridge from our 1, 2 and 3 bedroom luxurious Mackinac Island suites. Each features bay windows in dining area, sliding glass doors leading to private balcony or patio, well appointed living room with fireplace. Private bath with Jacuzzi and separate shower. Fully equipped kitchens include microwaves and coffeemakers. Available May 22 through October 15. *Website: www.yesmichigan.com/lakebluff*

Nightly $225-$245 (1 Bedroom); $325-$365 (2 Bedroom); $425-$475 (3 Bedroom)

HOUGHTON LAKE • CHEBOYGAN • BOIS BLANC ISLAND

INCLUDES: BURT LAKE • CARP LAKE • GAYLORD • GRAYLING •
HARRISON • HIGGINS LAKE • LEWISTON • MULLET LAKE

Houghton Lake is where fishing enthusiasts and vacationers thrive on one of Michigan's largest inland lakes. Enjoy hunting, boating, water skiing, cross-country skiing, and snowmobiling. Ice fishing for walleyes, bass and bluegill is so good it merits its own annual event. Each year, the Tip-Up-Town U.S.A. Festival (held mid to late January) offers a variety of events including contests, parades and games for the entire family.

Known as the "Alpine Village", **Gaylord** has more to offer than just great downhill and x-country skiing or groomed snowmobile trails. Try their championship golf courses or terrific year around fishing. Nearby, in the Pigeon River State Forest, roams the largest elk herd east of the Mississippi.

Grayling's historical logging background is preserved at Crawford County Historical Museum and Hartwick Pines State Park. Grayling is also the area for canoeing and trout fishing enthusiasts. In fact, the area is known as the Canoe Capital of Michigan. It is the spot for the internationally famous Weyerhaeuser Canoe Marathon which takes place the last week of July. During this event, up to 50 teams of paddlers attempt to finish a gruelling 120-

mile course which can take up to 18 hours to complete. This event is considered one of the most demanding endurance races in any sporting event. Televised broadcasts reach over 150 countries worldwide. The popular AuSable River Festival takes place the week of the Marathon. The festival abounds with numerous activities which include a major parade, juried art shows, antique car shows, ice cream socials, special canoe tours, and several amateur and youth canoe races.

Cheboygan continues the chain of great year around fishing, skiing, snowmobiling, swimming and golf. Be sure to visit Cheboygan's Opera House built in 1877. This restored Victorian theater still offers great entertainment on the same stage that once welcomed Mary Pickford and Annie Oakley.

Seeking an island retreat without all the crowds? **Bois Blanc Island** is your spot. Referred to as Bob-lo by the locals, this quiet, unspoiled island is only a short boat ride from Cheboygan and Mackinac Island. One main road (unpaved) takes you around the Island (cars are permitted). Great for nature hikes, private beaches, boating and relaxing. Here is a community of century homes and a remote lighthouse. While visiting, stop at the Hawk's Landing General Store or the Bois Blanc Tavern and meet some of the warm and friendly year around residents. The island is accessible via ferry boat service (runs several times per day). Be sure to call ahead and reserve a spot if you plan on bringing your car (Plaunt Transportation: 231- 627-2354).

BOIS BLANC ISLAND

BOIS BLANC ISLAND RETREAT
GRAM & LINDA MCGEORGE

(616) 846-4391
PRIVATE COTTAGE

★ EDITOR'S CHOICE ★

Secluded, four bedroom, waterfront cottage on quiet protected bay. Surrounded by white pines and cedar forest. Beautiful view of Lake Huron and the Straits Channel. Cottage offers all the conveniences in a private setting — just bring groceries and fishing pole. Relax, fish, hike, swim, explore. Mackinac Island 30 miles by boat. Open May-Nov. Car ferry. No pets/smoking.

Weekly $675-$875   (Call for off-season weekend rates)

Editor's Note: Comfortable and clean cottage with renovations completed in 1995. Nice island retreat with natural grounds and sandy beach.

BURT LAKE

MILLER'S GUEST HOUSE ON BURT LAKE   (231) 238-4492
JESS & PAM MILLER   PRIVATE HOME

★ EDITOR'S CHOICE ★

Spacious Burt Lake cottage. Built to exacting standards for our personal friends and family. Available for up to 4 non-smoking guests. Complete kitchen, private sandy beach. Brilliant sunsets, quiet wooded atmosphere. Ideal for swimming, sailing, kayaking, bicycling. No pets. Open year around. *Website: www.upnorthlakes.com*

Weekly $950 ($550 off-season)

Editor's Note: Upstairs and above the garage ... this cute, very comfy and really well-maintained lodging was a very nice discovery. Very good choice for the area. See our review in this edition.

SHARON PRESSEY   SUMMER (TOLL FREE) (866) 313-6543 • WINTER (772) 229-1599
PRIVATE COTTAGES

One and 2 bedroom cottages on 150' of Burt Lake's west shore. CATV, gas grills, rowboat, complete kitchens, bedding provided, decks overlooking lake. Sandy bottom for great swimming, beautiful sunrises, wooded setting. Great walleye and bass fishing. Great location 20 minutes north of Petoskey, 20 minutes south of Mackinaw City. Pets OK with approval. Open May-October. *Website: my.voyager.net/~yesserp*

Weekly $550-$1,000 ($400-$575 off-season)

CARP LAKE

STARRY NIGHTS RESORT   (231) 537-3100
VICKIE POWELL   COTTAGE RESORT

Open Year around. On Paradise Lake. Great for reunions and family fun. Located 6 miles south of Mackinac Bridge. Shop till you drop and relax on our sandy beach or take a boat out. Cottages sleep 6, equipped kitchens, private baths, TV. Snowmobile, downhill and cross-country trails nearby. Pets OK.

Weekly $375-$450

CHEBOYGAN & MULLETT LAKE

LAKEWOOD COTTAGES SUMMER **(231) 238-7476** • WINTER **(248) 887-5570**
KEITH R. PHILLIPS COTTAGE RESORT

Clean comfortable 2-3 bedroom cottages located on Mullett Lake, with lake frontage. Screened porches, CATV, carpeted, fully equipped kitchens, showers, picnic tables, grills, boats and motors for rent. Buoys for private boats, swimming, fishing, 24' pontoon boat and evening bonfires. Pets allowed. Open May-Sept.

Weekly $435-$515   Nightly $65-$75

THE PINES ON LONG LAKE   **(231) 625-2121 • (231) 625-2145**
COTTAGE RESORT

Year around resort. 1-3 bedroom cottages face the lake. Private showers. All have stoves, refrigerators, limited utensils, gas heat, blankets/pillows (bring linens). Pets allowed ($10 add'l).

Weekly $325   Nightly $60 (2 night minimum)

VEERY POINTE RESORT ON MULLETT LAKE   **(231) 627-7328**
FRED SMITH & DEBBIE SOCHA COTTAGE/MOTEL RESORT

Lakefront cottages, open year around. Fully furnished (except linens—linens available), includes microwave, CATV/HBO & Disney. Picnic area. Motel with efficiencies (some with A/C) across from lake, beach privileges. Docks. Good fishing, x-country skiing, skating and snowmobiling. Ask about pets.

Weekly $350-$1,200 (Motel: $25-80 Nightly)

GAYLORD

ACORN CABIN   (989) 731-1887 • EMAIL: pineconeacc@core.com
SANDY SNOOK PRIVATE CABIN

An "Up North" getaway with access to Ostego Lake. Short drive to 25 area golf course and shopping. Downtown Gaylord 10-minutes away. Two-bedroom/1bath (sleeps 5-8), features CATV, VCR, fireplace, full kitchen, washer/dryer, charcoal grill, garage. Pets OK. Open year round. *Website: www.pineconevacations.com*

Weekly $700

BEAVER CREEK RESORT   **(877) 295-3333**
THE NATURAL   **CABIN RESORT**

Year round all season resort. Family getaways, golf getaways, or just time to enjoy and relax. Beautiful 1 and 2 bedroom, fully furnished log cabins. 200' waterslide. 18-hole adventure golf course. No pets. Website: www.beavercreekresort.org

Nightly $53-$185

Editor's Note: Excellent golfing and family fun at this impressive resort featuring rustic-contemporary accommodations.

HOFFMAN CEDAR HOME   **(734) 439-7230 • EMAIL: devcat1@aol.com**
PRIVATE HOME

New cedar home on wooded lot. Minutes from top rated golf courses. Large deck with 8 person hot tub and gas grill. Fully furnished, central AC, CATV and VCR. Fully equipped kitchen with microwave, dishwasher. Washer/dryer. Five bedrooms (sleeps 12) with 2.5 baths. No pets/smoking. Weekends negotiable.

Weekly $900

MARSH RIDGE   **(800) 743-PLAY**
HOTEL/TOWNHOUSE/CHALET(LODGE) RESORT

★ EDITOR'S CHOICE ★

A golfer's paradise in Gaylord's golf mecca. Unique decor and themes throughout. Jacuzzi rooms, king and queen size beds, microwaves, refrigerators. Townhouses with full kitchen. Outdoor Thermal Swimming Pool, Pro Shop. Jac's Restaurant and more on premises. No pets.

	Hotel/Suites	Townhouses/Lodge
Nightly	$89 (and up)	$120 (and up)

Editor's Note: Beautifully landscaped golf resort. Popular for executive retreats and conferences.

PORCUPINE LAKE COTTAGE   **(586) 415-8330**
PRIVATE COTTAGE

Two-bedroom cottage (sleeps 6), nestled on 40-acre private beach property on Porcupine Lake (8 miles from Gaylord). Living room includes TV and VCR. Fully equipped kitchen also includes dishwasher and microwave. Washer/dryer. Gas grills and picnic table near campfire ring. Available year around. *Website: www.porcupinelakecottage.com*

Weekly $700

POINTES NORTH　　　　　　　　　　　　**(989) 732-4493**
BETSY BERRY　　　　　　　　　　　　　　**PRIVATE HOMES**

Five private, lakefront vacation homes for day, week or month rental. Sizes vary from 3 to 4 bedrooms. Properties vary from sophisticated country to cozy, log cabin and chalet styling. All are set in secluded locations and come fully furnished and equipped, including rowboat, CATV and telephone. No pets.

Weekly　　　$700-$1,200

Editor's Note: Betsy's lodgings are very comfortable with good locations.

TREETOPS SYLVAN RESORT　　　　**(888) TREETOPS • (989) 732-6711**
　　　　　　　　　　　　　　　CONDO/CHALET/EFFICIENCY RESORT

Standard, deluxe accommodations—condominiums, efficiencies and chalets. 81 holes of championship golf, 19 downhill ski runs and 14 km. of groomed, x-country trails. Dining room, grill and sports bar on premises. Plus indoor/outdoor pools, spas, fitness center, state licensed day care, Edelweiss Ski and Sports Shop.

Nightly　　　$115 (and up)

GRAYLING

BORCHERS BED & BREAKFAST　　　**(800) 762-8756 • (989) 348-4921**
MARK & CHERI HUNTER　　　　　　　　　**BED & BREAKFAST**

★ EDITOR'S CHOICE ★

The friendly hosts at Borchers invite you to enjoy a unique riverfront experience on the banks of the AuSable. Six rooms, twin/double beds (shared baths) and queen beds (private baths). Full breakfasts. Canoe rentals. Smoking permitted on porch. Open year around. *Website: www.canoeborchers.com*

Nightly　　　$59-$69 (shared bath); $64-$89 (private bath)

Editor's Note: This delightful retreat will make a great place to begin your AuSable River vacation.

PENROD'S AUSABLE RIVER RESORT　　　　　　　**(989) 348-2910**
　　　　　　　　　　　　　　　　　　COTTAGE/CABIN RESORT

Established resort on the AuSable River. Noted for its planned river canoe/kayak trips. 13 rustic cabins, most set along the river. All include TV, gas heat, grill and shower. Some with kitchens. Non-kitchen cabins include coffeepot, toaster and dishers. Mountain bike rentals. Opened spring-fall.

Weekly　　　$330-$540　　　　Nightly　　　$55-$90

Editor's Note: One of the area's best noted spots to begin an AuSable River trip. Cabins are clean but rustic with very basic amenities.

TWIN PINE LODGE BED & BREAKFAST　　　**(989) 344-9707**
EMAIL: **twinpinelodge@attglobal.net**
BED & BREAKFAST

Two rooms, each with private entrance overlooking our stocked trout pond and 20 secluded acres on the famous Au Sable River "holy water." *Website: www.twinpinelodge.net*

Nightly　　$75-$100

TWIN PINE LODGE - AU SABLE　　　**(989) 344-9707**
RIVER HOLY WATER　　EMAIL: **twinpinelodge@attglobal.net**
COTTAGES & LODGE

Enjoy premier fly-fishing, bird hunting, cross-country skiing, golf or just relax on 20 secluded, wooded acres along the famed Au Sable River mainstream. Two private cabins and lodge guest rooms accommodate 10 guests Historic Lodge offers luxurious bed and breakfast. No smoking. *Website: www.twinpinelodge.net*

Weekly　　$350-$2,400　　Nightly　　$50-$350

HARRISON

LAKESIDE MOTEL & COTTAGES　　　**(989) 539-3796**
BOBBIE & GARY SAGER　　MOTEL/COTTAGE RESORT

Modern, air conditioned waterfront cottages. Private beach, picnic pavilion/grills, and campfire hearths. One room cottage (2 people) and two bedroom cottages (up to 5 people) available. Renting April-November. Boat/canoe rental also available. No pets. *Website: www.lakesidemotel.com*

Weekly　　$375-$475 (+ tax)

SERENDIPITY INN　　　**989-539-6602**
BILL & LORI SCHUH　　BED & BREAKFAST

Four unique guest rooms, with private baths, provide comfortable, luxurious accommodations. Nestled on 16 wooded acres, walking trails, perennial/herb gardens. Relax in the outdoor Jacuzzi or by the fireplace in the common area. Large suite with fireplace, clawfoot tub. Corporate rates. Smoke free. AAA 2 diamonds.

Nightly　　$55-$175

SNUG HAVEN LAKESIDE RESORT　　　**(989) 539-3117**
EMAIL: **snughaven@charter.net**
COTTAGE RESORT

Fully furnished housekeeping cottages on all-sport Budd Lake. Located on 150 ft. of sandy beach, all cottages have decks, picnic tables and gas grills. Pontoons and fishing boats available for rent. Excellent bass, muskie and pan fishing. *Website: www.snughaven.com*

Weekly $600-$1,200 (peak season, fall/spring discounts); Nightly $75-$150

HIGGINS LAKE

BIRCH LODGE   **(989) 821-6261**
COTTAGE RESORT

50 year old resort on the shores of Higgins Lake. The 9 cottages (2-3 bedrooms with kitchenettes) are simply furnished, maintained in great condition and sit in a semi-circle facing the water. Sandy beach. Gathering room features TV with VCR. Open July-August.

Weekly $610   Nightly $100

Editor's Note: Well established area resort...family owned for over 50 years. Clean, simply-furnished cottages.

CEDAR SHORE CABINS   **(810) 629-6657**
RICK DIXON   **Email: reservations@higginslake.com**
PRIVATE HOME/COTTAGES

Enjoy one of the most beautiful lakes in the world! At the Cedar Shore, you can choose the cottage that's right for you. We have small, medium, or large depending on your needs. Four cottages are located on 150 ft. of lakefront on the northwest shore of Higgins Lake. There is a gravel road that separate some of the cabins from the beach. *Website: www.higginslake.com*

Weekly $1,000-$2,800

Editor's Note: Seven cottages, diverse size and amenities offered, from small cottage to spacious home, are all nicely decorated, comfortable and clean.

MORELL'S HIGGINS LAKE COTTAGE   **(989) 821-6885**
PRIVATE COTTAGE

Overlooking the south end of beautiful Higgins Lake, this immaculate, cozy cottage sits on a nicely wooded lot, is fully furnished w/equipped kitchen, two bedrooms and nursery. Cottage sleeps 5-6. Includes rowboat and a 4000 lb. hoist. No pets.

Weekly $954 (Summer. After Labor Day thru Memorial Day — special rates)

REZNICH'S COTTAGES
(989) 821-9282
COTTAGE RESORT

Clean, comfortable 3, 2 bedroom cottages on Higgins Lake. Carpeted floors, private bath, gas heat and equipped kitchen. BBQ, picnic table and rowboat included in rental price. All cottages are close to the water, one directly overlooks the lake and features knotty pine interior. No pets.

Weekly $625-$700

HOUGHTON LAKE

BAY BREEZE RESORT & MOTEL
MANFRED & DIANE BOEHMER
(989) 366-7721
COTTAGE/MOTEL RESORT

2 large cottages (sleep 6) and spacious kitchenette motel rooms with 2 double beds on Houghton Lake. Private sandy beach, CATV, picnic tables, BBQ grills, horseshoes, boat dockage. Linens provided. Pontoon, boat/motor, wave runners and bicycle rentals available. Open year around.

Weekly $385-$600   Nightly $50-$95 (seasonal rates)

BEECHWOOD RESORT
RICK & ROCHELLE JURVIS
(989) 366-5512
COTTAGE RESORT

★ EDITOR'S CHOICE ★

6 cabins completely renovated or newly built in Sept. 1999 on north shore of Houghton Lake. Exceptionally clean, carpeted. Three rustic log cabins with fireplaces (one, three bedroom; two, two bedroom); three newly built with knotty pine interiors (2 bedroom). All feature quality double beds, sleeper sofas, color TV, private bath/shower, refrigerators, stoves, equipped kitchens, gas BBQ, picnic tables. Coin operated laundry, sea wall, dock, boats, play areas, fire pit, lighted walkways. Minutes from public launch, state land and towns. Handicap friendly. No pets.

Weekly $650 and up

Editor's Note: Quality renovations made to this long-time Houghton Lake resort make this a standout. Fresh, attractively styled. Highly recommended for the area.

THE CREST
(989) 366-7758
COTTAGE/EFFICIENCY RESORT

Lakefront lodgings (3 cottages/3 efficiencies) feature nicely maintained, very clean facilities inside and out! Furnishings in good condition and comfortable. Complete kitchens, picnic table and grill. Ping pong, horseshoes, basketball, paddlewheeler and swim raft. No pets.

Weekly $305-$485

DRIFTWOOD RESORT   RESERVATIONS: (800) 442-8316 • (989) 422-5229
BOB & SHEILA BLESSING   CABIN RESORT

Modern lakefront resort on 2 wooded acres on the north shore. 7 housekeeping cabins (4 log cabins with fireplaces and microwaves) include porches, swings, color TV, full kitchens, electric coffeemakers, 14 ft. boat, picnic table and grill. Excellent playground with basketball, volleyball, horseshoes, swings, etc. Motor and paddle boat rental. Open all year. No pets. *Website: www.driftwoodresort-fun.com*

Weekly $500 and up

HIDEAWAY RESORT
(989) 366-9142
MARYANN PRZYTULSKI   COTTAGE RESORT

A clean and well kept resort on Houghton Lake features 4 cottages (2 bedrooms) with full kitchens. 3 cottages directly face the water. Sandy swimming beach. Rowboat included, dock available. No pets.

Weekly $400-$425

MILLER'S LAKESHORE RESORT   RESERVATIONS: (248) 652-4240
DOUG MILLER   EMAIL: doug@millerslakeshoreresort.com
COTTAGE/CHALET RESORT

Open all year. Good swimming, fishing, hunting, snowmobiling and ice fishing. New chalet with fireplace. Modern lakefront housekeeping cottages. Large unit with fireplace. Boats with cottages. Motor rentals. Dockage. Safe sandy beach. Large playground. Grill and picnic tables. Ice shanty. On snowmobile trails. Located at Tip-Up-Town, Zone 10. 306 Festival Drive. Visitors by approval. No pets. Reservations: Doug Miller, 3639 Pierce, Shelby Twp., MI 49316. *Website: www.millerslakeshoreresort.com*

Weekly $440-$620

MORRIS' NORTHERNAIRE RESORT
(989) 422-6644
Email: northernaire@i2k.com
COTTAGE RESORT

Two bedroom housekeeping cabins on Michigan's largest inland lake. Dock, 14' boat included. Cabins feature all kitchen items, microwave and drip coffeemaker, bathroom/shower, HBO TV. Open all year. Hunting, fishing, snowmobiling, cross-country skiing, water activities. No pets. Mobile Travel Club quality rated. *Website: www.morrisresort.com*

Weekly $330-$700   Nightly $55-$150

REFLECTIONS ON THE LAKE **(989)366-6784**
Email: stay@reflectionsonthelake.com
MOTEL RESORT

Along 180 ft. of sandy beach, motel features one and two bedroom units, some with kitchenettes. All rooms with queen or double beds, microwaves, refrigerators, coffeemakers, telephones and CATV's. All kitchenettes include eating and cooking utensils. Recreation area with swimming beach, boat dock, fire pit, paddle boat, gas and charcoal grills. Pontoon and fishing boat rentals. No pets/smoking. Open year around. *Website: reflectionsonthelake.com*

Weekly $350-$800   Nightly $55-$90

SONGER'S LOG CABINS **(989) 366-5540**
BILL & JILL SONGER COTTAGE RESORT

★ EDITOR'S CHOICE ★

Open year around, these clean and well maintained log cabins are located on the north shore of Houghton Lake with 150' lake frontage. Each two bedroom cabin features fully equipped kitchens, cable TV, private baths, and screened porches. Several have natural fireplaces. Paddle boat, pontoon boat, tether ball, swimming and more. No pets (except for fall).

Weekly   *$675-$775 (summer)   Nightly $100-$120 (winter)
*Rates reduced in winter

Editor's Note: Nothing fancy, just clean and cozy log cabins by the water. A nice choice for the area.

TRADEWINDS RESORT **(989) 422-5277 • EMAIL: tradewinds@i2k.com**
PAUL & KIM CARRICK COTTAGE RESORT

Year around cottages are carpeted, fully furnished with equipped kitchens, private bath/showers, double beds, CATV. Boats included. Motors and pontoon boats available. Spacious grounds with sandy beach. Horseshoes, volleyball, shuffleboard, playground on premises. Provide your own linens and paper products. *Website: www.tradewindsresort.org*

Weekly $475-$525 (off-season rates available)

WOODBINE VILLA **(989) 422-5349 • EMAIL: lpress@i2k.com**
COTTAGE RESORT

Staying at The Woodbine Villa is like taking a step back in time. Experience the charm of the Old Fashion Log Cabins, yet still enjoy all the amenities of home. 9 fully equipped, two-bedroom log cabins. Pontoon boat rental, fishing boats, motors. Nearly 300 ft. beach frontage. Sauna. Expanded cable and much more. MC and Visa accepted. Open year around. *Website: www.woodbinevilla.com*

Weekly $875 (June-Aug.); $595 (Sept.-May); Nightly $95-$125

LEWISTON

GORTON HOUSE BED & BREAKFAST **(989) 786-2764**
LOIS & TOM GORTON **BED & BREAKFAST**

Relaxing, peaceful Cape Cod on Little Wolf Lake. Antique "theme" rooms. Canoe, boats, putting green, 1920 pool table, fireplaces. Gazeboed outdoor hot tub. Bountiful breakfast, chocolate chip cookies. Garland Golf package. XC skiing, snowmobiling, antiquing, mushroom hunting, nearby golf courses. Gaylord 20 miles. Six rooms with private baths. Open all year.

Nightly $75-$130

PINE RIDGE LODGE (989) 786-4789 • EMAIL: PINERIDG@NORTHLAND.LIB.MI.US
DOUG & SUZAN STILES **LODGE**

Grand 7 bedroom log lodge located in the AuSable Forest. Perfect for family holidays, work retreats and couples getaways. Unlimited recreation. Cross-country skiing and mountain biking on-site. Snowshoe rentals, outdoor hot-tub, pool table, fireplace, dart boards and wet bar. Full breakfasts served. Lunch/dinner service upon request. First class amenities with rustic charm. Open year around.

Nightly $54-$89

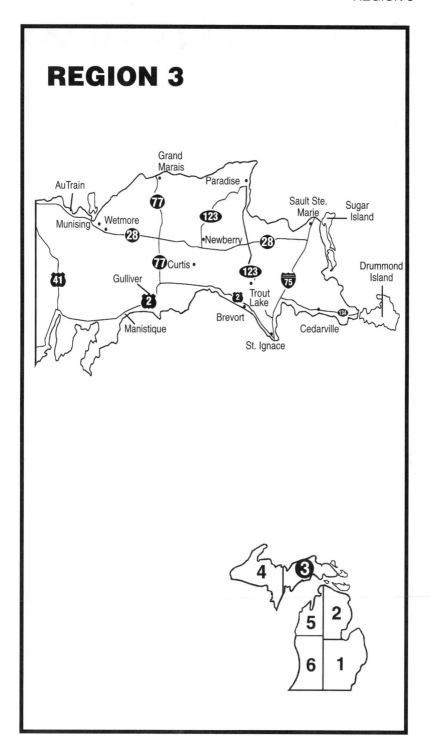

REGION 3

Grand Marais

AuTrain

Paradise

Sault Ste. Marie

Sugar Island

Munising

Wetmore

77

123

28

•Newberry

28

Drummond Island

41

77 Curtis •

Gulliver

123

75

2

Trout Lake

2

Brevort

Manistique

Cedarville

St. Ignace

4 **3**

5 **2**

6 **1**

ST. IGNACE • SAULT STE. MARIE

INCLUDES: BREVORT • CEDARVILLE • DRUMMOND ISLAND • SUGAR ISLAND

St. **Ignace**, established in 1671 by the Ojibwa, Huron, and Ottawa tribes, is the third oldest community in the United States. The French Father, Jacques Marquette, was the first priest at the Mission of St. Ignace and became famous for his travels of the Great Lakes and Mississippi River. He is buried outside a 150 year old church which is now a museum in the Father Marquette State Park, located at the base of the Mackinac Bridge. Native American pow-wows are still held outside the mission church. Some are open to the public with the most popular being held Labor Day Weekend. Be sure to see the Marquette Mission Park and the Museum of Ojibwa Culture where you'll learn about Native Americans at the Straits of Mackinac.

An hour's drive north is **Sault Ste. Marie** (meaning the Rapids of St. Mary), the oldest community in Michigan. The Indians once considered this area their summer gathering and fishing place and the first Jesuit missionaries arrived in 1641. It is often referred to as the Gateway to the North.

Starting at the Sault, you will see the Great Rapids white waters as Lake Superior feeds into Lake Huron. The Soo Locks, an engineering marvel, were built in 1855 to raise or lower vessels up to 1,000 ft. in length through these white waters. Take a boat tour through the Locks, experience the feeling and wonder at the ingenuity of man.

Afterwards, walk the path to historic churches and homes and visit the Tower of History. Of course, you must take time to relax and enjoy one of Lake Superior's many sandy beaches. For all those wanting to give Lady Luck a try, this is also the home of The Kewadin Casino, one of the largest casinos in this region. In winter, this area becomes a snowmobilers' heaven. It's also the spot for many winter festivals and outdoor events.

There are several good restaurants in the Sault Ste. Marie area. *Antler's* has been a favorite among vacationers for years. The atmosphere here is fun and laid back and the decor a taxidermist's fantasy with numerous stuffed wildlife found throughout. Expect loud whistles, bells and plenty of good hamburgers (the menu is a fun read, too). If you have a taste for Mexican, try *The Palace Restaurant* or, for an Upper Peninsula flavor, *Abner's Restaurant* is the spot for a traditional "Yooper's" menu which includes, of course, their special pasty. A quieter atmosphere, with good Italian food can be found at *Ang-gio's Restaurant.*

Accessible by ferry, **Drummond Island** is a wilderness paradise. Its natural beauty and wildlife are protected by state and federal laws. The island features over 110 miles of hiking and snowmobile trails and is a wonderful experience for those seeking peace and quiet in natural surroundings. But don't expect total wilderness here. Excellent golfing and refined accommodations are available at the popular Druummond Island Resort. It served as the Domino Pizza's executive retreat for several years and is now opened to the public.

BREVORT

BREVORT LAKE COTTAGE   **(517) 881-7311 • EMAIL: kwenco1@aol.com**
WENDY KUSLER   **PRIVATE HOME**
Lakefront log home on 140' of Brevort Lake frontage. 2,600 sq. ft. home offers 3 bedrooms, 2 full baths, den, 1st floor laundry, gourmet kitchen, dishwasher, large greatroom with stone fireplace, extensive deck overlooking the lake. Satellite TV, VCR, ceiling fans. Beautiful year-round. No smoking/pets.
Weekly: $1,500-$1,950

CEDARVILLE

ISLAND VIEW RESORT, INC.   **(906) 484-2252 • (800) 854-0556**
LARRY & JACKIE   **COTTAGE RESORT**
Two and 3 bedroom cottages with carpeting, showers, electric heat and ranges, refrigerators, dishes and cooking utensils. Linens furnished except towels and wash cloths. Fish cleaning house and freezer. Children's playground. Good swimming area. Great fishing. Boats and pontoon available. Major credit cards.
Website: www.islandviewresortinc.com
Weekly $600-$715

DRUMMOND ISLAND

BRETT'S HIDE-A-WAY   **(508) 533-6087 • EMAIL: b.basa@verizon.net**
BRETT DAVIS   **PRIVATE COTTAGE**
Log cottage built in 1993. Located in a quiet wooded lot 300 ft. from the road. Fully equipped and furnished. Satellite TV, VCR, ceiling fan. Hot tub.
Website: http://members.bellatlantic.net/~vzeqhxz
Weekly $600   Nightly $125 ($100 off-season; 3 night min.)

CAPTAINS COVE RESORT
DRUMMOND ISLAND REALTY

(906) 493-5344
COTTAGE RESORT

Nine remodeled, 1- 2 bedroom cottages in a wooded area on Gold Coast Shores in the heart of Potagnnissing Bay. Some lakefront cabins with fireplaces. All are completely furnished light housekeeping cottages, automatic heat, bathrooms with showers. Boat included. $100 refundable deposit. No pets.

Weekly $370-$450 (4 people)

CHANNELVIEW CONDOMINIUMS
LARRY HARMON

(906) 493-5885
Email: lharmon@starband.net
CONDOMINIUMS

Relax on the deck, watch the Great Lakes freighters passby. Walk on our sandy beach. Condos feature 4 bedrooms/3 baths (sleeps 10), fireplace, CATV, VCR, full kitchen. Linens provided. Whirlpool tub, hot tub, garage, boat dock. Campfire pit. No pets/smoking. *Website: www.channelviewcondominiums.com*

Weekly $1,200-$1,650

DRUMMOND ISLAND GETAWAY
JAMES & LARRY GOLDMAN

(616) 850-8360 • (616) 240-GOLD
PRIVATE HOME

★ EDITOR'S CHOICE ★

3,000 sq. ft. cedar home on 7.8 private acres. 300 ft. of shoreline on Sturgeon Bay. 10 rooms, fireplace, CATV, VCR. Excellent swimming, boating and water sports. Fantastic snowmobiling in winter. No smoking. Pets allowed. Open year around.

Weekly $2,450 (plus tax)

Editor's Note: Luxury home overlooking Sturgeon make ... a picture-perfect view. Pricey, but well worth it.

DRUMMOND ISLAND RESORT

(800) 999-6343
HOME/LODGE RESORT

★ EDITOR'S CHOICE ★

On 2,000 acres of beautiful woods and waters. Challenging golf at *The Rock*, one of the best courses in the Midwest. Eight homes with fireplaces, full kitchens and 1-5 bedrooms. The Lodge offers 40 rooms. Restaurant on premises. Boats, pontoon rentals.

Nightly $114-$600 (specials starting at $59 nightly)

Editor's Note: Former Domino Pizza executive retreat. Standard hotel rooms to luxurty condos and rustic cabins. Excellent golf and vacation resort.

FORT DRUMMOND MARINE & RESORT (906) 493-5471
BLAINE & KAREN TISCHER COTTAGE RESORT & PRIVATE HOMES
Three cottages on Whitney Bay with equipped kitchens and baths. Linens
included. Dock, fish cleaning house. Also, two private homes with washer/
dryer. One home is spacious (sleeps 10) with hot tub, fireplace, CATV/VCR.
Second home is on a private island, sleeps 6, TV/VCR. Year around.
Weekly $340-$1,300

PAPIN'S LOG CABIN RESORT (906) 493-5254
EMAIL: rbpapin@hotmail.com
CABIN RESORT
Family run resort where friendliness is guaranteed.Located on the shores of Scott's
Bay. Breathtaking sunset views. Log cabins with fully equipped kitchens with
microwaves, TV, private showers. Bed linens and blankets are also provided.
Some with fireplace. *Website: www.papinsresort.com*
Weekly $270-$1,000

ST. IGNACE

BALSAM'S RESORT & MOTEL (906) 643-9121 • SEPT.-JUNE (313) 791-8026
STEVE & SARA MAKOWSKI COTTAGE/MOTEL RESORT
Close to many U.P. attractions. 40 acre woods, sandy Lake Michigan beach,
playground, nature trails and streams. Real log cabins equipped and furnished.
Motel rooms include microwave and fridge. CATV. Pets allowed. Open June-
October. *Website: www.balsamsresort.com*
Weekly $650 (in-season) Nightly $45-$95
*Editor's Note: Clean, rustic lodgings in a wooded setting along the Hiawatha
National Forest. See our review in this edition.*

COTTAGE ON THE STRAITS (651) 646-2915 • (651) 690-0590
JIM & DIANNE MASTERS PRIVATE COTTAGE
Old world charm, modern amenities, and a spectacular view of the Mackinac
Bridge and Island from 100 ft. of private lakeshore. Antiques, wicker, quilts,
fireplace, screened porch. Sleeps 6. Close to shops, restaurants, ferry. Open
year around. No pets/no smoking. *Website: www.upnorth.biz*
Weekly $950 June-Aug. (Call for other rates/times)
*Editor's Note: Clean and cozy interior decor. Owners had fun styling the kitchen
with memorabila from the '50's. Exterior wood deck offers a great view of the
lake and Bridge.*

ISLAND VIEW COTTAGE **(906) 643-6198 • Email: mmgang@nmo.net**
MIKE & JOANNE MCMAHON **PRIVATE COTTAGE**

On Lake Huron overlooking beautiful Mackinac Island. Two-bedroom cottage sleeps up to six and has a fully equipped kitchen, TV, DVD player, gas grill and laundry. Located conveniently to many of the Eastern U.P.'s well-known attractions. Rented May-Sept. No pets/smoking.

Weekly $600

Editor's Note: Cute, immaculate cottage. Nicely maintained with updated kitchen. Sits a bit back from the lake. See our review in this edition.

SAULT STE. MARIE

RIVER COVE CONDOS /HOUSEBOAT RENTAL, **(906) 632-7075**
SCENIC & FISHING CHARTERS **CONDOS/HOUSEBOAT**

★ CONDOS: **E D I T O R ' S C H O I C E** ★

Waterfront, two bedroom condos completely furnished in nautical themes. Handicap access. Also, 34 ft. live aboard dockside houseboat, rented nightly. Great view of passing ships. Two miles from Kewadin casino and Soo Locks. Open May-December. No pets/no smoking. Charters available. *Website: www.rivercove.com*

Weekly $600-$1,100   Nightly $99-$189

Editor's Note: The Tiptons' special touches will make you feel welcomed. Great spot to watch the big ships pass. Contemporary condos. Houseboat is a unique alternative.

SUGAR ISLAND

BENNETT'S LANDING **(906) 632-2987**
COTTAGE RESORT

This fishing resort located on the shores of Big Lake George, has been newly remodeled including a new general store. Cabins are fully equipped. Rent boats, motors, bait. Propane for RVs. Open April 1-Oct. 18.

Weekly $375;   Nightly $65 (rates based on 2 people)

PARADISE • GRAND MARAIS

INCLUDES: BLANEY PARK • CURTIS • GULLIVER • NEWBERRY • TROUT LAKE

As you travel along M123, stop at Hulbert and plan a trip to the Tom Sawyer River Boat and Paul Bunyon Timber Train, or the Toonerville Trolley and River Boat. Both offer 4-1/2 hour round trips to the Tahquamenon Falls with commentary on fauna, flora and various points of interest. Then on to **Paradise**, only 10 miles from the second largest waterfall east of the Mississippi River. It is sometimes called Little Niagara, for here lies Tahquamenon Falls in all its glory. Not far away is Whitefish Point, site of an Audubon Bird Observatory. When you're in the area, be sure to tour the Great Lakes Shipwreck Museum. This is where you will find the "Graveyard of the Great Lakes" and the first Lighthouse of Lake Superior.

Grand Marais is the Eastern Gateway to the Pictured Rocks National Lakeshore. This lovely, unspoiled village offers it all — ladyslippers and trillium, white-tailed deer, black bear, Canadian lynx, moose and — even our own bald eagle resides in this beautiful Upper Peninsula wilderness. As might be expected, boating, fishing, hunting, skiing, and snowmobiling are the thing to do in this area. The Grand Marais Historical Museum, Pictured Rocks Maritime Museum, and the AuSable Lighthouse are some of its attractions. But, of course while you are here, you must be sure to explore their many scenic overlooks including the Log Slide, Munising Falls, Sable Falls and don't forget the unforgettable Tahquamenon Falls and the beautiful Pictured Rocks along Gitche Gumee (Lake Superior). This area is a photographer's dream—bring your camera!

If you're in the **Gulliver** area, enjoy a casual meal at *Fisher's Old Deerfield Inn* which features an informal log cabin atmosphere and quaint dining room.

CURTIS

MANILAK RESORT   **(800) 587-3285 • Email: manilak@direcway.com**
CHALET/HOME RESORT

Relax in luxury. Two miles north of Curtis, 13 chalets or ranch-style homes (sleep 1-8). Carpeted, fireplaces, full baths, fully equipped kitchens, linens, charcoal grills, picnic tables and decks. Overlooks Manistique Lake. Includes rowboat. Activity area. Laundry. Pontoon boat rentals. Open year around. No pets.*Website: www.manilakresort.com*

Weekly $510-$1,177

Editor's Note: A mix of old and new accommodations. The new lodgings look very nice.

THE LOON'S NEST RESORT

(906) 586-3525
COTTAGE RESORT

Nestled along the south shore of Big Manistique Lake on 12 acres of North Country woods, 3 miles west of Curtis. This is a perfect getaway spot with a beautiful setting. There is abundant wildlife, fishing and a great centrally located base to see many UP sightseeing attractions. One, 2 and 3 bedroom cottages include private bath with showers, fully equipped kitchens, CATV, dock and firepit. Also included, 14 ft. aluminum boat. Bring linens. Open all year. No pets, Call or write for a free color brochures. *Website: www.loonsnestresort.com*

Weekly $325-$625   Nightly $65-$125

Editor's Note: Small to medium size lodgings. Clean with nicely maintained exteriors and interiors.

SUNSET PINES RESORT
KAY

(800) 586-3199
CABIN RESORT

Lovely woodland/lakeside setting. Spacious grounds, secluded, quiet. Playground, swim area. Comfortable, very clean, attractively furnished 1-4 bedroom cabins. Fireplace, TV, laundromat (seasonal), grills, posturepedic beds, carpeted. Open year around.

Website: www.curtismi.com/members/sunsetpines/resort.htm

Weekly $495-$745 (Off-season rates available - spring, fall, midweek)

SUNSET POINTE RESORT   (877) 586-9531 (AM) • (906) 586-9527 (PM)
MIKE SODER   CABIN RESORT

NEWLY REMODELED in 2004! Secluded location on Manistique Lake, 3 miles north of Curtis. Newly Remodeled - 4 spacious cottages on 260' of lake frontage. 2-3 bedroom cottages, fully equipped kitchens. 27" Dish TV, VCR/DVD. 40' deck overlooking lake with gas or charcoal grills. Winter packages include

cottages and snowmobile. Outboard motor, pontoon rentals available. Pets OK.
Visit our on-line store at, www.fishandhuntshop.com. *Visit our resort's Website: www.sunsetpointeresort.com*

Weekly $425-$750
Nightly $89-$150

Editor's Note: Clean, basic cottages with private baths/

showers. Nice sitting/play area for adults and children overlooking the lake.

TRAILS END RESORT   (906) 586-3515
TIM & CARMEN   Email: carmentim@hotmail.com
                                                        CABIN RESORT

Five, 2 bedroom housekeping cabins, private showers and cable TV. Linens included (bring towels and washcloths). A 14 ft. aluminum boat included with rental (motors available). Campfire site. Open year around. Pets O.K. Great fishing for walleye, pike, perch and smallmouth bass.

Weekly $400 - $650

Editor's Note: Traditional cabins with nicely maintained exteriors. We found their location appealing ... at the end of a quiet lane overlooking Cooks Bay on Big Manistique Lake.

GRAND MARAIS

HILLTOP MOTEL & CABINS
(906) 494-2331
CABIN/MOTEL RESORT

Five, renovated motel units (2 with kitchenettes). Also 9 furnished house-keeping cabins, 5 are brand new. All include gas heaters, showers and CATV. Outdoor fireplace, grills, picnic and play area. Open year around.

Nightly $50-$90

THE RAINBOW LODGE
(906) 658-3357 • EMAIL: www.rbl2hrt@up.net
RICHARD & KATHY
CABIN/MOTEL RESORT

All new, modern cabins. Full housekeeping services. Each cabin sleeps up to 6 and features a complete kitchen. Linens are furnished ... all you need to do is come! 3-4 day minimum stay required. Canoe, fishing, snowmobile. Open year around. *Website: www.exploringthenorth.com/twoheart/rainbow.html*

Weekly $267-$510

Editor's Note: Remote setting. Very clean, basic lodgings. Rooms lite by gaslight, electricity supplied by on-site generator. A true wildnerness experience.

SUNSET CABINS
(906) 494-2693 • EMAIL: sunset3@jamadots.com
CRAIG WINNIE
CABIN RESORT

Four, newly remodeled, fully furnished cabins (1- 3 bedrooms), along the banks of the old Sucker River overlooking Lake Superior. Equipped kitchens, private bath, full and king si ze beds, CATV. Fire pits, charcoal grills, decks and picnic tables. Open year around. Pets O.K.

Nightly $80-$90   Weekly $480-$540

Editor's Note: If Sunset's other cabins are as appealing as the small, one-bedroom we visited, we are impressed. Fully renovated in 2003. Simply furnished but still comfortable. Park-like setting.

GULLIVER

FISCHER'S OLD DEERFIELD
(906) 283-3169
MARILYN
COTTAGE/MOTEL RESORT

On Gulliver Lake, 21 up-to-date lakeside motel units and housekeeping cottages feature pine paneled walls, bath with shower and automatic heat. Enjoy the private, shallow, sandy beach. Stroll among the well groomed grounds and wooded nature trails. Restaurant, lounge, gift shop, fish cleaning on premises. Open May through November. No pets.

Call for Rates

TOP OF THE LAKE   **(906) 283-3361 • EMAIL: nancy@topofthelake.com**
WALLY & NANCY WARNER   **PRIVATE COTTAGE**

★ EDITOR'S CHOICE ★

Secluded woodland, all-season home. A private, short path through the woods leads to miles of sugar sand beach. Cottage features two bedrooms, fireplace, washer/dryer, full kitchen with dishwasher, water softener. Direct TV, VCR, DVD. No pets/smoking. Open April-December. *Website: www.topofthelake.com*

Weekly $800

Editor's Note: Spacious, beautifully maintained home tucked in the woods. A short path takes you to a fabulous stretch of beach. Highly recommended. See our review in this edition.

NEWBERRY

NORTHCOUNTRY CAMPGROUND & CABINS   **(906) 293-8562**
CATHY CLEMENTZ   **EMAIL: cclementz@lighthouse.net**
       CABINS, LODGE/CAMPGROUNDS

Located on 76 acres, 4.5 miles N. of Newberry on M-123, 1/16th mile to snow-mobile trails. Campground includes 2 room log cabins with rustic charm and modern conveniences, plus Little Lodge. Lodge accommodates a group of up to 6 and has full kitchen, CATV and more. Bedding provided for all units. Two are partially barrier free. Open May 15 through snowmobile season.

Weekly $435-$625   Nightly $65-$100

PARADISE

BIRCHWOOD LODGES   **(906) 492-3320**
STEVE HARMON   **CABIN RESORT**

★ EDITOR'S CHOICE ★

8 modern but rustic log cabins on Lake Superior. Two lakefront cabins with fireplaces. All units carpeted with well furnished kitchens. TV/VCR and movie rentals. Individual picnic tables and grills. All units spotlessly clean, you can bring your mother, and affordable. Shallow all-sand beach with inner tubes, bikes and playground. Paradise is the center of numerous tourist and natural attractions. Check out this year around resort and its accommodating owner since 1981. Late June to September, by-the-week rentals only. No overnights. No pets. *Website: www.harmonsbirchwoodresort.com*

Weekly $360 - $725 (2 people)   Nightly $55-$90

Editor's Note: Simple but comfortable and clean. Steve does a nice job with upkeep. Great sandy beach.

TROUT LAKE

TROUT LAKE RESORT

(906) 569-3810
CABIN/HOUSE RESORT

45 minutes from the Mackinac Bridge in the eastern U.P. Property overlooks Trout Lake. Cabins are well spaced for privacy with a spectacular view. Fully equipped kitchenettes with microwave, color TV. Fishing boat is included. Open year around. *Website: www.troutlakeresort.com*

Nightly $95 (cabins); $125 (house)

TWIN CEDARS RESORT

(906) 569-3209
COTTAGE/MOTEL RESORT

Located in the heart of Hiawatha National Forest, on beautiful Frenchman's Lake — resort provides private setting. Completely furnished, two bedroom cottages, small cabin and plush motel accommodations. Three cottages are lakefront. All, except one, have lake views. Recent additions: individual decks, complete with grill, table/chairs. Boat use included with stay. Large stone patio on water's edge with built-in firepit. Twin Cedars is a small resort and a memorable place, surrounded by Upper Peninsula atmosphere. Close to points and ports of historical interest.

Three of the great lakes, entertainment, and premium shopping. Smoking units available. Sorry, no pets. Well established, family owned and operated.

Call for Rates (Portions of off-season, motel units reduced to $50 for 1 person)

Editor's Note: Nice location, friendly owners. Traditional cottages. The hotel-type accommodations located on the back lot compare to some of the nicer motel rooms we've seen.

AUTRAIN • GARDEN • MANISTIQUE
MUNISING • WETMORE

Just north of **Manistique** you'll find Palms Books State Park, home of the amazing Kitch-iti-kip (Big Spring). It's one of the most unusual water sites in the Upper Peninsula. Take a wooden raft out to the middle of the crystal clear water and watch as more than 23 million gallons of water erupt daily from the lake's bottom.

Looking for a well-preserved ghost town? Then you'll enjoy Fayette Historic Townsite in **Garden**. On the north side of Lake Michigan, Fayette was once a bustling industrial community from 1867 to 1891. Today there are 19 structures standing with a visitor's center, museum exhibits and walking tours .

For you fishermen, stop at either Big Bay de Noc or Little Bay de Noc, rated in *USA Today* as one of the top 10 walleye fishing spots in the country. With nearly 200 miles of shoreline, the bay hosts perch, smallmouth bass, northern pike, rainbow trout, salmon and fishing tournaments. You'll also find uncongested and challenging golf courses, and even a Las Vegas style gambling casino called "Chip-in-Casino". In the winter there are pow-wows and dogsled races.

In **Munising**, take a cruise along the shores of the world famous Pictured Rocks — Miner's Castle, Battleship Rock, Indian Head, Lovers' Leap, Colored Caves, Rainbow Cave and Chapel Rock. Most of these can only be seen from the water. Visiting **Au Train,** you will walk in the footsteps of Hiawatha for, according to Longfellow, here lies his home. Es'ca'naw'ba, from the Indian Eshkonabang, means flat rock. Longfellow's Hiawatha tells of the rushing Escanaba River, sometimes referred to as the land of the Red Buck.

While in the Munising/Au Train area, for good family dining at very reasonable prices, check out *Sidney's* in Munising. Just west of Autrain, *The Brownstone,* is one of the area's more popular restaurant with laid-back UP atmosphere and really great food. Another excellent restaurant is the *Camel Riders* restaurant (2 miles east of county highway 450) reservations are recommended. Just west of Manistique at Highway 2 and 13, *Maxie's* provides a simple but homey Yooper's atmosphere with pretty good steaks.

AUTRAIN

COLEMAN'S PARADISE RESORT **(906) 892-8390**
BILL & MICHELLE COLEMAN **COTTAGE RESORT**
On the west side of AuTrain Lake, this resort offers 1-3 bedroom, furnished cottages. Three bedroom cottages have fireplaces. Large deck overlooks sandy beach. Great swimming. Playground, with horseshoes, volleyball, badminton, basketball. General store and bait shop. Boats and motors available. *Website: www.colemansresort.net*
Weekly $295-$600

DANA'S LAKESIDE RESORT **(906) 892-8333** • EMAIL: info@danasresort.com
AMY HERSTAD **COTTAGE RESORT**
Located in Hiawatha National Forest on the west shore of AuTrain Lake, 3 miles south of M-28. Minutes away from Lake Superior sand beaches, Pictured Rocks National Lakeshore, Grand Island National Recreation Area and Kewadin Casino. Modern 2 and 3 bedroom housekeeping cottages with cable TV hookup. Sand beach, playground, basketball court, shuffleboard. Recreation building with pool table, pinball and video games, air hockey. Washer and dryer available. Boat, motors, kayaks, canoes, and pedal boat available. Lighted boat dock and screened-in fish cleaning house. Campfires in the evenings. Pets welcome. Open all year. *Website: www.danasresort.com*
Weekly   (beginning at) $410

NORTHERN NIGHTS **(906) 892-8225**
HERB & DEBBIE BLACKSTOCK **COTTAGE RESORT**
Cabins on west shore Autrain Lake. 175' of sandy beach. Cottages 1-4 bedroom, all with a view. Bait shop, rec room, washers/dryers available. Boats, motors, canoes, kayable, paddle boats available. Lighted boat dock. Fish claning house. Campfires. No pets. Open all year. *Website: www.cabinsnorth.com*
Call for Rates

NORTHWOODS RESORT **(906) 892-8114** • EMAIL: edkuivanen@chartermi.net
ED & PAM KUIVANEN **COTTAGE RESORT**
Located on the northside of Autrain Lake, in the Hiawatha National Forest, 2 miles from Lake Superior, on a paved road. 1-5 bedroom, housekeeping cottages. Beautiful sandy beach, boats, motors, bait, canoe and kayak livery. Open year around. Small pets welcome. *Website: www.exploringthenorth.com/ northwoods/resort.html*
Weekly $425-$900

PINEWOOD LODGE BED & BREAKFAST   **(906) 892-8300**
JERRY & JENNY KRIEG   **BED & BREAKFAST**
Massive log home overlooking Lake Superior. Relax on decks, gazebo, atrium, great room. Enjoy the sauna and stop at our craft store. Walk miles of sandy beach. Tour Pictured Rocks, Grand Island, Hiawatha National Forest, Song Bird Trail, Seney Wildlife Refuge. Full breakfasts, 5 rooms, private baths. *Website: www.pinewoodlodgebnb.com*
Nightly $105-$140
Editor's Note: On M-28. Country-styled rooms give a rustic, woodsy feel with all the modern conveniences.

SEACOAST COTTAGE   **(800) 555-6792 • (877) 307-6710**

PRIVATE COTTAGE
Lakefront, comfortable, 3 bedroom A-frame located 3.5 miles west of AuTrain/13 Miles west of Munising. Seacoast cottage rests on the shores of mighty Lake Superior. Accommodates 4 adults. Features new furnishings, fully equipped kitchen, CATV, stereo, linens

provided. Open year around. *Website: ww.seacoastcottage.com.*
Weekly $700 and up   Nightly $110 and up

GARDEN

THE SUMMER HOUSE   **(906) 644-2457**
MIKE & NANCY RANGUETTE   **BED & BREAKFAST**
Built in 1874, this two-story farm house has been restored and decorated in Victorian style. It is located on the picturesque Garden Peninsula, just 7 miles from Fayette State Historical Park. Enjoy golfing, swimming, hunting, fishing, hiking and snowmobile trails. Explore area shops or just relax! 4 rooms.
Nightly $45-$75

MANISTIQUE

MOUNTAIN ASH RESORT
(906) 341-5658
COTTAGE RESORT

On beautiful Indian Lake, 2-4 person cabins or 2-3 bedroom deluxe cabins. Fully furnished (except bath towels). Boat included, individual fire pits. Picnic tables, BBQ grills. Grat fishng and water sports. motor and pontoon rentals. Nearby golfing, salmon fishing and casinos.

Weekly $275-$650   Nightly $45-$95

WHISPERING PINES RESORT
(888) 772-1786 • (906) 573-2480
MIKE HOLM
CABIN RESORT

Four modern, fully equipped, two-bedroom cabins on Thunder Lake. One large cabin with fireplace, deck, TV, sleeps eight. Bed linens, boats and canoe included. Fish cleaning shed, docks, firepit, barbecue, horseshoe pits, picnic tables. No pets. Open May-December. *Website: www.manistique.com/resorts/whisper/home.htm*

Weekly $350-$450

MUNISING

JOHNSON COTTAGE
(906) 387-4971
PRIVATE COTTAGE

Immaculate, tastefully decorated, 3 bedroom cottage on 16 Mile Lake, 8 miles south of Munising. Gas fireplace, wood burning stove, TV/VCR, indoor sauna, 2 bathrooms, screened porch. Enjoy all-sport lake, snowmobiling, fishing. Paddleboat and BBQ provided. Cross-country skiing, restaurant within 5 miles. Pets OK with approval. Open all year.

Weekly $800   Nightly $150

RUSTIC RETREAT
(906) 387-4971
PRIVATE LOG COTTAGE

★ EDITOR'S CHOICE ★

Newly renovated, loft-styled log cabin tucked away in the Hiawatha National Forest on all-sport 16 Mile Lake. Very comfortably furnished. TV/VCR. Linens provided. Sun porch with swing. Includes use of rowboat, paddle-boat, BBQ grill, fire pit, wood burning sauna. Swimming beach. Open March-October. Pets O.K. with approval.

Weekly $650   Nightly $125

Editor's Note: Beautifully maintained and very comfortable. Great north country ambiance. Very good price. Highly recommended. See our review in this edition.

WHITE FAWN LODGE   **(906) 573-2949 • EMAIL: hannah@net-link.net**
SANDRA & SCOTT BUTLER   CABIN/LODGE RESORT
In the heart of Hiawatha National Forest, lakeside and wooded area cabins.
Rooms, suites or apartment units. All have microwaves, refrigerator, coffee
makers and color TV's. Community building. Enjoy ATV, hiking and snow-
mobile trails, hunting, fishing, canoeing and waterfalls. Located 2 hours from
Mackinac Bridge/3 hours from Green Bay.
Weekly $375-$450   Nightly $50-$125

WETMORE

CABIN FEVER RESORT   **(800) 507-3341 • (906) 573-2372**
RICK & COLLEEN JOHNSON   LOG CABIN RESORT
On 30 acres, these log cabins are fully carpeted and completely furnished
with log furniture. Each has housekeeping facilities (1 or 2 bedrooms), fully
equipped kitchen and private bath w/shower. Use of boat included. Excellent
snowshoeing, x-country ski and snowmobile trails nearby.
Nightly   *$60 (and up) *based on 3 night minimum

REGION 4

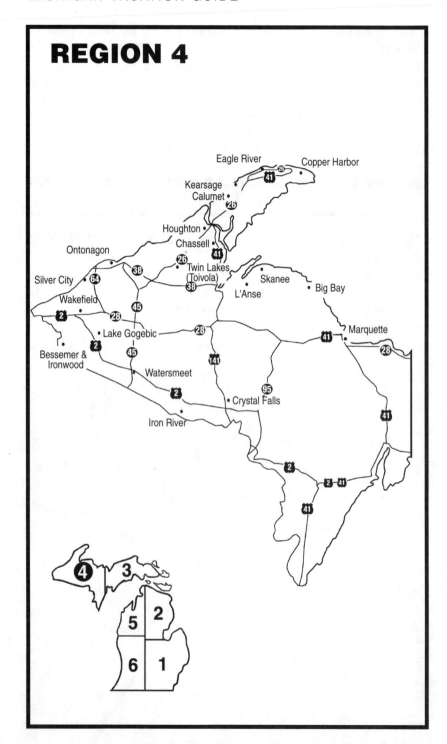

MARQUETTE • KEWEENAW PENINSULA • SILVER CITY

INCLUDES: AHMEEK, BIG BAY • CALUMET • CHASSELL • COPPER HARBOR •
EAGLE RIVER • HOUGHTON • KEARSARGE • L'ANSE • LAURIUM •
ONTONAGON (PORCUPINE MTNS. & LAKE OF THE CLOUDS) • PEQUAMING •
SKANEE • TOIVOLA (TWIN LAKES)

Marquette, one of the oldest cities in the Upper Peninsula, was initially founded in the 1840's by French settlers to serve the iron-ore mining and lumber industries. Visitors to the area will enjoy the 328-acre Presque Isle Park with its extensive cross country and hiking trails or its International Food Festival in July, hosted by Northern Michigan University. There are plenty of historic sites and outdoor activities to fill your day. As you leave Marquette for Copper Country, you'll want to stop at the *Mt. Shasta Restaurant* in the Champion/Michigamme area where several scenes from the 1950's movie, *Anatomy of a Murder,* were filmed. Here you'll find pictures of Jimmy Stewart, Lee Remick and other cast members adorning the walls.

Thrill to a genuine underground adventure—The Arcadian Copper Mines not far from **Houghton/Hancock**. Take a tour and see the geological wonders created eons ago deep inside the earth. Here, too, is a mecca for rock hounds. Then on to the Quincy Mine Hoist (the Nordberg Hoist), the largest steam-powered mine hoist ever manufactured. Not only is the hoist of great interest, but so is the lore of the Quincy Mining Company. You'll have to visit the area to learn more about it.

In **Calumet,** visit Coppertown USA's Visitor Center. It tells the story of mines, communities and the people of the Keweenaw Peninsula. Theater buffs must stop at the Calumet Theatre and walk with the "Greats" — Bernhardt, Fairbanks, and Sousa. While visiting the area, you'll want to stop at *The Old Country House* just two miles north of Calumet known for its fresh Lake Superior fish, prime rib and homemade bread.

Looking to explore a ghost town? Then travel further north to Mandan, between Delaware and Copper Harbor. In the woods, a block or two south of US-41, you'll find what's left of the town, once a bustling community in Michigan's early copper days. A small sign marks the road.

Then continue on, all the way to **Copper Harbor**, at the tip of the peninsula. Here you'll find a charming little village where everything is less than four blocks away. Stop at the Laughing Loon Gift Shop and from there take a tour into the countryside to view the untouched, towering Estivant Pines. Before the tour, stop for breakfast at the *Pines Restaurant* and taste one of their wonderful cinnamon rolls, a local institution , or *Johnson's Bakery* for great rolls and coffee. The aroma alone from these tasty places will add 10 lbs.

Your trip to Copper Harbor is not complete until you dine at the *Keweenaw Mountain Lodge* which provides well prepared meals in a wilderness setting. Once you've replenished yourself, take a tour of historic Fort Wilkins found almost at the tip of the Keweenaw Peninsula on the shoreline of Lake Superior. It was initially built in 1844 to maintain peace in Michigan's Copper Country. Life at the Fort was very difficult with raging waters, frigid winters and heavy snows taking its toll. Much of the Fort's history is retold through museum exhibits, audio-visual programs and costumed interpretation.

Feeling a little more adventurous? You may want to enjoy the Keweenaw Underwater Preserve where a variety of historic sunken shipwrecks can be found. Rent or bring your sea kayak or boat to explore the Keweenaw Water Trail, located along Michigan's northernmost shoreline of Lake Superior.

For a day-long or even overnight trip, take the boat ride to Isle Royale National Park, one of America's few island national parks. There are over 160 miles of hiking trails with varying levels of difficulty. The park offers an amazing,   roadless land of wildlife, unspoiled forests, refreshing lakes, and scenic shores. You will find massive waves exploding along rugged coastlines, lighthouses, rolling hills, thimbleberries, vast pines and hardwood forests. Best of all, you can view both the spectacular sunsets and sunrises no matter where you are. Here is vacation land at its very best.

For your next adventure head south, back through the Keweenaw and west to **Silver City**. Get ready to experience one of Michigan's biggest and most impressive wilderness retreat, the beautiful Porcupine Mountains. In the Porkies you'll find 80 miles of marked hiking trails in the 58,000 acres of mountainous terrain and more than a dozen rustic trailside cabins. Backpacking the "Porkies" is a challenge reserved only for the strong of heart. For those seeking less challenging experiences but still wanting to savor the beauty of nature, there are driving tours. You might also enjoy the 1/4 mile hike up to The Lake of the Clouds overlook with a wonderful, panoramic view of the lake's clear waters surrounded by forest (this is a particularly breathtaking view in the fall). Of course, the Porkies also has excellent Alpine and cross-country skiing along with terrific snowmobiling, fishing, and swimming.

Ready for another ghost town? Perhaps one of the UP's biggest and most interesting is Nonesuch, which covers a number of acres in the southeast corner of the Porkies. Park interpreters often provide guided tours of the site.

AHMEEK

SAND HILLS LIGHTHOUSE INN
906-337-1744
BED & BREAKFAST

★ EDITOR'S CHOICE ★

In the magnificent Keweenaw Peninsula, this 1917 inn is listed on the National Registry of Historic Places. Enjoy 8 Victorian-themed rooms featuring queen or king beds, private baths, A/C, whirlpool bathtubs, balcony overlooking Lake Superior. Open year round. No pets/smoking. *Website: www.sandhillslighthouse.com*

Nightly $132.50-$196.10 (includes tax)

Editor's Note: Picturesque location and unique, theatrical styling of its Victorian rooms make this an interesting choice. See our review in this edition.

BIG BAY

BIG BAY POINT LIGHTHOUSE B&B
JEFF & LINDA GAMBLE
(906) 345-9957
BED & BREAKFAST

★ EDITOR'S CHOICE ★

A secluded retreat. Seven rooms with private baths. Living room with fireplace. Sauna. 1/2 mile of lakeshore and 50 wooded acres for walking. Spa packages. Ideal area for hiking, mountain biking, snowmobiling, cross-country skiing and more. Open year around. Full breakfasts. *Website: www.bigbaylighthouse.com*

Nightly $117-$185 (May-Oct.); $99-$160 (Nov. -Apr.)

Editor's Note: This B&B represents one of the few surviving resident lighthouses in the country. A truly unique experience. Highly recommended.

THUNDER BAY INN
DANA & JOLIE DEMAY
(906) 345-9376
INN

Built in 1911 and renovated by Henry Ford in the 1940's. The Inn was used for filming scenes from "Anatomy of a Murder". 12 guest rooms furnished with antiques. Historic lobby with fireplace. Pub and restaurant on premises. Conference facilities. Gift Shop. Open year around. Private and shared baths. Continental breakfasts.

Nightly $70-$120

Editor's Note: This is a classic inn with well maintained rooms that definitely reflect Henry Ford's styling of the 1940's ... lot's of history here!

CALUMET

CALUMET HOUSE B&B
GEORGE & ROSE CHIVSES

(906) 337-1936
BED & BREAKFAST

In the Keeweenaw Peninsula, built in 1895, B&B features original woodwork, upright piano and antique furniture. Breakfast served in the formal dining room which has an original butler's pantry. Guests can view television in the drawing room by a cozy fire with their evening tea. No smoking/pets. Adults only.

Nightly $30-$35

CHASSELL

THE HAMAR HOUSE

(906) 523-4670
BED & BREAKFAST

1903 Victorian, set on spacious grounds, features 3 rooms with adjoining sunroom and shared bath. Children welcome. Parking for snowmobiles and trailers. Close to shops, lakefront, ski/snowmobile trails. Open year around. Check or cash only.

Nightly $48-$64 (summer); $48-$58 (winter)

MANNINEN'S CABINS

(906) 523-4135 (W) • (906) 334-2518 (S)
CABIN RESORT

The 7 housekeeping cabins, located on 60 acres of land, are very accessible. The cabins, on Otter Lake (well known for outstanding fishing), come with boats. Freezer service. Open May 15-Oct. 1.

Call for Rates

NORTHERN LIGHT COTTAGES
MARGE WICKSTROM

(906) 523-4131
EMAIL: margewickstrom@hotmail.com
COTTAGE RESORT

Three fully furnished cottages on Chassell Bay. Two bedrooms sleep up to 6, bed linens and towels provided. Sandy beach, swimming, fishing, docking space. Boats, sauna and campfire site are available. Rent weekly (Saturday to Saturday). Open May-August. Six miles to Michigan Tech. University.

Weekly $300 (and up)

COPPER HARBOR

BELLA VISTA MOTEL & COTTAGES   (877) 888-8439 • (906) 289-4213
BECKY BRAUN, MIKE & JUDY JUKURI   COTTAGES/MOTEL RESORT
In Copper Harbor, 22 smoking/non-smoking, pet-free motel rooms with beautiful, scenic Lake Suprior frontage and views. 8 housekeeping cottages feature kitchens or kitchenettes. Dogs OK in cabins 1-4, only. CATV. Open mid-May to mid-October. *Website: www.bellavistamotel.com*
Nightly $45-$75

LAKE FANNY HOOE RESORT   (906) 289-4451 • (800) 426-4451
COTTAGES/CHALET/MOTEL/CAMPGROUND RESORT
Lakefront rooms and cottages with kitchenettes and private balconies on Lake Fanny Hooe. Modern campground with rustic and full hook-up sites. Amenities include clubhouse, sandy swimming beach, boat/snowmobile rentals, gift shop/camp store, laundromat, LP gas, playground, fishing, hiking, cross-country skiing, snowmobiling. *Website: www.fannyhooe.com*
Nightly $69-$89

KEWEENAW MOUNTAIN LODGE   (906) 289-4403
CABINS/LODGE RESORT
Log cabins and main lodge nestled in the pines south of Copper Harbor. One, 2 or 3 bedroom cabins, most with fireplaces, and motel rooms. Scenic golf course, hiking trails, tennis court, restaurant and lounge. Discover the tradition.
Nightly $80-$100
Editor's Note: Picturesque comfort in a wilderness setting. Older cottages are basic but comfortable and clean. The restaurant prepares excellent meals.

EAGLE RIVER

EAGLE RIVER'S SUPERIOR VIEW   (906) 337-5110
PAUL   PRIVATE HOME
Three bedroom vacation home overlooking Lake Superior and the Sand Dunes. Sleeps 9 comfortably, 1-1/2 baths, fully equipped kitchen, modern decor. Linens provided. Fireplace, washer/dryer. Full porch. Excellent snowmobiling, skiing, swimming beach and play area. Call for free brochure.
Weekly $650   Nightly $100

HOUGHTON

CHARLESTON HISTORIC INN   **(800) 482-7404**
JOHN & HELEN SULLIVAN   **BED & BREAKFAST**
Circa 1900 Georgian architecture. Ornate woodwork, library with fireplace, grand interior staircase, antique and reproduction 18th Century furniture. King canopy beds, private baths, TV's, telephones, A/C, sitting areas. Suites, some with fireplace, private verandas. Deluxe continental breakfast. Major credit cards. Smoking limited. Children 12+ welcome. AAA approved. *Website:www.charlestonhouseinn.com*
Nightly $118-$168

KEARSARGE

BELKNAP'S GARNET HOUSE   **(906) 337-5607**
                                             BED & BREAKFAST
Enjoy the huge porch and 3 acres of this beautiful mining captain's Victorian home. Unchanged throughout the 1900's. Original fireplaces, fur room, leaded/beveled glass pantries, fixtures, woodwork and servants' quarters. 5 rooms (private/shared baths) are decorated with Victorian theme. Full breakfast. Open mid-June through mid-September. Adults only.
Nightly $60-$90

L'ANSE-PEQUAMING

FORD BUNGALOW   **(906) 524-7595**
ALVIN BRINKMAN, MGR.   **PRIVATE HOME**
★ EDITOR'S CHOICE ★
Henry Ford's summer home. Spacious retreat (over 5,000 sq. ft.), sitting 30 ft. above the shores of Lake Superior in a densely wooded area. 9 bedrooms/6 full baths (sleeps up to 16). Fireplace, linens provided. Rocky/pebble beach. No pets/restricted smoking.
Weekly (7 nights) $2,600; 2 Nights $950; 3 Nights $1,350
Editor's Note: An historic home with plenty of ambiance. Located on a very quiet, private back road with a bluff overlook.

LAURIUM

LAURIUM MANOR INN   **(906) 337-2549** • **EMAIL: innkeeper@laurium.info**

BED & BREAKFAST

★ EDITOR'S CHOICE ★

Opulent 1908 antebellum mansion has 41 rooms, 13,000 sq. ft. (including a ballroom), 5 fireplaces, hand painted murals and gilded leather wall covering. This elegant mansion offers 17 bedrooms (15 private bath, 2 shared bath), whirlpool tubs, king and queen size beds. Tour this mansion and relive the unforgettable wealth that once was Copper Country. No smoking/pets.

Nightly $59-$139 private bath
            $55-$99 shared bath

Editor's Note: Elegant and inviting ... premiere Victorian styled B&B.

MARQUETTE

WHITEFISH LODGE   **(906) 343-6762** • **EMAIL: whitefishl@aol.com**
KAREN & STEVE PAWIELSKI   **LODGE/COTTAGES**

★ EDITOR'S CHOICE ★

A quiet retreat in the U.P. northwoods on the picturesque Laughing Whitefish River. 2 and 3 bedroom lodgings, each completely furnished throughout including kitchens, bedrooms (queen beds) and baths. Enjoy our outdoor decks, grills, excellent walking and biking trails from door. Great fall colors! Five minutes from Lake Superior and close to Pictured Rocks. Open year around. On snowmobile trail and close to x-country ski trails. Gas available on property. 17 miles east of Marquette and 21 miles west of Munising, off M-28. *Website: http://members.aol.com/whitefishl/*

Weekly $350-$675   Nightly $60-$135

Editor's Note: Rustic, secluded, scenic location. Dirt roads ... 4-wheel drive cars recommended in winter. Amiable owners. We enjoyed our stay in their clean accommodations.

ONTONAGON & SILVER CITY (PORCUPINE MTNS. & LAKE OF THE CLOUDS)

A CABIN UP NORTH   (906) 885-5481 • Email: acabinupnorth@yahoo.com
LINDA   PRIVATE COTTAGE

Nestled on 3-1/2 acres and 1,000 ft. private beach, this 2,200 sq. ft. log cabin has 3 bedrooms, 2 baths (sleeps 8 comfortably), jacuzzi tub, satellite TV, VCR, fireplace and full kitchen with dishwasher. Back deck overlooks Lake Superior. No pets. No smoking. Open year around. *Website: www.acabinupnorth.com*

Nightly   beginning at $225

LAKE SHORE CABINS   (906) 885-5318
                                                         CABIN RESORT

Lake Superior beachfront, unique 2-bedroom cabins with private sandy beach, screened porches and swing. Also, 3-bedroom loft cabin, fully equipped kitchen, living room bathroom, screened porch and fireplace. TV, sauna. No pets. To mils from Porkies on M-107. Open year around.

Nightly $79-$128

Editor's Note: Simple but well maintained traditional/rustic cabins. Great beach. A definite "Up North" feel. Cabins with 1/2 baths. Main shower in sauna room.

MOUNTAIN VIEW LODGE   (906) 885-5256
RICK & JENI VARECHA   COTTAGE RESORT

★ EDITOR'S CHOICE ★

Contemporary lakeside cottages, 1 mile from Porcupine Mountains. Ski hill 3 miles. On snowmobile trail. Two bedroom cottages with queen beds. Fully equipped kitchens including dishwasher and microwave. CATV with videoplayer, fireplace. Pets allowed in specific cottages. *Website: www.mountainviewlodges.com*

Nightly $124-$139/2 people

Editor's Note: Built in 1994, these cottages are well designed, very clean and comfortable. Highly recommended for the aera. Great view of Lake Superior.

PETERSON'S CHALET COTTAGES &   **(906) 884-4230 • EMAIL: petcot@up.net**
VACATION HOMES (CHUCK/WENDY PETERSON)   **CHALET/HOME RESORT**

★ EDITOR'S CHOICE ★

On the shore of Lake Superior. 13 chalets with kitchenettes (some with fireplaces) and vacation home (with whirlpool). CATV, phones. Sandy beaches, grills, picnic tables and Porcupine Mountain, gift shop on premises. Major credit cards. Open all year. Some non-smoking units. No pets.

Nightly $85-$130 (Cottages); $300 (Homes)

Editor's Note: Lodgings vary in style and amenities from small to large homes and chalets. All well maintained and comfy...something for everyone.

TOMLINSON'S RAINBOW LODGING   **(906) 885-5348 • (800) 939-5348**
BOB & NANCY TOMLINSON   **CHALET/MOTEL RESORT**

Overlooking Lake Superior and Porcupine Mountains. We offer our guests a variety of accommodations, all extremely well maintained with all the amenities of home. We have a two bedroom Lake Superior beach front home. Chalets, 1 with a 2-person hot tub. Kitchen equipped family suites, country decor motel units and much more.

Call for Rates

Editor's Note: Chalets and motel look very well maintained.

SKANEE

GABE'S SUMMER SUITE COTTAGES   **(906) 524-6619**
BETTE & JOSEPH GABE   **COTTAGE RESORT**

Three charming cottages on private grounds along beautiful Huron Bay. Attractively furnished, meticulously-cleaned. Each lodging features two bedrooms, equipped kitchens, private bath, DDS Satellite TV, fireplace. BBQ grills, picnic tables and outdoor furniture. Safe, sandy beach, dock and fish cleaning area. Open year around. No pets/smoking.

Weekly $385-$465

Editor's Note: Well maintained with attractive interior in excellent condition. Located on quiet, very spacious grounds.

AURORA BOREALIS RESORT
ARLENE & HAROLD RIPPLE

(906) 524-5700
COTTAGE RESORT

★ EDITOR'S CHOICE ★

Four comfortably furnished cottages on the shore of Lake Superior offer a unique experience in the Upper Peninsula. They offer a variety of styles from a 150 year old log building to a traditional cedar sided dwelling. Kitchen facilities are complete and all linens, except beach towels, are provided. Three of the cottages are designed to accommodate wheelchairs. The grounds are lovely with many gardens, and a gazebo is available for use in inclement weather. You are invited to enjoy all of the property including the sandy beach and dock. Open April-December. No pets/no smoking. *Website: www.uppermichigan.com/aurora*

Nightly $65-$85

Editor's Note: From historic to new lodgings, all are nicely appointed, clean and comfy. Unique/fun wood carvings hidden on wooded grounds. A very nice choice for the area.

TOIVOLA /TWIN LAKES

KRUPP'S ALL SEASON RESORT

(906) 288-3404
COTTAGE RESORT

Nine units, 1-3 bedroom, modern, lakefront housekeeping cottages with full kitchens. Boating, fishing, swimming, hunting, ATV, snowmobiling. Golf course and state park nearby. Four RV sites available/full hook-up. Open year around. Groceries and fuel on premises. Pets accepted with stipulations. Major credit cards accepted.

Weekly $250-$550

TWIN LAKES RESORT

(906) 288-3666
COTTAGE RESORT

6 summer homes/cottage, comfortable housekeeping, 2/3 bedrooms. Relaxing, scenic atmosphere. Sandy swimming beach, boats, fishing. Near golf course. Bring your own kayak, canoe, sailboat for quiet sports. Hiking, near state park. Centrally located for exploring the beautiful, historic Keweenaw Peninsula. Open late May to October. Limited pet policy. Reservations appreciated.

Weekly $400-$790

IRONWOOD & SURROUNDING AREAS

INCLUDES: BESSEMER • CRYSTAL FALLS • IRON RIVER • IRONWOOD •
LAKE GOGEBIC • WAKEFIELD • WATERSMEET

Ironwood is known as *The Big Snow Country*. But don't let that fool you, it is more than just winter fun. Here among unspoiled forest and mountains are miles of trout streams and hundreds of spring fed lakes. Visitors will enjoy their vacation on the famous Cisco Chain of Lakes, in Bergland/Marenisco. Bring your camera! Here stands "The World's Tallest Indian"—HIAWATHA. He towers 150 feet over downtown Ironwood. Also, don't miss the Copper Peak Ski Flying Hill in the Black River Recreation Area, 10 miles northeast of Ironwood.

Lake Gogebic is the area's largest lake, with 13,000 acres of prime fishing water. In June, September and throughout the season, fishing tournaments are held. Families will enjoy all sorts of summer fun, sight-seeing, hiking and water sports. Further northeast we come to the Porcupine Mountains Wilderness State Park (15 miles west of Ontonagon).

BESSEMER

BLACKJACK SKI RESORT
(800) 848-1125
CONDO/CHALET RESORT

Trailside lodging units offer ski-in, ski-out convenience. Cozy fireplaces, new TV systems, complete kitchens and saunas in every building. Longest run over 1 mile. PSIA Ski School, Kinderkamp and nursery. Lodgings range from studio to 1-3 bedroom. Special package rates available.

Nightly $49-$109 (per person, per night) Call for special package rates

BIG POWDERHORN LODGING
(800) 222-3131 • (906) 932-3100
CONDO/CHALET RESORT

Luxury to budget conscious private chalets and condos. Ice rink, horse-driven sleigh rides, x-country skiing, pool, special events, trailside decks, and live entertainment. NASTAR, ski school, ski shop, rentals, Kinderschool and cafeteria. 3 restaurants and lounges, sauna/whirlpool, and fireplace. Credit cards accepted. Call for special package and off-season rates.

Nightly   Beginning at $62 ($13 ea. add'l person)

CRYSTAL FALLS

THE LISTENING INN   (906) 822-7738 • EMAIL: carol@thelisteninginn.com

BED AND BREAKFAST

Beautiful handcrafted log lodge on 560 acres of giant pines, open meadows, fabulous hardwood trees. Enjoy miles of trails with rolling terraine and abundant wildlife.

Hiking, cross-country ski trails on-site. Close to George Young Challenge and Blue Ribbon trout streams. Common area includes satellite TV, VCR, game room. Suites feature fireplace, private bath, Jacuzzi tub. Extended stay rooms also available. Full country breakfasts. Open year around. No smoking/pets. Major credit cards accepted. *Website: www.thelisteninginnc.om*

Nightly $89-$109   Weekly $450

IRON RIVER/IRON COUNTY

LAC O'SEASONS RESORT   (800) 797-5226

RANDY & NANCY SCHAUWECKER   COTTAGE RESORT

10 min. from downtown Iron River on Stanley Lake, close to Ski Brule, snowmobile trails. Indoor pool, sauna /whirlpool. 2-3 bedroom cottages, some log, electric heat, full kitchens. Some with fireplaces. Porch, grills with each unit. Boats rentals. No pets. *Website: www.lacoseasons.com*

Weekly $610-$1,510 (plus tax)

PRIVATE LAKE RESORT **(739) 289-2351** • EMAIL: **gaillarner@hotmail.com**
STEVE & GAIL LARNER   PRIVATE COTTAGE

Private lake, 3-bedroom surrounded by 200 acres of forest. Greatroom with fireplace, recreation room with wood stove, piano and bumper pool, full kitchen. TV (no cable) and VCR. No pets/smoking. Excellent bass, walleye and perch fishing. Rented May 25-Sept 25. *Website: www.privatelakeresort.com*

Weekely: $1,060 (6 people)

IRONWOOD

BEAR TRACK CABINS   **(906) 932-2144**
                                     CABIN RESORT

Deep within the west end of the Ottawa National Forest, adjacent to a designated national scenic river. Cabins include kitchens, showers, woodburning stoves, linens. Authentic Finnish wood sauna on premises. Minutes from 5 waterfalls, Lake Superior beach, hiking/mountain biking trails. Located in a true wilderness setting.

Nightly $68-$146

BLACK RIVER LODGE   **(906) 932-3857**
                LODGE/SUITES/CONDOS/TOWNHOUSES/RESORT

Located on Black River Scenic Byway, minutes from 3 ski areas, snowmobile trails, Copper Peak, 5 waterfalls and Black River Harbor. Open year around. Diverse lodgings, indoor pool, hot tub, restaurant, bar, game room. Smoking/non-smoking/pet units. *Website: www.westernup.com/blackriverlodge*

Weekly $300-$680   Nightly $45-$130 (summer); $63-$299 (winter)

Editor's Note: Located in a great four-seasons region, Black River offers very competitive rates, nice amenites and clean accommodations. Good choice for economic-minded outdoor enthusiasts.

RIVER ROCK RETREAT   **(906) 932-5638**
                                     PRIVATE LOG CABIN

Massive log cabin that sets the highest standard for log cabin construction with many special features including hand-hewn red pine logs. Snowmobile right outside your door and snowshoeing. Fully equipped and furnished, 3 fireplaces, 3 baths, 3 living areas, complete kitchen, jacuzzi, sauna, phone, BBQ. Open year around.

Call for Rates

LAKE GOGEBIC

GOGEBIC LODGE   **(906) 842-3321**
BERQUIST FAMILY   **CHALET/COTTAGE RESORT**

CHALETS: ★ EDITOR'S CHOICE ★

West side of Lake Gogebic, cottage and chalet accommodations. Cottages feature private bath, AC, CATV, equipped kitchens, and more! The Lodge includes sauna/whirlpool, dining room/lounge. Boat and motor rentals available. Enjoy hunting, fishing, swimming, snowmobiling and skiing. Credit cards accepted. Pets allowed, extra charge.

Weekly $400-$1,200   Nightly $70-$225

Editor's Note: Very good location. Great for fishing/outdoor enthusiasts. Excellent restaurant on-site. The chalets built are in very nice condition and rate an Editor's Choice.

MALLARD COVE & TEAL WING   **(800) 876-9751**
SNOW COUNTRY REAL ESTATE   **PRIVATE HOMES**

★ EDITOR'S CHOICE ★

Mallard Cove: Four bedroom, two baths with cedar sauna. Accommodates 8. Features phone, fireplace, Weber grill, fully equipped kitchen with dishwasher, linens, towels. Excellent waterfront view. Lakeside deck and boat dock. Groomed snowmobile trails and skiing nearby.

Teal Wing: Contemporary, spacious lakeside home on Lake Gogebic. Four bedrooms, two baths (sleeps 8). Fully furnished and equipped including microwave, phone, TV/VCR, stereo. Includes use of boat dock. Also overlooks Lake

Teal Wing

Gogebic and is located on snowmobile route. Available year around. Pets O.K. Private setting on the lake. *Website: www.snowcountryhomes.com*

Weekly $1,095 (Summer)   Nightly $225 (Winter) (Seasonal Discounts)

Editor's Note: Tom and Arlene Schneller, owners, have designed and decorated these homes with comfort and style.

NINE PINE RESORT
RON & JOANN MONTIE

(906) 842-3361
COTTAGE RESORT

A family resort, centrally located in "Big Snow Country". Snowmobile right to your door. Modern, carpeted housekeeping units (sleep 2-8) with TV. Boats and motors available for rent. 1 cottage with fireplace. Linens provided. Restaurants nearby. Open year around. Major credit cards. Pets allowed.

Weekly $400-$995 (up to 4 people)

SOUTHWINDS COTTAGE (906) 575-3397 • EMAIL: pat@pathansonhomes.com
MARLINE & PAT HANSON PRIVATE COTTAGE

Cozy, clean 2 bedroom cottage on Lake Gogebic with 220 ft. of sandy beach. Private dock. Sleeps 6. All new carpet and furnishings. Fully equipped kitchen with microwave and grill. Private, very quiet. Lovely wood deck overlooks the lake. Rent year around. Snowmobile/watercraft rentals available. No pets.

Weekly $650

SUNNYSIDE COTTAGES
SUE GROOMS

(906) 842-3371
COTTAGE RESORT

★ EDITOR'S CHOICE ★

Set along 450 ft. of Lake Gogebic, these 8 well maintained, comfortably furnished lodgings feature fully equipped kitchens including microwaves, knotty pine interiors, satellite TV, private baths, bedrooms with 1 to 2 full size beds. Doorwalls lead to private deck. Campfires-charcoal grills. *Website: www.sunnysidecottages.net*

Weekly $650-$750

Editor's Note: Spotless cabins with a "luxurious" feel. We continue to be very impressed.

THE TIMBERS RESORT   (906) 575-3542 • EMAIL: ldaniels@portup.com
DAVID & LINDA DANIELS COTTAGE RESORT

Focused on family vacationing, open year around. Located on the north end of Lake Gogebic. Eleven furnished cottages with most of the amenities of home. Enjoy nightly bond fire, playground, trampoline, swim area, laundromat, fish cleaning house, bait, boat and motor rentals. Pets welcome.*Website: www.thetimbersresort.com*

Nightly $60-$260

WEST SHORE RESORT

(906) 842-3336
COTTAGE RESORT

450 ft. on Lake Gogebic. Great fishing for walleye or hunting for bear and deer. All cabins are 2 bedrooms, sleep 6, bath (towels and linens provided). Boat launch on site, docks and boat lifts. Boat and motor rentals. Pets welcome. Open year around.

Weekly $475 (dbl. occ. - $50 each add'l person) Summer Rates
Nightly $70 (dbl. occ. - $10 each add'l person) Summer Rates

Editor's Note: Small but very clean, comfortable accommodations — reasonable prices make this a good choice.

WHITETAIL LODGING (906) 842-3589
PHIL BERCOT **COTTAGE RESORT**

★ EDITOR'S CHOICE ★

Four fully furnished lodges on the east shore of Lake Gogebic. Two hold 4 people, one 8 and another 10. All include knotty pine interiors, full baths, queen size beds, linens, complete kitchens and gas fireplaces. Includes dock space and boatlifts . Fish cleaning house, children's cedar playground set, campfire pits. Great walleye, smallmouth bass and perch fishing, deer and upland bird hunting. Gorgeous fall colors. Snowmobile trail access from the resort. Pets OK. Open all year.
Website: www.whitetaillodging.com

Weekly $750-$1,500; Nightly 125-$250 (May 1-Nov. 3); $45 (per person-winter)

Editor's Note: Fully renovated, nicely furnished cottages with fresh, appealing interiors. Clean and comfortable.

WAKEFIELD

INDIANHEAD MOUNTAIN RESORT (800) 3-INDIAN
 CONDO/CHALET RESORT

Condos, chalets and lodge room with varied amenities including phones, color TV's and/or CATV, VCR's, dishwashers, washers/dryers, Jacuzzi or sauna. Two restaurants, 2 cafeterias, 5 cocktail lounges, indoor pool and spa, health/ racquet club, full service ski shop, child care, Kids 12 and under free. Pets allowed in some units. *Website: www.indianheadmtn.com*

Nightly $75-$498 (from basic lodge room to 5 bedroom chalet)

WATERSMEET

THE ARROWS   (906) 358-4390 • EMAIL: the arrows@portup.com
DENVER & CAROLE YAKEL   COTTAGE/HOME RESORT

Six ultra-modern homes and luxury vacation homes with fireplaces, satellite TV's, double whirlpools, dishwashers, microwaves, washers and dryers, phones, decks, piers and more. On Thousand Island lake on the Cisco Chain in the Upper Peinsula. Sleep up to 15 each. Boat, motor, deluxe boat and pontoon rentals. Snowmobile from door and x-country nearby. Great off-season discounts. LVD casino coupons. *Website: www.watersmeets.org/thearrows*

Weekly $520-$1,435

Editor's Note: Cottage interiors in good condition. The newer homes are very nice. Beautiful, natural setting. Excellent fishing and boating.

CROOKED LAKE RESORT   (906) 358-4421 • Email: crookedlake@portup.com
                                          COTTAGE RESORT

On Crooked Lake in Sylvania Perimeter/Wilderness Area. Motors allowed. Six modern, 2 and 3 bedroom housekeeping cottages. Everything furnised except personal towels. Each cottage comes with a boat or canoe. Dock space available for rent. Motor rental, bait, gas available. Open May 15-November. Pets allowed.

Weekly $555-$850

JAY'S RESORT   (906) 358-4300
                                          COTTAGE RESORT

Lakefront cottages on Thousand Island Lake. Ten, 1-4 bedroom housekeeping cottages, including 2 new log units. Many with fireplaces. Complete kitchen, color TV, sleeps up to 15. Lund boats, deluxe boats and pontoons. Spacious grounds with play area. 20% seasonal discounts. Pets with permission, extra charge. Handicap access.

Weekly $500-$1,650

Editor's Note: Cottage exteriors new — the natural grounds were well groomed. Cute play area for children.

LAC LA BELLE RESORT   (906) 358-4390 EMAIL: the arrows@portup.com
THE YAKELS   HOME/MOBILE HOME/COTTAGE RESORT
Located on Thousand Island Lake on the beautiful Cisco Chain in Michigan's Upper Peninsula. A very modern, four-bedroom home with two baths, dishwasher, satellite TV, VCR, washer and dryer, large deck, pier. Also a modern, two-bedroom mobile home right on the water with pier. Picnic tables, grills. Boats, motors, deluxe boats and pontoon rentals. Fantastic sunsets. Snowmobile from door. LVD canio coupons. *Website: www.watersmeet.org/laclabelle*
Weekly $565-$1,100

VACATIONLAND RESORT   **(906) 358-4380**
BILL & JAN SMET   **EMAIL: vacationland@myvine.com**
                                                COTTAGE RESORT

Fourteen beautifully maintained lakeside cottages located on the Cisco Chain of 15 Lakes. Less than a mile from the Sylvania Wilderness Area; a choice location for cross-country skiing, snowshoeing, hiking and biking. One thousand feet of waterfront with a beautiful swimming beach, raft and diving board. Outside our back door is access to over 2,000 miles of meticulously groomed snowmobile trails. Enjoy horseshoes, tennis and basketball court, sauna, and playground. Vaulted ceilings, skylights, fireplaces, dishwashers, glass doors, and Color DVD/VCR TVs are just some of the features in our cottages. *Website: www.vacationlandresort.com*
Weekly $290-$1,560   Nightly $60-$312

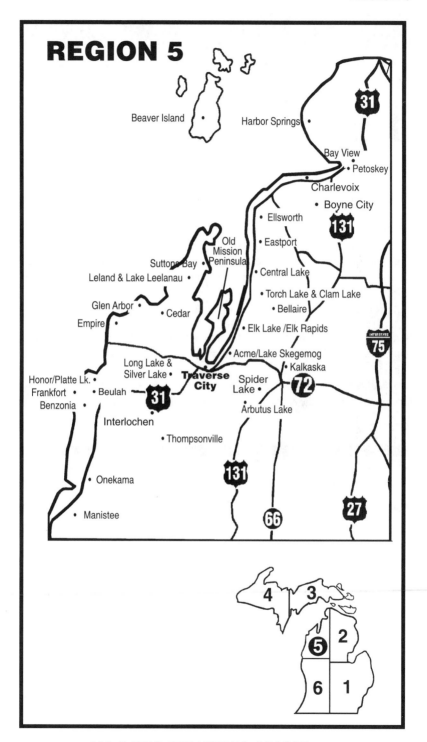

REGION 5

Beaver Island
Harbor Springs
31
Bay View
Petoskey
Charlevoix
Boyne City
Ellsworth
131
Old Mission Peninsula
Eastport
Suttons Bay
Central Lake
Leland & Lake Leelanau
Torch Lake & Clam Lake
Glen Arbor
Bellaire
Cedar
Empire
Elk Lake /Elk Rapids
75
Acme/Lake Skegemog
Long Lake & Silver Lake
Traverse City
Spider Lake
Kalkaska
Honor/Platte Lk.
72
Frankfort
Beulah
31
Benzonia
Arbutus Lake
Interlochen
Thompsonville
131
Onekama
Manistee
66
27

4 3
5 2
6 1

BOYNE CITY • CHARLEVOIX • PETOSKEY

INCLUDES: BAY VIEW • EASTPORT • ELLSWORTH • HARBOR SPRINGS
• LITTLE TRAVERSE BAY • ODEN

The scenic area of **Boyne, Charlevoix, Harbor Springs**, and **Petoskey** offers superb sight-seeing, unique shops, fishing, sailing, and some of the best downhill and cross country skiing in Lower Michigan.

Five linear miles of flower-lined streets, a drawbridge, and two lakes have earned "Charlevoix the Beautiful" its name. The village has become the center for the arts complete with galleries and shops. The spring offers Petoskey Stone and other fossil collectors hours of treasure hunting along its many sandy beaches. Don't forget to visit Petoskey's unique shops in the historic Gaslight District. Harbor Springs' scenic beauty compares to few and includes the very scenic 31 mile route to Cross Village through the Tunnel of Trees. Harbor Springs also features several interesting shops where you'll want to take time to browse. We can't overlook Boyne's high-peaked hills, that provide the scene for some of lower Michigan's finest downhill skiing.

Some outstanding restaurants in the area include *The Rowe Inn* (Ellsworth), *Tapawingo* (on St. Clair Lake) and *Pete and Mickey's* at the *Edgewater* (Charlevoix). For other good fixin's in Charlevoix, try homestyle cooking at *Darlene's*, dine on the lake at *Round Table Restaurant* or, for a Friday night fish-fry, tasty hamburgers, pasties, or Mexican there's the *Lumberjack Saloon*.

BAY VIEW

THE GINGERBREAD HOUSE	(231) 347-3538
MARY GRULER	BED & BREAKFAST

Pastel hues, white wicker and floral gardens provide a romantic setting for this 1881 renovated Victorian cottage situated in the heart of Bay View, a National Historic Landmark. All rooms with view of Little Traverse Bay, private entrances and baths, A/C. Deluxe continental breakfast. No smoking/pets. Open mid-May-October. 4 rooms.

Nightly $115-$175

BOYNE CITY/BOYNE MOUNTAIN

DEER LAKE BED & BREAKFAST　　　　　**(231) 582-9039**
SHIRLEY & GLENN PIEPENBURG　　　　　**BED & BREAKFAST**

★ EDITOR'S CHOICE ★

Contemporary waterfront B&B on Deer lake in quiet country setting. An all season resort area near Boyne Mountain. Features five rooms with private baths, individual heat and A/C. Enjoy full breakfast by candlelight on china and crystal. Personalized jewelry class available.

Nightly　　　$95-$115

Editor's Note: Beautiful setting. Impressively designed interior with gracious hosts. You won't be disappointed.

HARBORAGE CONDOMINIUMS　　**(231) 582-2000 • (888) 285-2111**
RICK SMITH (HARBORAGE PROPERTY RENTALS)　　　　　**CONDOS**

Two and 3 bedroom condos close to Lake Charlevoix and near a full-service marina. Completely equipped and beautifully decorated.

Weekly　　　$1,700-$2,000 (prices exclude holidays)

R & H CHALET　　**(734) 676-1405 • EMAIL: brichards@trenton-mi.com**
BARB　　　　　**PRIVATE CHALET**

Beautiful three bedroom, two full bath chalet, located on Deer Lake at Boyne Mountain in Northern Michigan. All conveniences of home. Fireplace, equipped kitchen, CATV, VCR. 120' lake frontage with beach and dock. Weekly rentals during summer, weekend rentals during ski season. Open year around. No pets.

Weekly　　　$1,000　　　Nightly　　　$200

Editor's Note: Cozy chalet, comfortably styled and competitively priced.

BAY SPRINGS CONDO　　**(734) 675-2452 • (734) 675-2873**
CHRIS SCHADE　　　　　**PRIVATE CONDO**

Spacious, 3-level condo overlooks Lake Charlevoix. Furnished (with linens), sleeps 6. Features king/queen beds, full kitchen, microwave, dishwasher, 4 baths, fireplace, sauna, private beach and dock, balcony, patio, CATV, VCR, washer/dryer. Minimum 1 week. $775 non-refundable deposit per week. No pets. References.

Weekly　　　$ 1,550 ($75 cleaning fee)

THE LANDINGS　　**(800) 968-5115 • (231) 547-1222**
VACATION PROPERTY RENTAL AND MGT. CO.　　　　　**CONDO RESORT**

Two bedroom/2 bath condos on the shores of Lake Charlevoix in the heart of northwest Michigan's recreational playground. Sandy beach, heated pool, boat slips. Only minutes from Boyne Country Championship Golf. An excellent rental value, located in Boyne City. Call early for best availability.

Weekly　　　$1,800

NANCY SERRA

(248) 625-8705
PRIVATE CHALET

★ EDITOR'S CHOICE ★

In prime golf area. Overlooks Lake Charlevoix. Only steps to beach. Conveniently located 2 blocks from marina. Chalet features 3 bedrooms (4 twin, 1 full, 1 queen). All amenities including CATV, BBQ, washer/dryer and linens. Weekly rentals. $300 deposit. No pets. Rental season May-October.

Weekly $750

Editor's Note: Lovely chalet with contemporary Indian motif ... very appealing. Spacious lot with view of lake somewhat obstructed by homes. Good price for the area.

WATER STREET INN
MAIN RENTAL OFFICE

(800) 456-4313
INN/CONDOS

On beautiful Lake Charlevoix, 27 suites with lake views feature living room, dining area, separate bedroom, kitchenettes, gas fireplaces, whirlpool bath, CATV, king size beds. Boating, shopping, fishing or just relaxing and just minutes from ski hills, snowmobile trains, sledding, ice skating and more.

Weekly $1,200   Nightly $75-$200

Editor's Note: Good location and well decorated rooms make this a nice choice.

WOLVERINE/DILWORTH INN
MAIN RENTAL OFFICE

(800) 748-0160 • (231) 582-7388
INN

Built in 1912, the Historic Wolervine Dilworth Inn has 24 rooms with A/C, private baths, suites (multi-rooms), phone and CATV. Inn offers continental breakfast and banquet facilities for weddings and special events. Open year around.

Nightly $129

CHARLEVOIX

AARON'S WINDY HILL GUEST LODGE

(231) 547-6100 • (231) 547-2804
BED & BREAKFAST

Victorian home with a huge riverstone porch. Homemade buffet-style breakfast. Eight spacious rooms have private bath (some with A/C). Two rooms accommodate up to 5. One block north of drawbridge, one block east of Lake Michigan. Children welcome. Open May - Oct.

Nightly $75-$140

ABIDE (231) 547-3545 • EMAIL: beth@stayatabide.com
PRIVATE COTTAGE

Enjoy the magical world of an Earl Young stone 'mushroom' home. Charming, one bedroom cottage across from Lake Michigan's sandy beach, park, lighthouse and breath-taking sunsets. Two blocks to town. Amenities: fireplace, linens/towels, CATV, VCR, equipped kitchen. Pets OK. No smoking. Open May-Oct. *Website: www.stayatabide.com*

Weekly $1,000

BOULDER PARK COTTAGES (231) 547-6480 • EMAIL: charlevoixOK@aol.com
JOAN CHODAK PRIVATE COTTAGES

2 charming stone cottages (1 and 3 bed-room) are located in Earl Young's Boulder Park on 2 acres of land in a park-like setting. Only 800 ft. to Lake Michigan. Includes: linens, dishwashers,  microwaves, phones, VCR, CATV and fireplaces. Outdoor furnishings, campfire, flowers abound. 50% deposit. Pets allowed.

Weekly *$1,200 (1 bedroom); *$1,700 (3 bedroom)
*Plus clean-up. Off-season rates available

Editor's Note: Part of Charlevoix's history. These 2 cottages are built in the style of Earl Young's boulder homes and are located on a quiet side street

THE BRIDGE STREET INN (231) 547-6606
BED & BREAKFAST

Built in 1895, this Colonial Revival home retains the charm of yesteryear. Relax on its sweeping porch with view of Lake Michigan. Seven guest rooms - floral rugs on wooden floors, antique furnishings, plush beds. Breakfast/coffee served on the porch or lounge. *Website: www.bridgestreetinn-chx.com*

Nightly $90-$145 (May to October)

CHARLEVOIX COUNTRY INN (231) 547-5134
BED & BREAKFAST

Visitors will feel welcomed as they enter this 1896 country decor inn. Relax and get acquainted in the common room, balcony or porch while watching boats and Lake Michigan sunsets. 8 bedrooms/2 suites, all with private baths. Continental breakfast buffet. Late afternoon beverage, wine and cheese social.

Nightly $90-$145

HIDDEN VALLEY RESORT

(231) 547-4580 (Leave Message)
COTTAGE RESORT

Quiet, unspoiled resort on 620 ft. of Nowland Lake with natural shoreline. Each cottage has been renovated to retain knotty pine charm and modern conveniences. 1 bedroom (sleeps 4 with pullout), private bath, equipped kitchen, TV, screened porch. Sandy beach, excellent fishing lake.

Weekly $700-$900 (call for 3-4 night rates)

SUE HUMMEL

(248) 855-3300 • (248) 363-3885
PRIVATE CONDOS

Lakefront condos sleep 2-8+ with 1-2 baths, A/C, fireplace, 2 person Jacuzzi and CATV. Designer furnished. Includes linens and towels. Within walking distance to Charlevoix, marinas, beach. Heated pool. Lots of skiing within 1/2 hours. Available year around. 50% deposit.

Weekly $400-$1,200   Nightly $100-$200 (summer rates)

LARRY KISH

(517) 349-5474 (HOME) • (517) 482-7058 (WORK)
PRIVATE HOME

Lake Charlevoix home. 4 bedrooms/2 baths, 128 ft. water frontage, 600 sq. ft. deck, dock, raft, 5 sliding glass doors, lots of windows. Dishwasher, washer/dryer, TV/VCR and stereo. Vaulted ceiling. Fabulous view. Available year around. No pets.

	July & Aug.	June & Sept.	Oct - May
Weekly	$2,975	$2,275	$1,575

LAKEFRONT LOG LODGE
SHARON & AL FROST

(231) 536-2851
PRIVATE HOMES

These 2 spacious, 7 bedroom vacation homes with serene setting offers a spectacular view of Lake Charlevoix. Features 7 full baths, large modern kitchens, CATV, fireplaces, docks, campfire area and swing sets, 3 decks and 200 ft. of sandy beach. Large Jacuzzis. Sleeps up to 28—great for 3 or 4 families. Only 50 ft. from Lake Charlevoix and 5 minutes from town. Great swimming and fishing. Near Boyne Mountain. Available year around. 50% deposit. No pets. *Website: www.greatrentals.com/mi/2211.html*

Weekly $4,000-$6,000 per home (off-season rates available)

POINTES NORTH INN

(231) 547-0055
CONDO RESORT

1-2 bedroom suites with lofts and full or partial kitchens. Indoor/outdoor pool. CATV, A/C, VCR and Jacuzzi whirlpools in all units. Located in downtown Charlevoix. Pets allowed - call for information. Corporate, off-season rates available.

Nightly $240-$325 (2-night min.)

EASTPORT

EDEN SHORES **(313) 417-0331**
GREG & CONNIE SOVIAK **PRIVATE COTTAGE**

Cute cottage sits in a private, wooded area. Cozy, quiet, clean. Bright sunroom with lots of windows. Short drive to Traverse City and Charlevoix's fine shopping and dining. Nestled betwee Torch Lake and Lake Michigan, steps to sandy beach. Updated with full kitchen. Linens provided. No pets/smoking.

Weekly $575

ELLSWORTH

THE HOUSE ON THE HILL B&B **(231) 588-6304**
CINDY & TOM TOMALKA **EMAIL: innkeeper@thehouseonthehill.com**
BED & BREAKFAST

★ EDITOR'S CHOICE ★

This ultimate hostess overlooks peaceful St. Clair Lake. 53 acres with on-property activities including hiking, canoeing and kayaking. Walking distance to gourmet restaurants Tapawingo and Rowe Inn. Evening social hour. Full breakfast. Seven rooms/private bath - king or queen bed. Winter packages. Open all year.

Nightly $150-$200

Editor's Note: Picturesque B&B with beautifully designed rooms. An excellent choice for the area. Highly recommended.

HARBOR SPRINGS

HAMLET VILLAGE **(231) 526-2754 • (800) 678-2341**
C/O LAND MASTERS **HOME/CONDO RESORT**

★ EDITOR'S CHOICE ★

Contemporary country styling located in the secluded, rolling hills of Harbor Springs. Slope side condos features ski-in/ski-out access to Nubs Nob. Condos offer 1-4 bedroom + loft. Homes/chalets (between Boyne Highlands and Nubs Nob) vary in size. A few miles from beaches/marinas/golf. Prices vary based on season and size of accommodation. Full range of pricing options available.

Weekend Pkgs: Beginning at $300

Editor's Note: Scenic locations and well maintained properties make Hamlet Village accommodations a good choice. You Nubs Nob fans will love their condo's ski-in/out privileges.

HOUSE ON THE HILL
ZULSKI BROTHERS

(231) 539-8909
PRIVATE VACATION HOME

★ EDITOR'S CHOICE ★

New home situated on 400 secluded acres. Fully furnished, three bedroom getaway. Close (1/2 hour and less) to golf, skiing, beaches, shopping and dining. Access to groomed snowmobile trails. Scenic views, wildlife and miles of hiking trails. Satellite TV. No pets/smoking. *Website: www.mivg.com/houseonthehill*

Weekly $800

Editor's Note: Spacious, well-designed and abundantly comfortable home resting on secluded, scenic grounds overlooking woods and walking trails. Highly recommended.

KIMBERLY COUNTRY ESTATE
RONN & BILLIE SERNA

(231) 526-7646
BED & BREAKFAST

This colonial plantation style B & B welcomes its guests with a lovely veranda and terrace overlooking the swimming pool and Wequetonsing Golf Course. On several secluded acres. Features 6 exquisitely decorated rooms, some with fireplace, sitting area and Jacuzzi. 4 min. to Boyne Highlands or Nubs Nob.

Nightly $155-$275

THE VERANDA BED & BREAKFAST

(231) 526-0202
BED & BREAKFAST

★ EDITOR'S CHOICE ★

Delightful B&B is as warm and inviting as a Norman Rockwell painting. Guests are treated to a full gourmet breakfast in the morning, and wine with appetizers in the evening. Convenient to shops, restaurants, tennis courts, and beaches. Open year around. 6 rooms. *Website: www.harborspringsveranda.com*

Nightly $125-$295

Editor's Note: Lovely accommodations. Highly recommended. See our review in this edition.

TROUT CREEK CONDOMINIUM RESORT   **(800) 748-0245 • (231) 526-2148**
CONDO RESORT

★ E D I T O R ' S   C H O I C E ★

Family resort with beautifully furnished condos (accommodate 2-10). Each with full kitchen, fireplace, washer/dryer. Enjoy indoor/outdoor pools, spas, fitness center, tennis courts, trout ponds, nature trails, and picnic/playground. Nubs Nob, Boyne Highland Ski areas within one mile. Minutes to premium golf courses, beaches, shopping, restaurants, boating, bike trails and casino. Centrally located to Harbor Springs, Petoskey, Mackinaw, and Charlevoix. 24-hour on-line reservations. Ask about Big 4 Golf Package, romantic, ski, spring and fall package. Sorry, no pets.

Website: www.troutcreek.com

Nightly $110 (and up)

ODEN

WINDJAMMER MARINA   **(231) 347-6103**
HOUSEBOATS

On Crooked Lake, the 40 ft. Royal Capri sleeps 8 includes head with hot water, shower, refrigerator with freezer, gas stove/oven, dishes and utensils. The 28 ft. Riviera Cruiser sleeps 4 and has stove, ice box, porta potty, hand pump water system, dishes and utensils. Deposit required. Rates do not include gas. No linens.

Weekly $1,500 (40 ft.); $750 (28 ft.)

PETOSKEY & WALLOON

EL RANCHO ALANSON   **(586) 777-6808 • EMAIL: donapp@ameritech.net**
LOT 42   RV (RECREATIONAL VEHICLE)

Located 10 minutes from Petoskey. Three bedroom Park Model RV, 12'x35'. Completely carpeted and furnished, ceiling fans, satellite TV, VCR. Full size bath/kitchen. 80 acre resort grounds feature swimming pool, tennis/basketball courts, shuffleboard, horseshoes. Waterfront and skiing nearby. Open year round. No pets/smoking.

Weekly $400   Nightly $65

BARBARA OR MARTHA MOYERS   (303) 499-4089 • EMAIL: martymoyers@attbi.com
PRIVATE COTTAGE

Walloon Lake frontage on 6 acres of mature forest. 2,304 sq. ft. home features 4 bedrooms, 2 baths (sleep 10), full kitchen with dishwasher and microwave, plus mini-kitchen on lower level. TV/VCR, phone, fireplace. Deck overlooking trees and lake. On 200 sq. ft. of shoreline. Firepit and sandy beach. Large dock with sandy bottom at end of dock. No weeds, gradual slope, swimming rafts. No pets/smoking.

Weekly $2,300 (late June-Aug.) Off-season rates & shorter says in the fall.

THE TERRACE INN   (800) 530-9898 • Email: info@theterraceinn.com
BED & BREAKFAST

Historic inn features 43 unique rooms decorated with original antiques and one-of-a-kind art. All with private baths. Continental plus breakfast. Deluxe

rooms include A/C. Jacuzzi suite available. Complimentary bicycles, showshoes. Private Lake Michigan beach just 150 yards away. Tennis courts.TV room with CATV/VCR. Enjoy special seasonal programs, including Murder Mystery, Sleigh Rides, Jazz, Women's Only Pamper and Victorian weekends. Spa packages. Lovely dining room featuring fresh Michigan produce and eclectic menus. Open year around. No smoking/pets. *Website: www.theterraceinn.com*

Nightly $59-$109

WILDWOOD ON WALLOON   (231) 582-9616
MAIN OFFICE - RESERVATIONS   CONDO RESORT

Lovely townhouse community near the borders of Walloon Lake. Enjoy 3 professionally designed holes of golf and two carefully sited tennis courts private beach. Contemporary units vary in design and sleep 6-12, up to 5 bedrooms, 2 bath with fully equipped kitchens. Amenities frequently include fireplace, TV/VCR. No pets.

Weekly (summer) $1,500-$1,900

Editor's Note: On well groomed grounds surrounded by trees, the units we visited varied in decor but maintained a very comfortable, contemporary theme.

TRAVERSE CITY & SURROUNDING AREAS

INCLUDES: ACME • ARBUTUS LAKE • BELLAIRE • BENZONIA • BEULAH • CEDAR • EAST BAY • ELK LAKE/ELK RAPIDS • FRANKFORT • GLEN ARBOR • GRAND TRAVERSE BAY • HONOR • INTERLOCHEN • KALKASKA • LAKE LEELANAU • LAKE SKEGEMOG • LELAND • LONG LAKE • NORTH PORT • OLD MISSION PENINSULA • PLATTE LAKE/PLATTE RIVER • SILVER LAKE • SPIDER LAKE • SUTTONS BAY • THOMPSONVILLE • TORCH LAKE • WEST BAY

From beautiful sunsets and lazy days on a sandy beach to the rush of down-hill skiing—**Traverse City** and the surrounding areas have a variety of fun and exciting activities in a setting of blue water, rolling hills, and natural beauty. Dining, shopping, entertainment, and even gambling will fill your days and nights.

One of the City's biggest events is the annual Cherry Festival, held the week of July 4th. Thousands of people come to the area to enjoy parades, concerts, fireworks, air shows, Native American pow-wows and crafts along with other family activities. If you're interested in coming by, we highly recommend you plan well in advance for this very popular event.

Enchanting **Interlochen** is a wonderful place to visit throughout the year. You'll want to stroll along its cool waters, scented pines and natural grounds. Here you'll find the internationally known Interlochen Center for the Arts and the Interlochen Fine Arts Camp. Here gifted young artists (ages 8-18) develop their creative talents with concentrated studies in their specialized areas of theatre, painting, sculpturing, music and more. In addition to over 750 student performances yearly, the Interlochen Center for the Arts also hosts a variety of nationally known music and recording artists. From classical and folk to jazz, blues and pop, the diversity of music continues to attract area residents and visitors from across the world. For performance and ticket information, call (231) 276-6230.

Want to try something a little *lifting*? Get a really scenic view of the Traverse City area from a hot-air balloon. You'll be awed by views of **Elk and Torch Lakes, East and West Grand Traverse Bay**, Manitou and Fox islands, to name a few. Contact the area Chamber of Commerce (see Chamber section of this book) for further information.

The 70,000 acre Sleeping Bear Sand Dunes National Lakeshore is another must see while visiting the area. Drive south along M-22 through the charming communities of **Leland** and **Glen Arbor**. The Pierce Stocking Scenic Drive (closed in mid-November) is a relaxing and enjoyable car tour. Of course, hiking the dunes in the park has become a fun challenge for youngsters of all ages. And, if you still have energy after getting to the top, take a short walk across the sand to a wonderful overlook of Lake Michigan.

The **Leelanau Peninsula** and **Old Mission Peninsula** are known for their beautiful scenery. They're also known as *wine country*. Winery tours and tasting have become a popular day time diversion for many. Check out our "Michigan Wineries" section for further information.

Feeling like Lady Luck is on your side today? Then put on that lucky hat and head out to one of two area casinos. The Leelanau Sands Casino is 20 miles north of Traverse City near **Suttons Bay**; and the Turtle Creek Casino is four miles east of **Acme** in Williamsburg. Our Michigan "Casinos" chapter provides phone numbers and addresses of casinos in this area and throughout Michigan.

Take a ride on the Malabar, a two-masted schooner. Then drop by The Music House north of Traverse on US-31 (Acme) to enjoy a unique museum where history, education and entertainment combine.

Just about time to eat? There are many popular restaurants in the area. Just a few: *Poppycock's* (on Front Street in downtown Traverse City) is known for inventive dinner entrees, fresh pastas and unique salads (we personally recommend their Front Street Salad). Others include *Hattie's Grill* or *Boone's Prime Time Pub* (Suttons Bay); *Trillium* (Grand Traverse Resort); *Boone's Long Lake Inn; Sweitzer's by the Bay* (Traverse City); *Scott's Harbor Grill* (M-22 on Sleeping Bear Bay Beach); *LeBear* (M-22 in Glen Arbor); *Bluebird* (Leland); or *Stubbs* (Northport). *Windows* (on West Bay Shore Drive, north of Traverse City), though pricey, has developed a reputation for preparing some of the area's finest cuisine. *Spencer Creek Fine Dining* in the **Torch Lake** area (also higher priced) prepares creative and diverse fare with a very distinctive Italian flavor and, being on Torch Lake, the view is wonderful.

For tasty and inexpensive "eats" give *Art's Tavern* a try (**Glen Arbor**) for breakfast, lunch or dinner. Their special 1/3 pound ground chuck burger with bacon, blue cheese along with homemade chili (not too spicy) is quite good. For good pizzas and burgers in a country-styled family restaurant, try *Peegeos Restaurant* in the **Spider Lake** area. *Mabel's* (in Traverse City, on Front Street) is known for freshly prepared baked goods and traditional homemade meals. For a fun 50's decor atmosphere and to re-discover the taste of good old-fashioned hamburgers, *Don's Drive-In* is definitely a dandy choice.

We can't forget the *Grand Traverse Dinner Train* for a truly unique dining experience. You'll enjoy a four-course lunch or five-course gourmet dinner while touring the scenic Boardman River Valley area. For additional information on the dinner train, call (231) 933-3768.

ACME

GRAND TRAVERSE RESORT **(800) 748-0303 • EMAIL: info@gtresort.com**
AND SPA **CONDO RESORT**

★ EDITOR'S CHOICE ★

Along Grand Traverse Bay. Studio, one-, two- and three-bedroom condos with kitchens, some with whirlpool baths, fireplaces. Three restaurants, three golf courses, full-service spa, health club, beach club, indoor-outdoor tennis, indoor-outdoor pools, shopping gallery, children's center, x-country skiing, ice skating. *Website: www.GrandTraverseResort.com*

Call for Rates

Editor's Note: Premier resort. Excellent accommodations with abundant amenities.

ARBUTUS LAKE

MAC'S LANDING RESORT **(231) 947-6895**
COTTAGE RESORT

14 cottages (1-3 bedrooms, sleeps 2-8) on 700 ft. of beautiful lakefront property. Scenic setting and sandy beach. Features docks, great swimming, raft, boats and motors, campfire pits, playground, volleyball and horseshoes. Bring linens. Open June-Sept. Pets allowed.

Weekly $390-$870

PINEVIEW RESORT **(231) 947-6792 • EMAIL: tc1pinevue@aol.com**
COTTAGE RESORT

12 cottages (some fireplaces) on 400 ft. of lake front, 2-3 bedrooms (sleeps 5-8). Fire pit on beach, lounge deck and dock on lake. Enjoy volleyball, shuffleboard, horseshoes and playground. Boats, motors, pedal boats and pontoons available for rent. Open June-Sept. Pets allowed.

Weekly $680-$898

SHADY CREST RESORT **(231) 947-9855 • EMAIL: shady@traverse.net**
COTTAGE RESORT

Eight very clean and comfortably furnished cottages. 1-3 bedrooms that sleep 4-10. Kitchens with all the extras, bath with shower. Cable with TV's in some cottages, ceiling fans. Linens and towels are not provided. Deck overlooking lake and beach area. Playground and laundry. Boat included with cottage, kayak and paddle boat available. Dock space available. Motor and pontoon rental, bait and pop available. Open all year. Pets welcome.

Weekly $400-$625 (Summer) Nightly & off-season rates available)

Editor's Note: Friendly owners making a real effort at updating this older resort. Simple but very clean cottages.

BELLAIRE

CLARE TAYLOR (517) 394-4162 • EMAIL: mirman@myexcel.com
(AT SCHANTY CREEK RESORT) PRIVATE CHALET

On a secluded lot in the wooded, rolling hills of Schuss Village. Lodging features 3 bedrooms/2 full baths, fully equipped kitchen with microwave, ski storage area, electric heat, CATV, telephone. Linens provided. Use of hot tub, pool and sauna at Schuss Village Lodge. Available year around.

Weekly $500 Nightly $150-$250

GRAND VICTORIAN B&B INN (800) 336-3860
STEVE AND GLENDA SHAFFER EMAIL: info@grandvictorian.com
BED & BREAKFAST

1895 Victorian mansion built by lumber barons. On National Register. Inn features antiques, 3 fireplaces, etched glass and wicker-filled porch/balconies overlooking park. Elegant breakfast. Close to golf and skiing. 4 rooms w/private baths. No smoking.

Nightly $115-$135

SHANTY CREEK RESORT (231) 533-8621 • (800) 678-4111
ROOM/CHALET/CONDO RESORT

Four season resort on the lake. 3 championship golf courses including *The Legend* by Arnold Palmer. 41 downhill slopes, 31 km of x-country trails. Tennis, mountain biking, health club, beach club and indoor/outdoor pools. Fine dining, live entertainment. 600 rooms, condos and chalets some with full to partial kitchens, fireplaces, Jacuzzis. Great swimming. No pets.

Golf Get-a-way Packages (starting at) $59 (per person/per night)
Ski Season Packages (starting at) $72 (per person/per night)

SOCHA'S CHALET (TOP OF SCHUSS, MT. SHANTY CREEK RESORT)

(734) 663-3766 (EVE)
EMAIL: gs@gsgold.com
PRIVATE CHALET

Private chalet nestled in a secluded setting with 3 bedrooms, 2 full baths, sleeps 7-9. Contemporary design with decks off of upstairs bedrooms and wrap around decking off of family and dining room. Full kitchen, washer and dryer. Accessibility to the indoor/outdoor pools, sauna and hot tub at Schuss Village. TV/VCR/DVD, fireplace (wood provided), linens and maid service included. No pets/smoking. Available April-November.

Weekly $850   Nightly $200

BENZONIA

CRYSTAL-RENTALS, INC.   (800) 221-0928 • EMAIL: vacation@crystal-rentals.com
PRIVATE HOMES/COTTAGES

Seasonal and year round homes and cottages in Benzie County. Waterfront properties on Crystal Lake, Lake Michigan, Platte Lake, Long Lake, Bear Lake, Betsie River and Platte River. Visit our Website for pictures, occupancy and prices. *Website: www.crystal-rentals.com*

Weekly $800-$2,800 (Daily rates available)

HANMER'S RIVERSIDE RESORT   RES: (800) 252-4286 • (231) 882-7783
JOHN HANMER   COTTAGE RESORT

Eleven very clean cottages (accommodates 2-12 people) with A/C overlooking the beautiful Betsie River. Indoor pool, spa, canoe/kayak rentals. Open year around. Nearby summer activities, winter skiing at Crystal Mountain, snowmobile trails. Fall salmon and spring steelhead fishing. *Website: www.hanmers.com*

Weekly $500-$910   Nightly $75-$135

Editor's Note: Small, family-friendly resort. Traditional cottages with some very nice amenities like A/C, enclosed pool and hot tub. Their small, one room cabin was our favorite with gas fireplace and cute styling. See our review in this edition.

BEULAH

NORTHERN RENTALS MGT.   (888) 326-2352 • EMAIL: gold@coslink.net
PRIVATE HOMES/CONDOS/COTTAGES

For your "get-away" in beautiful Northern Michigan, we offer beachside cottages, secluded riverside retreats, and spacious homes located at Crystal Mountain Resort. Enjoy skiing, golf, miles of sandy beaches and much more...all in your backyard while visiting scenic Benzie County.

Weekly $995-$2,595

CEDAR

WINGED FOOT CONDO (AT SUGAR LOAF RESORT)   **(616) 846-3978**
JEANNE & JERRY SHERMAN   PRIVATE CONDO

Modern, contemporary, 2 bedroom (sleeps 7) condo on 18th fairway at Sugar Loaf Resort. Fireplace, full kitchen, TV, linens, pools. Overlooks golf course, ski hills (Palmer Course on premises). Lake Michigan beach 1 mile, Leland 6 miles, Traverse City 22 miles. Other nearby activities: Horseback riding, casino, boating. No pets. Open year around.

Nightly $150

CENTRAL LAKE

RIVER'S EDGE   **(248) 377-2382**
BETTY   PRIVATE COTTAGE

Two bedroom (sleeps 6) cottag on Hanley Lake. Near golf and skiing. Complete kitchen with refrigerator, stoves, microwave, breadmaker, TV/VCR, gas grill, fire pit, screened porch. Includes use of fishing boats. Pets OK with security deposit.

Weekly $600   Weekend $300

ELK LAKE/ELK RAPIDS

CEDARS END ON ELK LAKE   **(231) 322-6286**
DEAN & SHARON GINTHER   Email: Dean_Ginther@tamu-commerce.edu
    PRIVATE HOME

Spacious 3 bedroom, 2 bath home on 450 ft. of private east Elk Lake frontage. Furnished, dishwasher, microwave, cookware, 2 fireplaces, dock with boat mooring. 50 acres of woodland attached. Excellent swimming, hiking, biking, boating and fishing. No linens. No pets.

Weekly $2,000 (off-season $1,000)

ELK RAPIDS BEACH RESORT   **(800) 748-0049**
    CONDO RESORT

Luxury condos overlooking Grand Traverse Bay, just minutes from Traverse City. Heated pool (in the summer), in room Jacuzzi and full size kitchen. No pets. Call about our free night during the fall color season. *Website: www.elkrapidsbeachresort.com*

Weekly $1,295 (dbl. occ., summer)   Call for Off-Season Rates

Editor's Note: Small condominium resort. Attractive units sit across a quiet section of road with direct access to private, fabulous sandy beach.

WATER'S EDGE RESORT   (231) 264-8340
COTTAGE/EFFICIENCY/MOTEL RESORT

Come to the "water's edge" of beautiful Elk Lake ... where your family is treated like ours! For your comfort and enjoyment, we offer cottages, units with full kitchens, motel-type accommodations. Also sandy beach/children's play area, two docks, rowboats, a paddleboat, picnic tables, gas grills. Bring linens. No pets.

Weekly $525-$800

WANDAWOOD RESORT & RETREAT CENTER   (231) 264-8122
COTTAGE/DUPLEX RESORT

On Elk Lake, 17 cottages with lakefront and orchard settings. Each varies in size from small 1 bedroom cottage to duplex and 5 bedroom homes. Full kitchen/bath facilities. Nine beach areas with docks plus 2 swimming rafts. Boats, canoes and paddle boards available. Area for field sports and a paperback book library for those quiet times. Open Memorial Day to mid-November.

Weekly $380-$1,165

WHISPERING PINES   (616) 329-1937
JERRY McKIMMY   PRIVATE HOME

Three bedroom lakefront ranch, walkout lower level on the west side of Elk Lake (100 ft). Features C/A, washer/dryer, microwave, dishwasher, CATV/VCR. Linens provided. Boat lift. Sleeps up to 10 people. No smoking/pets. Available year around.

Call for Rates

WHITE BIRCH LODGE   (231) 264-8271 • EMAIL: WBLodge@aol.com
CONDO/LODGE RESORT

CONDOS ★ EDITOR'S CHOICE ★

Year around resort on Elk Lake. Packages offer 3 meals a day plus waterskiing, wind surfing, sailing, tennis, children's programs and more. Accommodations range from simple lodge rooms to deluxe condominiums. Children 2-12 half price. Call for brochure. *Website: www.whitebirchlodge.org*

Weekly $595-$1,065 (per person)

Editor's Note: A fun family resort. Beautiful grounds and plenty of activities for all ages. We recommend their lovely condominiums as your lodging of choice

FRANKFORT

THE HUMMINGBIRD   (314) 965-4598 • EMAIL: gerriemich@aol.com
PRIVATE COTTAGE

Three bedroom/2 bath cottage located on two lakes (one lake is a conservancy). Equipped kitchen, attic and ceiling fans, washer/dryer, patio. Linens included. 400 ft. from water, sandy beach, fishing boat, trolling motors, canoe, paddle boat, lounge chairs. No pets/smoking. Open summer-Labor Day

Weekly $1,000-$1,300

LAKEVIEW LOFT (231) 352-5566 • EMAIL: bayer@benziecounty.com
RICHARD & BILLIE BAYER PRIVATE UPSTAIRS COTTAGE
Close to Lake Michigan, Crystal Lakes and Plattes. Private setting with deck
and views of Lake Michigan and woods. Full kitchen with microwave. Linens
included. Two twin beds, full kitchen, living room, private bath with tub,
shower, CATV/VCR. Available year around.

Nightly $75 (call for weekly rates)

GLEN ARBOR

THE HOMESTEAD (231) 334-5000
MAIN OFFICE RENTALS CONDO/HOME RESORT

★ EDITOR'S CHOICE ★

A resort on Lake Michigan surrounded by the Sleeping Bear Dunes. Restaurants, shops, golf, tennis, pools, x-country and downhill skiing, meeting centers, four small hotels, vacation homes and condominiums. Open May-Oct;
Christmas week and winter weekends.

Nightly $82-$800 (Weekly rates/package plans available)

Editor's Note: Secluded location in a scenic setting... a favorite of ours for years

THE GLENS OF LEELANAU (313) 881-5693 • Email: ckegs@realmatrix.com
CATHY KEGLER PRIVATE VACATION HOMES
Three luxury homes: *Aspenglen* (3 bedrooms/2baths), steps from swmming;
Cherry Glen (4 bedrooms/2 baths) with Glen Lake frontage; *Settler's Glen*
(5 bedrooms/4 baths), 300 ft. to Glen Lake. Homes include A/C, CATV,
VCR, fireplaces, full kitchens with microwaves, dishwashers. No pets/smok-
ing. *Website: http://escape.to/theglens*

Weekly $2,095-$2,595

WHITE GULL INN (231) 334-4486 • EMAIL: gullinglen@aol.com
BILL & DOTTI THOMPSON BED & BREAKFAST
Older 2-story home on a lovely wooded lot in Glen Arbor. Nestled between
Sleeping Bear Sand Dunes and the lake shore of Sleeping Bear Bay. Walking
distance to shops, restaurants, tennis courts, hiking trails. Short drive to golf
courses and Glen Lakes. 5 rooms. Major credit cards accepted.

Nightly $85-$125

HONOR • PLATTE LAKE • PLATTE RIVER

AMERICAN RESORT #14   (734) 461-3374 • EMAIL: hockeydad39@aol.com
ROBERT & TAMMY WENCEL   **PRIVATE CABIN**
Two bedroom, one bath cabin on Little Platte Lake. Fully equipped kitchen, TV. Boat and dock included. Minutes from Lake Michigan, Sleeping Bear Dunes, Crystal Mountain, several golf courses, museums, lighthouses and many other family attractions. Open March-November. Pets allowed.

Weekly $350   Nightly $60

RIVERSIDE   **(231) 325-2121 • Email: bjweau-wh@centurytel.net**
                                                    PRIVATE COTTAGE
ALL SEASON FUN!! Fish, swim, canoe, hike, ski, sightsee, relax, enjoy ... BE 'UP NORTH'. Two-story home located on the beautiful Platte River in Honor, Michigan. 30 miles from Traverse City; 10 minutes from Lake Michigan and the National Lakeshore. 4 bedroom, 2 bath, full kitchen, CATV, DVD, VCR, deck, picnic table. Sleeps 6 adults/2 children. Dock. Non-smoking. No pets. Available all year.

Weekly $390   Nightly $70-$90

INTERLOCHEN

COTTAGES ON GREEN LAKE   **(231) 276-6756**
MARY MUELLER & MARK PAYNE   **2 PRIVATE COTTAGES**
Enjoy wooded, 2-1/2 acre lakefront (125'), sunset views, private setting, dock, swimraft, safe swimming with sandy bottom and two canoes. Both rentals smoke-free. Pets considered. Open May-September. Two rentals are:

Lake House is spacious, light and airy with living room, stone fireplace, enclosed porches (front/back), ktichen with microwave oven, dining room, outside patio, full bath, private bedroom with additional well-designed sleeping ror 6 people.
Weekly $750

One-Bedroom Cabin set back in the woods. This efficient and well-designed cabin includes private bath, full kitchen, capreting, living room-dining room combined. Sleeps 2-3.
Weekly $450

ELLIS LAKE RESORT   **(231) 276-9502**
KEITH & JOAN ATTWOOD   **LOG CABIN RESORT**
Log cabins, chalet and rooms on the lake. Kitchen facilities. some with Franklin fire-stoves. Includes private outdoor hot tub, boats, canoes, more. Linens included. Open year around. X-C skiing in winter. Resort featured in *Midwest Living Magazine*. Pets allowed. *Website: www.ellislakeresort.com*
Weekly $590-$1,160   Nightly $58-$225
Editor's Note: Clean, rustic-styled traditional log cabin resort for a simple vacation experience. Located just off US-31. Friendly owners. See our review in this edition.

INTERLOCHEN INTERLUDE **(734) 729-4941 • Email: iicottages@aol.com**
BARB POLICH   PRIVATE COTTAGES

Three charming cottages sleep 4-18 with private, sandy beach and dock. Property backs-up to state park, 1 mile to Arts Cener, 15 miles to Traverse City. CATV/VCR, stereo, phone, whirlpool tub, fireplace. Equipped kitchen w/dishwasher, grill. Linens included. No smoking/pets. Open all year. *Website: www.iicottages@aol.com*
Weekly $500-$1,200

INTERLOCHEN RETREAT   **(630) 752-9545**
JON & TERRI PENNER   EMAIL: **interlochenretreat@yahoo.com**
                                      PRIVATE HOME & APARTMENTS

Spacious lakefront retreat on 2 acres. Main House features 4 bedrooms/3 baths, custom kitchen, fireplace, covered porch, washer/dryer, gas grill. Two additional 1 bedroom apartments with new kitchens, deluxe baths. CATV, VCR, DVD. Pontoon boat option. Open year round. No pets/smoking. *Website: www.mivg.com/interlochenretreat*
Main House Weekly $1,750; Apartments Weekly $750-$945

JUDY'S PLACE   **(231) 263-5634 • (248) 626-2464**
                                             PRIVATE LOG HOME

★ EDITOR'S CHOICE ★

Log ranch-style home, built in 1992 on 1.12 wooded acres with sandy beach area on small, clean spring-fed lake. 5 miles to Interlochen, 20 miles SW of Traverse City. 4 bedrooms, 3 full baths, 2 air mattresses available. Full kitchen, stacked, full-size washer/dryer, A/C, ceiling fans. Well behaved pets O.K. with additional $25 charge. Prefer non-smokers. Photos available. Open year around. Everything provided except food, clothing and guaranteed good weather!
Weekly * $1,600   Nightly *$255   3-Nite Pkg.   * $720   (* and up)
Editor's Note: Quality home—packed with features and ambiance. Excellent location. Highly recommended.

KALKASKA

MANISTEE LAKE CABIN   **(248) 478-7365**
KATHY STACEY   **PRIVATE LOG CABIN**
Cozy 2 bedroom cabin on Manistee Lake in Kalkaska. Full kitchen, TV/ VCR. Centrally located between Traverse City and Grayling. Great family getaway! Bring linens. Sandy beach, excellent fishing, hunting, boat launch, water skiing and golf. Open spring through fall. No pets/smoking.
Weekly $675

LAKE LEELANAU

JOLLI LODGE   **(888) 256-9291**
COTTAGE/APT./LODGE RESORT
This homey retreat offers a great view of Lake Michigan from their 5 cottages, 11 apartments and 6 lodge rooms. Apartments (1-3 bedrooms) are newer. Cottages and lodge simply furnished but clean. Several steps down leads to pebbled beach. Tennis, rowboat, kayaking, volleyball and shuffleboard. Open year around. Major credit cards.
Weekly $750-$1,300

WEST WIND RESORT   **(231) 946-9457**
COTTAGE RESORT
Eleven cottages, 2 to 4 bedrooms (sleeps 4-10) some with fireplaces. Facilities have children's playground, hot tub. Paddle boards, kayaks and canoe rentals. Protected harbor. Open year around. No pets.
Weekly $975-$2,150 (Call for special off-season rates)

LAKE SKEGEMOG

JOHN KING   **(248) 349-4716 • EMAIL: jking1@peoplepc.com**
PRIVATE HOME
Luxury lakefront home on 200 ft. of sandy beach near Traverse City. 4 bedrooms, 2 baths, equipped kitchen, fireplace. Spacious deck overlooking Lake Skegemog which is part of Elk-Torch chain of 5 lakes. Rowboat. No smoking/pets. *Website: http://free.hostdepartment.com/jking1*
Weekly $1,500-$2,500
Editor's Note: Spacious lake home on scenic grounds. Good spot for the family vacation. See our review in this edition.

LELAND

MANITOU MANOR   **(231) 256-7712**
                                              BED & BREAKFAST

Beautifully restored 1900 farmhouse surrounded by cherry orchards and woods. King and queen size beds, private baths, on the main floor in the wing of the home. Huge parlor with fieldstone fireplace and TV. Full breakfast. Near sand dunes, bike trails, beaches, golf, x-country and downhill skiing. Non-smoking. No pets. Open all year. 5 rooms.

Nightly $95-$140

LONG LAKE

RON JONES OR FRED JONES   **(231) 946-5119 • (586) 286-1582**
                                              PRIVATE COTTAGE

Two bedrooms, queen beds and sleeper sofa. Sleeps 6. CATV/VCR, full kitchen. Private beach, dock, 12 ft. aluminum boat, BBQ grill, picnic table, outdoor furiture. Bring linens. 300 ft. from Gilbert Park. 8 miles from Traverse City. Pets allowed. Non-Smoking. *Website: http://groups.msn.com/ webpagescharterminet/longlakecottage.msnw*

Weekly $800 (includes tax)

LINDEN LEA ON LONG LAKE   **(231) 943-9182 • EMAIL: lindenlea@aol.com**
                                              BED & BREAKFAST

★ EDITOR'S CHOICE ★

"Enchanting spot on a crystal-clear lake...reminiscent of on Golden Pond," Fodor's B&B Guide. Lakeside bedrooms with window seats. Relax by the fire, listen for the loons. Peaceful sandy beach with row boat, paddle boat. Private baths. Full breakfast. Central A/C. 2 rooms. *Website: www.lindenleabb.com*

Nightly $95-$120

Editor's Note: Peaceful, picturesque surroundings and charming hosts make Linden Lea a very nice choice.

NORTHPORT

A NORTHPORT BAY RETREAT   **(231) 935-0111**
MICHAEL ANTON   **Email: info@antonco.com**
                                         PRIVATE HOME

22,000 sq. ft. luxury retreat on 6.5 acres. Ideal for group vacations or business conferences. 16 bedrooms, 19 bathrooms. AC, big-screen CATV, VCR, DVD, equipped kitchen with dishwasher. Dining room seats 64. 12-person hot tub. Fitness center, game room with pool table, foosball, air hockey. On 340 ft. of West Grand Traverse Bay. Near casino, wineries, Sleeping Bear Dunes. *Website: www.antonco.com*

Weekly $13,000-$15,400   Nightly $1,300-$2,050

OLD MISSION PENINSULA

BOWERS HARBOR BED & BREAKFAST   **(231) 223-7869**
                                     BED & BREAKFAST
1870 fully remodeled country farmhouse with private sandy beach is located in the Old Mission Peninsula. Open year around. Enjoy a gourmet breakfast in the dining room overlooking the Harbor. 3 rooms w/private baths. *Website: www.pentel.net/~verbanic*

Nightly $120-$150

CHÂTEAU CHANTAL BED & BREAKFAST   **(800) 969-4009 • (231) 223-4110**
                                       BED & BREAKFAST

★ EDITOR'S CHOICE ★

Old World charm in this fully operational vineyard, winery and B&B. Set on a scenic hill in Old Mission Peninsula, this grand estate features an opulent wine tasting room and 11 units, mostly suites, with private baths. Handicap accessible. Full breakfast. *Website: www.chateauchantal.com*

Nightly $135-$185 (in-season)

Editor's Note: Grand estate with a spectacular view of Old Mission Peninsula. You'll enjoy their "Jazz at Sunset" program.

SILVER LAKE

GERALD NIEZGODA   **(231) 943-9630**
     PRIVATE COTTAGE

Furnished cottage on Silver Lake, 80 ft. private frontage, 2 bedrooms (sleeps 4-6), sandy beach, swimming, fishing, sailing, skiing, outstanding view. 4 miles to Traverse City. Includes fireplace, CATV, VCR, microwave, boat and dock. Bring towels. Open all year. No pets/smoking.

Weekly $735 (Based on occupancy of 4)

SILVER LAKE COTTAGE   **(231) 943-8506**
RAYMOND PADDOCK & JILL HINDS   **PRIVATE COTTAGE**

Fully furnished 3 bedroom cottage accommodates 8 people and features full kitchen, fireplace, stereo, TV, grill and 2 decks. Also features dock, swim raft, canoe and rowboat. Open June-Sept. Pets allowed.

Weekly $750 (plus 6% Use Tax)

SPIDER LAKE

JACK & ROSEMARY MILLER   **(231) 947-6352**
     PRIVATE COTTAGE

Attractive lakefront log cottage on Spider Lake. Offers knotty pine interior, 2 bedrooms (with linens), fireplace, electric heat, TV and complete kitchen including microwave. This quiet, quaint hide-away is furnished with antiques, oak dining set, china cabinet, brass bed and marble top dresser. 13 miles from Traverse City. No pets.

Weekly $500 (May-Oct.)

MOONLIGHT BAY RESORT   **(800) 253-2853 • (231) 946-5967**
ROGER & NANCY HENDRICKSON   **COTTAGE RESORT**

7 cottages on wooded setting with direct Spider Lake frontage. 1-3 bedrooms. Fully equipped kitchens, CATV, ceiling fans, most cottages with fireplace or woodburning stoves. Rowboats, canoes, pedal boat included. Motor and pontoon boat rental available. Open year around. No pets. Website: www.moonlightbayresort.com

Weekly $520-$980

Editor's Note: Traditional cottages. Good beach area.

REGION 5

RED RANCH   **(231) 946-3909**
HAROLD MYERS   **PRIVATE COTTAGE**
Three bedrooms, ranch-style cottage with kitchen, dining area, living room with fireplace, enclosed porch facing the lake, 2 car attached garage. Located in a quiet, private area. Includes bedding, towels, microwave, washer, dryer, CATV, rowboat and dock, bonfire pit. Good fishing/swimming. $150 deposit.

Weekly $ 700 (Seasonal rates)

SUTTONS BAY

THE COUNTRY HOUSE   **(231) 271-4478 • (231) 943-9070**
                                     PRIVATE HOME
Fully furnished house in Suttons Bay offers A/C and 2 bedrooms (sleeps up to 6). It is centrally located to Lake Michigan and Lake Leelanau. No pets/smoking, please.

Weekly $750 (June-Aug.)   Daily $135

FIG LEAF BED AND BREAKFAST   **(231) 271-3995**
JHAKI FREEMAN   **BED & BREAKFAST**
Bring your camera! One-of-a-kind B&B features charming artistic embellishments throughout, and a 12 ft. natural waterfall. Waterfront park across the street. In Storybook Village of Suttons Bay. Classy and quaint shops, cafes within 2 blocks. Festive breakfasts! Casino, wineries, golf, skiing. Private and shared baths. Visa/MC.

Nightly $80-$145

INN AT BLACK STAR FARMS   **(231) 271-4970, EXT. 150**
CARYN ANDERSON   **EMAIL: innkeeper@blackstarfarms.com**
                                 BED & BREAKFAST

★ EDITOR'S CHOICE ★

160-acre year-round destination on the Leelanau Wine Trail combines B&B Inn, winery/distillery, creamery and equestrian center. Eight luxurious guestrooms with private baths. Sauna. Sumptuous gourmet breakfasts. Evening hospitality hour. Hiking and ski trails. On-site tasking room. Boarding for guest's horses. Smoke-free.

Nightly $130-$350
Editor's Note: Impressive rooms in an elegant setting. Winery and equestrian center add a distinctive touch.

ALL RATES SUBJECT TO CHANGE   231

SUTTONS BAY VILLAGE HOUSE   EMAIL: suttonsbayvillagehouse@comcast.net
PRIVATE HOME

1913 Victorian beauty with indoor pool, hot tub, sauna, pool table, updated kitchen with dishwasher, fireplace, 40" HD TV, laundry room, wrap around porch. In the heart of the Village of Suttons Bay (near Traverse City, Glen Arbor). Open year around. No pets/smoking. *Website: www.suttonsbayvillagehouse.com*

Weekly (seasonal) $1,100-$2,600

STRAWBERRY HILL HOUSE AND CABIN   **(314) 726-5266**
CINDY CURLEY   **EMAIL: cgcurley@hotmail.com**
PRIVATE LOG HOUSE/CABIN

Vintage north woods ambiance. Log house on peaceful bluff/shoreline, sleeps up to 6. Log cabin sleeps 2-3. Panoramic orchard and bay views, sand beach. Stone fireplace, antiques, screened porch. Beauty, comfort, and privacy. Furnished except linens. Non-smoking. No pets. Open May-November.

Weekly $1,200-$1,800 (House) ; $750-$900 (Cabin)

Editor's Note: Main home built in 1948, authentic log-style. Mix of older furnishings and family heirlooms. Small, 1-room cabin, simply furnished with basic amenities. Quiet, scenic setting.

THOMPSONVILLE

CRYSTAL MOUNTAIN   **(800) 968-7686 • (231) 378-2000**
MAIN OFFICE RENTALS   **CONDO/HOME/HOTEL RESORT**

★ EDITOR'S CHOICE ★

Family-owned resort featuring 36 holes of championship golf, 45 downhill slopes, 40km of nordic trails, kids' programs, lessons, lodging, mountain biking, indoor pool, fitness center, outdoor pool and water playground, hot tub, dining, IACC-approved conference facility. 28 miles SW of Traverse City on M-115. *Website: www.crystalmountain.com*

Call for Rates

Editor's Note: Premier family, all-season resort. Scenic grounds and beautifully maintained lodgings. Highly recommended! See our review in this edition.

TORCH LAKE

WAS-WAH-GO-NING   **(248) 644-7288 • (231) 264-5228**
JANE BLIZMAN   **PRIVATE COTTAGES**

Two secluded homes on 700 ft. of Torch Lake amid 25 acres of woods and fields. Each house has fireplace, color TV/VCR, CD, dishwasher, microwave, washer/dryer, dock with lift, picnic table, grill. No pets. *Website: www.torch-lake.com*

Weekly $1,500* (2 bedroom); $3,000 (5 bedroom)

TORCHLIGHT RESORT   **(231) 544-8263 • Email: knott@torchlake.com**
ROBERT & GLENDA KNOTT   COTTAGE RESORT

★ EDITOR'S CHOICE ★

Seven cottages with 150 ft. frontage on Torch Lake (part of the Chain of Lakes). Features sandy beach, playground, excellent boat harbor, beautiful sunsets. Located between Traverse City and Charlevoix. Near excellent golf courses and fine restaurants. Open May thru October. No pets.

Weekly $600-$1,950 (Off-season rates available)

Editor's Note: Friendly owners, clean, simple cottages in a lovely setting make this one an enjoyable retreat.

TRAVERSE CITY

BASS COVE   **(231) 946-5219**
                          EMAIL: **info@haroldsresort.com**
                                              PRIVATE COTTAGE

★ EDITOR'S CHOICE ★

Large vacation home with private, sandy Spider Lake waterfront. Has everything you need for 8-12 people: hot tub, pool table, pontoon boat, washer/dryer, CATV/VCR, fireplace 4 bedrooms/2 baths. Open all year. No pets/smoking. *Website: www.haroldsresort.com/harolds5.htm*

Weekly (summer) $2,600 (8-12 people); Nightly $200-$400

Editor's Note: Very picturesque view from the back deck. Spacious home, nicely maintained home with a slight 1960's flair. See our review in this edition.

THE BEACH CONDOMINIUMS   **(231) 938-2228**
                                              CONDO RESORT

These 30 luxury condos on Grand Traverse Bay feature private sun decks (sleeps 4), whirlpool baths, complete kitchen and 27" stereo CATV. Beautiful sandy beach, outdoor heated pool and hot tub plus daily housekeeping. Adjacent boat launch and close to championship golf. AAA discount, daily rentals, getaway and ski packages.

Nightly $89-$299

BROOKSIDE COTTAGES   **(231) 276-9581**
KEITH & TAMMY ENSMAN   COTTAGE RESORT

In the Traverse City/Interlochen area. 250 ft. lake frontage. 13 cottages vary in size (studio - 3 bedrooms) and sleeps 6. Includes fully equipped kitchens. Heated, in-ground swimming pool, game/recreational room. Motors and pontoon rentals. Open year around. No pets. 50% Deposit.

Weekly $440-$640 (off-season rates available

THE GRAINERY B&B (231) 946-8325 • EMAIL: THEGRAINERYBB@AOL.COM
RON & JULIE KUCERA BED & BREAKFAST

1892 Country Gentleman's farm on 10 quiet acres. Decorated in country Victorian tradition. A/C, coffee pot, refrigerator, CATV and outdoor hot tub along with 2 golf greens and a pond. Full country breakfast. 5 rooms/private baths (2 rooms feature Jacuzzi and fireplace).

Nightly $75-$139 (in-season); $55-$139 (off-season)

HAROLD'S RESORT (231) 946-5219 • EMAIL: info@haroldsresort.com
ROLF & KATHY SCHLIESS COTTAGE RESORT

★ EDITOR'S CHOICE ★

Seven log cabins sit upon a Private Peninsula overlooking beautiful Spider lake with sandy beach. Open all year. Honeymoon Cabin has a hot tub. Most have beautiful lake views. All have private bath and kitchen. No pets. *Website: www.haroldsresort.com*

Weekly (summer) $395 (Cabin 6); $800-$900 (Cabins 1- 5, 7)

Editor's Note: Friendly, cozy, picturesque resort with an excellent beach. Cottages kept in very nice condition.

KEN'S COTTAGE (231) 947-5948
PRIVATE COTTAGE

★ EDITOR'S CHOICE ★

One bedroom weekly rental. Large living room, private sandy beach-Grand Traverse Bay. Three blocks to downtown, one block to city tennis courts. Completely furnished, includes TV, kitchen, microwave, fold out couch, canoe, rowboat. New clients, $100 deposit. Available June 15-September 10.

Weekly $900 (July/Aug.) (June - $800)

Editor's Note: Small, private cottage with all the conveniences. Quiet setting, large windows with spectacular sunsets. This little gem is popular ... book early.

LEELANAU CHALETS (231) 218-6888 • EMAIL: tomncon@aol.com
CONNIE RICHARDS PRIVATE COTTAGES/CHALETS

8 lovely vacation rentals on Lake Leelanau and surrounding areas. 2-6 bedrooms. Some handicap friendly. Some pet friendly. Cozy to luxurious. Great for family reunions/large groups/year around. Watersports rentals on-site. No smoking. *Website: www.leelanauchalets.com*

Weekly $800-$5,000

RONALD MALLEK (231) 386-5041 • (954) 384-6363
PRIVATE COTTAGE

This charming, 1 bedroom (sleeps 3), English country cottage features a private patio, many gardens and sandy beach. Fully furnished with fireplace, linens and equipped kitchen. No pets/smoking.

Weekly $600

NORTH SHORE INN   **(800) 968-2365 • EMAIL: nshinn@pentel.net**
CONDO RESORT

Charming New England style condominium hotel. 26 luxury 1-2 bedroom beachfront units with full kitchens. Nightly, weekly, reduced off-season rates. Spectacular views of East Bay from front decks and balconies. 200' sandy beach, outdoor heated pool New golfing, skiing and casino.

Nightly $159-$239 (prime season); $59-$189 (off-season)

Editor's Note: Well maintained, attractively decorated. All rooms with water views. Very nice sandy beach.

THIS OLE HOUSE   **(231) 946-3842**
JIM & CONNIE LEGATO   **Email: thisolehouse@charter.net**
PRIVATE HOME

Well maintained older home, 3 bedrooms, (total 5 beds/sleeps 9). Features air conditioning, washer/dryer, CATV, VCR, phone and data jack for your laptop. A fully equipped kitchen and full line of linens provided. Quiet in-town location 2 blocks from the beach and volley ball courts on Grand Traverse Bay. Four blocks from the heart of the city for shopping and eating, leisure walks or bike rides along the bike path. Public lighted tennis courts 1 block. Available year around. No pets. Credit cards accepted. *Website: www.thisolehouse.com*

Weekly: $950 seasonally; Weekends $425 (Winter $600/weekly; $300/weekend)

Editor's Note: Unassuming 1930's home in quiet neighborhood setting. Full exterior renovation in 2000. Good price for the area.

RANCH RUDOLF   **(231) 947-9529**
LODGE/BUNKHOUSE RESORT

Packed with activities, the ranch offers restaurant and lounge with fireplace. Enjoy the hay rides, sleigh rides, river fishing, backpacking, horseshoes, hiking, tennis, swimming pool, badminton, volleyball and a children's playground. Visa and MC accepted.

Nightly $68-$210

Schoestring Resort (231) 946-9227 Email: info@shoestringresort.com

Cottage Resort

19 cottages, 1-3 bedrooms and 2 bedroom mobiles. An extended stay facility. A place more home than a hotel. Clean and well equipped with air conditioning, nicely furnished including linens, full kitchens or kitchenettes, CATV with 27" TV and complimentary coffee. Remote with amenities of the city and nature easily reached. 8 miles south of Traverse City. Open all year. *Website: www.shoestringresort.com*

Weekly $245-$500

Serenity Bay Acres (231) 946-5219 Email: info@haroldsresort.com
Rolf & Kathy Schliess

Private Cottage

Serenity means: 550' of private waterfront, 2 acres of private forest, no neighbors, beautiful lakeviews from all glass front of a chalet-style cottage. Deck with large cedar swing, dock with Pontoon Boat. One queen, 1 full, 4 twin beds. CATV, VCR, fireplace. No smoking/pets. Open all year

Nightly $160-$300   Weekly $1,500

Editor's Note: Nicely maintained, comfortable home with incredibly scenic view. See our review in this edition.

Tall Ship Manitou (800) 678-0383 • (231) 941-2000

Bed & Breakfast

Unique 'floating' B&B. Large traditional sailing vessel offers overnight accommodations with a 2-1/2 hour sunset sail, picnic dinner and hearty breakfast. Join the crew for a special evening on this 105 ft., two-masted topsail schooner. Shared toilets. Shower facilities on shore.. Reservations recommended. May-Sept.

Nightly $110-$192 (children 8-12 $53)

Traverse Bay Inn   (231) 938-2646
CONDO RESORT

All units are furnished with equipped kitchens including microwaves, A/C, CATV. Some rooms with whirlpool tub and fireplace. Pool, hot tub, gas grills and complementary bicycles. Swimming beach nearby. Pets O.K. Major credit cards accepted. *Website: www.traversebayinn.com*

Weekly $175-$1,175   Nightly $39-$199

Editor's Note: Clean, contemporary, well maintained units. Sizes vary significantly.

Whispering Waters   (888) 880-5557 • EMAIL: whisper@gtii.com
Bed & Breakfast Retreat   Bed & Breakfast

★ EDITOR'S CHOICE ★

Enjoy the tranquility of nature at our retreat surrounded by 42 acres of natural woods and streams. Explore hiking trails, relax in the outdoor hot tub, sit in the sauna, go tubing in the river. Main house with three rooms/two baths. Spring House addition with suite of four rooms including bedroom, bathroom, whirlpool, bathroom and sitting room overlooking a bubbling brook. One cabin for two on the river. Specially crafted interiors highlight nature. Full breakfasts. Personal growth workshops and massage available.

Nightly $80-$95 (Rooms); $150 Spring House; $150 Cabin (2 night min.)

Editor's Note: Lovely setting, creatively and tastefully decorated ... very comfortable for those seeking a quiet, back-to-nature retreat.

Wilkins Landing II   (231) 946-5219
Rolf & Kathy Schliess   EMAIL: info@haroldsresort.com
PRIVATE COTTAGE

★ EDITOR'S CHOICE ★

Glass front overlooks private Spider Lake waterfront with a large deck . Fieldstone fireplace, full kitchen, CATV/VCP, dock, paddleboat and pontoon boat. Near snowmobile, x-country ski and bike tails Available all year. *Website: www.haroldsresort.com/harolds5.htm*

Nightly $125-$200   Weekly $1,200 (2-6 people)

Editor's Note: Airy, spacious home, open windows and great deck to view the lake. Pontoon boat takes you to nice swimming area.

WILKINS LANDING III
ROLF & KATHY SCHLIESS

(231) 946-5219
EMAIL: info@haroldsresort.com
PRIVATE COTTAGE

★ EDITOR'S CHOICE ★

Quiet and secluded! Surrounded by private forest. Private Spider Lake waterfront, dock, pontoon boat across the street. Screened porch, deck, fireplace, jetted bathtub and queen log bed make this a great getaway! Open all year. Open year around. *Website: www.haroldsresort.com/harolds5.htm*

Nightly $125-$200   Weekly $1,100 (2-6 people)

Editor's Note: Very appealing cedar log home with fresh, open design. Lovely wooded setting.

WINTERWOOD ON THE BAY
R. SCHERMERHORN

(231) 929-1009
PRIVATE COTTAGE

Recently built beach house on East Bay. Sleeps 4 (2 bedrooms), bath, fully furnished kitchen, living/dining room with fireplace. Dishwasher, microwave, VCR and cable TV. Linens provided. Deck and private dock. Open year around. No pets/smoking.

Weekly $775

MANISTEE • ONEKAMA

The Cadillac area is an excellent stop for fishing and water sports enthusiasts with its two lakes (Cadillac and Mitchell) within its city limits, and many other lakes not far away. Wild and tame game are abundant at Johnny's Wild Game and Fish Park which also stocks its waters with plenty of trout. In February, come and enjoy the North American Snowmobile Festival.

On the shores of Portage Lake, with access to Lake Michigan, **Onekama** is a summer resort community with a charter-boat fleet, marina, white sandy beaches and lovely parks.

You'll definitely want to stop by to enjoy the lovely, historic Victorian port city of **Manistee**. The entire central business district of this community is listed in the National Register of Historic Places. You'll be delighted by the district's charming Victorian street lamps, museums, and shops. Stroll along the Riverwalk which winds along the Manistee River for more than a mile. Watch the boat traffic, stop at a restaurant, then take off your shoes and walk in the smooth sand of the beaches along Lake Michigan. The area also offers several challenging golf courses. Of course, you may prefer to take advantage of their charter-boat fishing or river-guide services. In winter, there's plenty of cross-country skiing and snowmobiling trails.

MANISTEE

LAKE SHORE BED & BREAKFAST   **(231) 723-7644**
WILLA BERENTSEN   **BED & BREAKFAST**

Enjoy relaxation on the shore of Lake Michigan. Spectacular sunsets, sunrises, freighters and stars. Delicious full breakfasts served at your leisure in our smoke-free new cedar home. Private deck at water's edge. 1 suite with private bath, sitting room.

Nightly $120 (plus tax)

MANISTEE BEACH   **(800) 666-9237 • info@manisteebeach.com**
FRANK MOORE   **PRIVATE CONDO**

Condo at Harbor Village along Lake Michigan shoreline. Overlooks marina. Next to indoor/outdoor pools and fitness center. Lake Michigan beach a two-minute walk away. Sleeps five, 1.5 baths, A/C, CATV, VCR, hot tub. Open year around. No pets/smoking. *Website: www.manisteebeach.com*

Weekly $700-$1,350   Nightly $125-$175

UP NORTH GETAWAY   **(248) 668-9925 • (989) 799-2412**
TREVOR & DENNIS WISNEWSKI   **PRIVATE CHALET**

★ EDITOR'S CHOICE ★

Nestled the Manistee National Forest on all-sports Pine Lake. Newly built, 2 bedroom chalet sleeps 8-10. Includes fireplace, TV, VCR, equipped kitchen with dishwasher, linens, outdoor firepit. Hiking, biking, winter skiing, boating, fishing, golfing, snowmobile and casino in area and more! Open year around. No pets.

Website: www.upnorthgetaway.com.

Weekly $780-$1,050
Weekend $365-$475

Editor's Note: Contemporary home comfortably styled. Breakthtaking lake view from beautiful great room. Very good value.

WOODLAND ACRES LAKEHOME (708) 460-3113 • Email: jbielecki1@AOL.COM
JOHN & BRIGID BIELECKI **PRIVATE CONDO**

★ EDITOR'S CHOICE ★

BRAND NEW LUXURY BEACHFRONT townhouse on the shore of LAKE MICHIGAN with 268' of private sandy beach! Huge, 3 bedroom, 3 bath, 2300 sq. ft. upscale home with living room, dining room, kitchen, master bath with 6 ft. tub, loft-den and ca-

thedral ceiling. The upstairs, full glass-walled veranda room overlooks the lake. Furnished and decorated to the nines! Enjoy the view and sunsets from your lakefront Jacuzzi on the deck. Stone fireplace, CATV, VCR, stereo, gas grill, washer/dryer. Vacation in style! Close to casino and world class golf. No smoking/pets.

Website: www.manisteelakefront.com

Weekly $1,500-$2,700 Nightly $300-$400

Editor's Note: This luxury, muti-level condo is packed with amenities. Scenic views with excellent Lake Michigan beach frontage. Highly recommended.

ONEKAMA

LAKE MICHIGAN BEACH CHALET (312) 943-7565
DONNA **PRIVATE CHALET**

An elegant, 3,500 sq. ft., 3 bedroom/3 bath home on Lake Michigan. This spacious home features fireplaces, fully equipped kitchen, living room/dining room and family room with pool table, 60" CATV, VCR and CD stereo. Lake and sunset viewing deck in addition to wraparound house deck with BBQ. Private setting. Weekly maid service and linens included. No pets.

Weekly $2,800-$3,500 Monthly $9,500

REGION 6

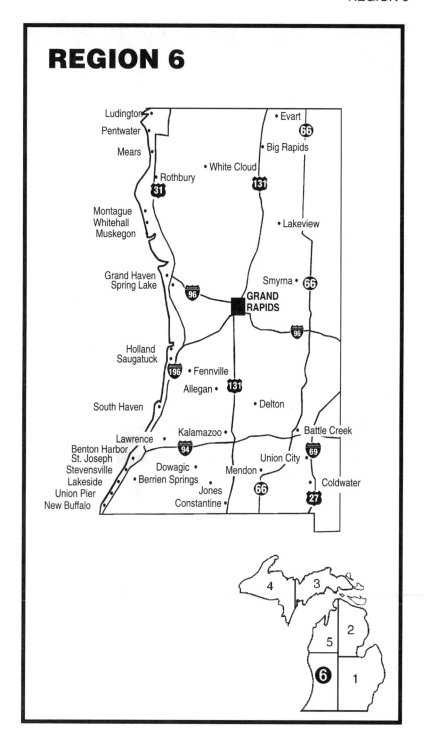

LUDINGTON • GRAND RAPIDS • HOLLAND & SURROUNDING AREAS

INCLUDES: BIG RAPIDS • EVART • GRAND HAVEN • LAKEVIEW • MEARS • MONTAGUE • MUSKEGON • PENTWATER • ROTHBURY • SMYRNA • SPRING LAKE • WHITEHALL

A boardwalk, stretching for 2-1/2 miles from downtown **Grand Haven** to its pier, is bordered by shops, eateries and sandy beaches. For a grand tour, hop on board the Harbor Steamer. For a spectacular sight, see the World's Largest Musical Fountain and visit Michigan's second largest zoo which has 150 species of animals, an aquarium, herpetarium, and more.

Grand Rapids, a unique blend of old and new, the city has many activities to keep you busy! Heritage Hill contains almost 100 historical homes. You'll also want to visit the John Ball Zoological Gardens, Roger B. Chaffe Planetarium, and the Voigt House, a Victorian home built in 1895.

People from all over come to **Holland's** special May event, the Tulip Time Festival; but there is much to see here throughout the year. Dutch Village should not be missed — and don't leave without seeing the Wooden Shoe Factory or Windmill Island.

Ludington's most visited attraction is, Historic White Pine Village, preserves Mason County's history. Visit the Big Sable Point Lighthouse, with daily tours. Enjoy some dune action at beautiful Hamlin Lake or Silver Lake, "home of the world's largest shifting sand dunes". The fall is a particularly breathtaking time. During this season, blue waters of Lake Michigan and white sands of the dunes sharpen the brilliant colors of changing leaves along the shoreline and trails. Bike through 22 miles of nature in Michigan's first linear state park, the Hart-Montage Bicycle Trail State Park. Several notable restaurants in the area include *P.M. Steamers* for a good view of marina activities or *Gibbs Country House* to indulge in their truly sticky, sticky buns and well prepared American cuisine in a family atmosphere.

With miles of sandy Lake Michigan beach, **Muskegon** is the place to book a fishing charter boat, Lake Michigan cruise, or rent a canoe or jet boat at one of many area marinas. You'll enjoy a full day of family fun at Michigan's Adventure Amusement Park & Wild Water Adventure (8 miles north of Muskegon, on U.S. 31). It's one of Michigan's largest amusement parks and features thrill rides, games and live shows for all ages.

Enjoy the New England charm of **Pentwater**, with its cozy cafes and double-decker bus. Stroll through the artisan galleries and little gift shops along Hancock and Second streets. Build a sand castle in the Silver Lake State Park which features a huge sandbox with 450 acres of dunes for off-road vehicles and 750 acres for pedestrians only.

Hungry? Try some of Pentwater's unique restaurants: *Historic Nickerson Inn* for a warm and charming atmosphere (reservations requested); the *Village Pub* for casual pizza, fish sandwiches and evening entertainment of comedy or jazz; the *Antler Bar* known for its special burrito; and *Gull Landing* serves up steak and seafood.

With plenty to do in this great lake playground, you will find the atmosphere relaxed, the people friendly, and the scenery beautiful.

EVART

WHITE GABLES B&B   (231) 734-6940
TERESE & JIM WHITTEN   BED & BREAKFAST
Treat ourself to a great night's rest in "the most expensive home in Osceola County" of 1887. Built during the Michigan Lumber Boom, this historic Queen Anne Victorian is still the "gem" of Evart. Come enjoy the simple pleasures of small town living. The peace and quiet here will melt your cares away. Convenient to mid-Michigan festivals, concerts, hunting, powerchuting, the Pere Marquette rail-to-rail and the Muskegon River. Smoke-free environment. Four guest rooms. Private and shared baths.
Nightly $49-$79; Family Suite $109 (Discounts for stays of 4 or more nights)

GRAND HAVEN

BOYDEN HOUSE INN BED & BREAKFAST   (616) 846-3538
                                                BED & BREAKFAST
1874 Victorian Home. Its eclectic decor represents our varied interests and welcomes guests. Cozy rooms, delightful breakfasts, books, flowers, walks on beaches and boardwalks. Air conditioned rooms feature TV, some with fireplaces, balconies and whirlpool tubs. 7 rooms/private baths.
Nightly $110-$150

KHARDOMAH LODGE
PATTY RASMUSSEN-RAVE & MO RAVE EMAIL: khardomahlodge@chartermi.net
(616) 842-2990
LODGE/SUITES/COTTAGES

★ EDITOR'S CHOICE ★

Established 1873. Historic site. Cottage-style facilities located 200 yards from Lake Michigan, nestled in wooded dunes. Lodge sleeps 35, partial A/C, TV and fireplace in great room. No in-room TV's or phones. Deck with gas grills and picnic tables. Suites sleep 4-6, offers Jacuzzi and fireplace or outdoor hot tub. Three bedroom cottage sleeps 7. Open year round. No smoking/pets. *Website: www.khardomahlodge.com*

Main Lodge (16 BR's), $625-$1,190/Nightly; $4,190-$6,290/Weekly ($55-$75/per room) Suites $125-$185/Nightly; $975-$1,100/Weekly. Cottage $135-$150/Nightly; $1,100/Weekly (Week stays in-season. Minimum weekends)

Editor's Note: Historic Lodge, set in a wooded commnity side street offers a beautifully preserved rustic 'up north' ambiance. Suites are spacious and lovely. See our review in this edition.

HARBOURFRONT CONDOMINIUM
LEE HASLICK
(616) 846-5545
PRIVATE CONDO

Prime Grand Haven location only steps from beach, downtown, musical fountain, fireworks, shipping channel, boardwalk. Newer efficiency condo furnished with stove, microwave, refrigerator, CATV, laundry in-room. Sleeps 4. Situated in historic Story and Clark Piano Factory. No pets/smoking. Open year around.

Weekly $620 (summer)   Nightly $80 (off-season)

LAKE MICHIGAN COTTAGES-GRAND SUMMIT   **800-870-3393**
MICHAEL MAY   **EMAIL: info@lakemichigancottages.com**
PRIVATE COTTAGES

Diverse selection of Lake Michigan vacation rentals in Grand Haven, Saugatuck, Holland and Muskegon. From small cozy beach cabins to luxurious homes, there's a rental to fit your budget. Rentals are directly on or have direct access to beautiful Lake Michigan beaches and shorelines. *Website: www.LakeM.com*

Weekly $595-$9,000

GRAND RAPIDS

CHICAGO POINT RESORT   **WINTER (517) 321-4562 • SUMMER (269) 795-7216**
DONALD STRAYER   **COTTAGE RESORT**
Spacious 2-4 bedroom cottages with breathtaking view of sparkling clean 'spring fed', 2,600 acre Gun Lake. Featuring 1,000 ft. of water frontage. Equipped for fun. Swimming, boating, fishing, golf, hiking, evening campires. Al Capone was known to have visited. No pets. *Website: www.chicagopointresort.com*

Weekly $600 (and up)

HOLLAND

BONNIE'S PARSONAGE 1908 B&B   **(616) 396-1316**
BONNIE MCVOY-VERWYS   **BED & BREAKFAST**
Enjoy our lovely, historic B&B. Situated in a beautiful neighborhood near downtown and Hope College. AAA approved. Featured in *Fodor's Best Upper Great Lakes*. Saugatuck resort 12 miles. Two rooms/private baths, third with shared bath. Full breakfasts served in formal dining room. Two nights minimum July/August/Holidays.

Nightly $100-$135

Editor's Note: Quaint B&B. Bonnie pays attention to decorating her antique-filled rooms. You'll be amazed at the detail used to create the right ambiance.

DUTCH COLONIAL INN B&B (616) 396-3664
PAT & BOB ELENBAAS BED & BREAKFAST

★ EDITOR'S CHOICE ★

1928 inn features elegant decor, 1930 furnishings and heirlooms. All rooms with tiled private baths, some with whirlpool tub for 2. Honeymoon suites for that "Special Getaway", fireplaces. Close to shopping, Hope College, bike paths, x-country ski trails and beaches. A/C. 4 rooms. Full breakfast. Corporate rates. *Website: www.dutchcolonialinn.com*
Nightly $110-$160
Editor's Note: Very welcoming innkeepers and lovely styling make this delightful inn a real treat.

EDGEWOOD BEACH (734) 692-3941
GERALYN PLAKMEYER PRIVATE COTTAGE

Located north of Holland, in Beach Front Association. Home has 2 bedrooms, 1 bath, fully furnished, equipped kitchen, fireplace, central heat and CATV. 150 ft. back from Lake Michigan, stairway to long sandy, private beach complete with sunsets and fire pit. Provide your own linens. Available June-Sept. No pets.
Weekly $500

ROSEWOOD POINTE RESORT (612) 501-2548
BRENT Email: rentals@rosewoodpointe.com
COTTAGE/HOME RESORT

Located in Holland. Four large, waterfront cottages and three homes ... including an 8 bedroom retreat house (sleeps 30). Resort features private, groomed beach, boat docks, fishing and beach volleyball. Great place for family reunions. No pets. Smoke-free. Open year around. *Website: www.rosewoodpointe.com*
Weekly $1,400 - $5,000
Editor's Note: Great beach. Comfortable accommodations in a cluster. Really nice for small groups or family reunions.

LAKEVIEW

LAKEVIEW COTTAGE (616) 874-9197 • EMAIL: bonewell3@yahoo.com
KELLY & JULIE BONEWELL PRIVATE COTTAGE

Private cottage on all-sports lake. Excellent fishing, lots of wildlife, great swimming, beautiful views. Three bedrooms (sleeps 7), one bath, fully equipped kitchen, TV, VCR, canoe. Provide your own linens. Available May-Sept. No smoking/pets.
Weekly $425 (Friday-Friday rental)

LUDINGTON

BED & BREAKFAST AT LUDINGTON   **(231) 843-9768**
GRACE & ROBERT SCHNEIDER   **BED & BREAKFAST**
Explore woods, trails, gardens and creek, shade tree canopy, tree-swing, camp-fires. Widely separated rooms enhance privacy. Popular barnloft ideal for families or honeymooners. Homey atmosphere. Big breakfast. Pet friendly. Open May 15-Nov. 7. *Website: www.carrinter.net/bedbkfst*
Nightly $45-$75 (and a 20% discount successive nights)

INN AT LUDINGTON   **(800) 845-9170**
KATHY & OLA KVALVAAG   **EMAIL: innkeeper @inn-ludington.com**
    BED & BREAKFAST

★ EDITOR'S CHOICE ★

The charm of the past meets the comfort of today in a picture perfect Queen Anne Victorian. Relax and feel at home in casual elegance. Breakfast is an event here. Cozy fireplaces, family suite. 6 rooms. Walk to shops, restaurants, beach. *Website: www.inn-ludington.com*
Nightly $100-$125
Editor's Note: Classicly styled Victorian home. Rooms more spacious than many. New owners. See our review in this edition.

LUDINGTON HOUSE B&B   **(800) 827-7869**
VIRGINIA BOEGNER   **Email: gypsyginger@webtv.net**
    BED & BREAKFAST

1878 Victorian. 8 rooms (capacity 21). Faily re-unions. Children wel-come. Private baths. AC/queen beds, whirlpools, fireplaces. Close to Lake Michi-gan, golf, canoeing, sand dune rides, horse-back riding, light-houses. Full, hearty breakfast. Carferry to Wisconsin. Murder mysteries. Special packages. Gift certificates. Pet-friendly. *Website: www.ludingtonhouse.com*
Nightly $70-$140

LAMPLIGHTER B & B (231) 843-9792 • RES. (800) 301-9792
BILL & JANE CARPENTER BED & BREAKFAST

Victorian Style, European Elegance and American Comfort are the hallmarks of "The Lamplighter Bed and Breakfast". Your stay in our individually decorated rooms with queen size beds, private baths, A/C, CATV and phones will be the most relaxing possible. 2 rooms feature a whirlpool for special occasions. All rooms as well as the common areas—parlor, living room and dining room— are decorated with original art and antiques. Full gourmet breakfasts are served either in our dining room or outdoors in the gazebo. AAA 3 Diamonds *Website: www.ludington-michigan.com*

Nightly $115-$145

Editor's Note: Charming accommodations, a nice choice for the area.

PARKVIEW COTTAGES (231) 843-4445
DENNIS & JILL COTTAGE RESORT

Nestled in shade trees, 2 blocks from Lake Michigan. Cottages sleep 2-8, feature knotty pine interiors, bath, equipped kitchen, gas heat, CATV, fieldstone fireplace. Large deck, grills and patio furniture. Across from public beach. No pets/smoking. Open May-Oct. *Website: www.parkviewcottages.com*

Nightly $70 (and up)

SCHOENBERGER HOUSE (231) 843-4435 • EMAIL: tschoenberg@hotmail.com
TAMAR SCHOENBERG BED & BREAKFAST

★ EDITOR'S CHOICE ★

This singularly beautiful neoclassical mansion, built by a lumber baron in 1903, has been home to the Schoenberger family for half a century. Included in *Historic Homes of America and Grand Homes of the Midwest*, this elegantly furnished B&B features exquisite woodwork, magnificent chandeliers, 5 fireplaces, music room with 2 grand pianos, an intimate library, the master bedroom suite and four other bedrooms, all with private bath. Minutes from Lake Michigan beach, city marina, car ferry and the majestic dunes of Ludington State Park. Smokefree. Visa/MC. *Website: www.schoenbergerhouse.com*

Nightly $145-$245

Editor's Note: Absolutely beautiful woodworking in his impressive home built by one of Ludington's early lumber barons make this a real visual treat.

TWIN POINTS RESORT   **(231) 843-9434**
JIM & BARB HUSTED   **COTTAGE RESORT**
Ten cottages (1-3 bedrooms) rest on 2 wooded bluffs overlooking lovely Hamlet Lake. Walk down to large and sandy swimming beach. Boaters can back
their trailers down with ease. Moor your boat in covered docks. Motors and
boats available for rent. Cottages are fully furnished and equipped. Most
have knotty pine interiors. Close to Ludington State Park.
Call for Rates

WILLOW BY THE LAKE RESORT   **(231) 843-2904 • RES. (800) 331-2904**
GORDON/DAVID BETCHER & MARTIN LUTZENKIRCHEN   **COTTAGE RESORT**
Attractive, clean, 1-2 bedroom cottages with equipped kitchens. Guests provide linens/towels. Beautiful view of sand dunes and sunsets from east shore
of Hamlin Lake. Sand box play area for children. Dockage/boat rentals available. Open May-October. No pets. *Website:www.hamlinlake.com/willow*
Weekly $475-$610

MEARS

THE LAKE HOUSE   **(313) 886-8996**
                                                       PRIVATE COTTAGE
Custom built (1997), 3 bedroom, 2 bath home. One door off of "private"
sandy Lake Michigan beach. 1,000 sq. ft. wrap-around and screened porch.
24'x26' great room. 17 ft. vaulted ceiling. Oak floors, outside hot and cold
shower, BBQ and more. Open year round.
Weekly $800-$1,200
*Editor's Note: Open styling offers plenty of room. Clean and comfortable. The
fabulous Lake Michigan beach is steps away, down a well-construced stairway.*

MONTAGUE

LIFE GUARD ROAD HOME (231) 893-2054 • Email: jeffreyckinney@yahoo.com
JEFF KINNEY   **PRIVATE HOUSE**
Year around Lake Michigan dune beach house adjacent to White Lake. Near
fishing pier and boat dock. 4 bedrooms (10 beds), 2 baths. Moonsets/sunsets.
Linens included. Washer/dryer, dishwasher, microwave, fireplace, CATV,
telephone, screened/sheltered porch. Close to Michigan Adventureland. No
pets. Open year around. *Website: www.angelfire.com/mi4/jeffk*
Weekly $700-$3,000

MUSKEGON

IDLEWILD RETREAT   **(616) 842-5716**
CAROLYN MILLER   **PRIVATE HOME/EFFICIENCY**

Beautiful home on Lake Michigan with adjoining efficiency with loft bedroom (sleeps 5/efficiency 4). Both have supplied kitchens, baths, linens, TV, phone and heat. Main cottage has dishwasher, washer, dryer and fireplace. Rented together only. Private beach on Lake Michigan. Available May-Dec. No pets. Call for Rates

PENTWATER

CANDLEWYCK HOUSE B&B   **(231) 869-5967**
JOHN & MARY JO NEIDOW   **BED & BREAKFAST**

★ EDITOR'S CHOICE ★

This 1868 farmhouse style inn offers a unique and comfortable getaway in the historic Lake Michigan port of Pentwater. Six rooms with private baths, A/C, CATV (2 with fireplaces and mini-kitchens). Walk to shops, restaurants and beach. Full country breakfast. Open May-November. *Website: www.candlewyckhouse.com*
Nightly $99-$139
Editor's Note: Cozy, comfortable and very welcoming. Colonial American decor with folk-art crafts add to the ambiance. A lovely stay.

HISTORIC NICKERSON INN   **(231) 869-6731 • EMAIL: nickerson@voyager.net**
HARRY & GRETCHEN SHIPARSKI   **BED & BREAKFAST**

★ EDITOR'S CHOICE ★

Offering guests exceptional hospitality since 1914. Completely renovated. Thirteen room with private baths and A/C. Three Jacuzzi suites with fireplaces and balconies overlooking Lake Michigan. Two blocks to beach and shopping district. Full breakfast included. Casual fine dining, cocktails.

Virtual tour: www.nickersoninn.com
Nightly $150-$250 (High Season); $100-$235 (Low Season)
Editor's Note: One of our favorites. Rooms are lovely and the historic inn is beautifully maintained. Highly recommended! See our review in this edition.

ROTHBURY

DOUBLE JJ RESORT RANCH **(231) 894-4444 • (800) DOUBLEJJ**
HOTEL/CONDO RESORT

★ EDITOR'S CHOICE ★

Open year-round. Enjoy horseback riding, championship golf, swimming, waterslide, snow tubing, dog sledding, children's program, dinner theatre and more. Room vary from bunkhouse to hotel rooms, log cabins and luxury condos. All inclusive packages available with meals and activities. *Website: www.doublejj.com*

Nightly   Standard Hotel: $69-$149; Condos: $99-$389

Editor's Note: Excellent horseback riding, top-rated golf course, beautiful grounds and friendly ranch hands too...Yee-ha!

SMYRNA

DOUBLE 'R' RANCH RESORT **(616) 794-0520**
CHALET/BUNK HOUSE/MOTEL RESORT

Lets go tubing on the Flat River! Great fishing too — pike and small mouth bass. Volleyball, horseback riding, golf, canoeing, hay rides. Each chalet has electric stove, refrigerator and all dishes. Chalets rent by week or day. For overnight stays, try the rustic western atmosphere of the Bunk House Motel.

Call for Rates

SPRING LAKE

MILL POINT CONDO #101   **(517) 783-3310 • EMAIL: scsoper@dmci.net**
SHIRLEY SOPER   **PRIVATE CONDO**

One bedroom waterfront condo at bridge into Grand Haven, Juncture Spring Lake and Grand River (Lake Michigan 3 miles). Sleeps 4. A/C, CATV, VCR, completely furnished, washer/dryer. Linens included. Patio, carport. Light, airy throughout. Handicapped accessible. Indoor/outdoor pool. River boardwalk bordering marina. Open year around. No pets.

Weekly: $850

ISLAND VIEW AT MILL POINT CONDO
LINDA & GRAM MCGEORGE

(616) 846-4391
EMAIL: mcgeorgeg@chartermi.net
PRIVATE CONDO

Private Grand River frontage condo minutes from Grand Haven. Enjoy facilities of the Holiday Inn steps away, including indoor/outdoor pools, hot tub, restaurant, tiki bar, exercise room. Condo amenities include two-bedrooms plus loft (sleeps 6), two baths, complete kitchen, A/C, CATV, VCR, dishwasher, laundry and linens. Relax on the private deck with a lovely sunset views, The Musical Fountain, Coast Guard Fireworks, Grand Island Marina, Holiday Inn Dockage. Covered, private parking with extra parking for friends. No pets/smoking. Open year round. *Website: www.greatrentals.com/mi/9681.html*

Weekly: $900-$1,100 (seasonal)

SEASCAPE BED & BREAKFAST
SUSAN MEYER

(616) 842-8409
BED & BREAKFAST AND COTTAGE

On a private Lake Michigan beach. Experience warm hospitality and "Country Living" ambiance at our nautical lakeshore home. Four rooms (private baths). Romantic fireplace suites. Full breakfasts served by firepla ce overlooking Grand Haven Harbor. Stroll or cross-country ski on dune trails. Separate Victorian cottage sleeps 8. No pets.

Nightly $140-$195

WATERFRONT CONDO
LARRY & JOYCE GOLDMAN

(616) 846-1541
PRIVATE CONDO

Waterfront condo adjacent to the new Holiday Inn. Rental includes use of indoor/outdoor pool and exercise room. Completely furnished, CATV, VCR, dishwasher, microwave, washer/dryer, A/C. Two bedrooms/2 baths. Children welcome. Sorry, no pets. 5 minutes to Grand Haven.

Weekly $1,200; 4 Nights $700; 3 Nights $600

WHITEHALL

MICHILINDA BEACH LODGE (231) 893-1895
COTTAGES/LODGE ROOMS

Modified American Plan resort with weekly activities and plenty to do. Well groomed grounds on scenic location. Cottages and lodge rooms offer private baths, most with sitting areas (no kitchens). Many rooms with lake views. Price includes breakfast/lunch. 49 rooms. Open May to early October. No pets.

Weekly $950-$1,500 (assumes 2 people)

Editor's Note: Well groomed, picturesque resort with plenty to keep families and couples busy. Rooms comfortable and clean.

SCENIC DRIVE HOME (231) 893-2054 • Email: jeffreyckinney@yahoo.com
JEFF KINNEY PRIVATE HOUSE

25 yards/35 stairs to 100+ ft. of private Lake Michigan sandy, shallow beach. Year around home with 2 fireplaces, 4 bedrooms (10 beds) and 2 baths. A/C, cable, sheltered/screened porch, open deck. Washer/dryer, dishwasher. Linens included. No pets. Near Michigan Adventureland. Open year around. *Website: www.angelfire.com/mi4/jeffk*

Weekly $700-$3,000

WHITE SWAN INN TOLL FREE: (888) 948-7926 • EMAIL: info@whiteswaninn.com
CATHY & RON RUSSELL BED & BREAKFAST

1880's Queen Anne home with screened porch. Gracious hospitality in a relaxing setting. Spacious rooms, mix of antiques and wicker furniture. Whirlpool suite. Walk to shops, restaurants, marinas. Near Hart-Montague Bike Trail. Gift shop on premises. Open year 'round. Delicious breakfast. Seasonal packages. *Website: www.whiteswaninn.com*

Nightly $95-$155

Editor's Note: Cozy B&B offering guests a welcoming atmosphere.

SAUGATUCK • KALAMAZOO • UNION PIER & SURROUNDING AREAS

INCLUDES: BATTLE CREEK • BERRIEN SPRINGS • COLDWATER • CONSTANTINE • DELTON • DEWEY LAKE • JONES • LAWRENCE • MENDON • NEW BUFFALO • ST. JOSEPH • SOUTH HAVEN • STEVENSVILLE • UNION CITY

Battle Creek, home of the cereal pioneers W. K. Kellogg and C. W. Post, has given this city the name of "Cereal Capital of the World". It is also the site of Fort Custer National Cemetery and the International Hot-Air Balloon Championship, which last for 8 days in June.

Kalamazoo — how very diverse. Whatever you wish to do or see, you'll find it here. Visit Victorian homes and quaint inns, tour museums and enjoy their community theaters. Stroll through their historic district. For additional galleries and antique shops stop at Lakeside.

Explore the village of **Saugatuck**. This enchanting, historical town earned its title as "The Art Coast of Michigan" with unique art galleries, shops and festivals. Stop at the city's 75-year-old drug store that makes the best hand-creamed sodas and shakes in the world. For a little fun and adventure, tour the dunes or take a dune ride. Cruise up the Kalamazoo River in the historic *Queen of Saugatuck*, a 67 foot-long stern-wheel riverboat. The water may make you thirsty, so head over to the Tabor Hill Wine Port and refresh yourself.

A visit to Saugatuck wouldn't be complete without a day at Oval Beach. Many travel magazines have recognized Saugatuck's main beach as one of the best in the world. In fact, MTV ranked it in the "Top 5" U.S. beaches. **South Haven** not only prides itself as the "Blueberry Capital of the World" it is also one of our major yachting and sport fishing ports**.** Explore the many parks and go hang gliding in the Warren Dunes State Park just south of **St. Joseph**. In the fall, harvest festivals and color tours are popular. May brings the Blossom Time Festival, celebrated for over 80 years. In mid-July the Venetian Festival turns the lakefront park and boulevard into a giant midway. You don't want to miss this one.

Getting hungry yet? Try out *Jenny's* on Lakeshore Road (between New Buffalo and Union Pier). Creatively prepared food and homey atmosphere featuring Great Lakes Indian art and high-beamed ceiling with skylights make this a worthwhile stop! Also, *Schu's Grill & Bar* on Lake Boulevard (St. Joseph) prepares excellent meals — their Blackout Cake is a wonderful treat. We understand the *North Beach Inn* serve's up very memorable blueberry pancakes or waffles. For casual dining on the water, give *Three Pelican's* (South Haven) a try.

BATTLE CREEK

GREENCREST MANOR   **(269) 962-8633**
TOM & KATHY VAN DAFF   **BED & BREAKFAST**

Grand French Normandy mansion on St. Mary's Lake is constructed of sandstone, slate and copper. Formal gardens include fountains and cut stone urns. A/C. Private baths. 8 rooms. Featured in "Country Inns Magazine" as Inn of the Month and Top 12 Inns of North America of 1992. *Website: www.greencrestmanor.com*

Nightly $95-$235

BERRIEN SPRINGS

PENNELLWOOD RESORT   **(269) 473-2511**
DAVID & JAMIE SPACEY   **COTTAGE RESORT**

One price includes everything—meals, lodging, recreation and entertainment. 40 cottages have 2 and 3 bedrooms. Bring beach towels, life jackets and tennis racquets. Enjoy fishing, pontoon rides, volleyball, softball, shuffleboard, square dancing. 2 heated outdoor pools. Reservations require deposit. No pets. *Website: www.pannelwoodresort.com*

Weekly $450 (per adult - children less)

COLDWATER

CHICAGO PIKE INN   **(517) 279-8744**
REBECCA SCHULTZ   **BED & BREAKFAST**

Turn of the Century reformed Colonial Mansion adorned with antiques from the Victorian era. 6 guest rooms in main house, two with whirlpools in Carriage House, all with private baths. Formal dining room, library, and reception room feature sweeping cherry staircase and parquet floors. Full country breakfast and refreshments.

Nightly $100-$195

CONSTANTINE

INN AT CONSTANTINE   **(269) 435-3325 • (800) 435-5365**
JAN MARSHALL   **EMAIL: jan@innatconstantine.com**
       BED & BREAKFAST

Located in Historical Village near antique centers. Inn features antique fireplace mantels, European antiques, in-ground pool. Rooms offers private bath (2 with Jacuzzi) and fireplaces. Full breakfast. Near Amish Shipshewana, Indiana. Canoeing, carriage rides, fishing on St. Joseph River/lakes. 5 rooms/ private bath. *Website: www.innatconstantine.com*

Nightly $85-$165

DELTON

KATIE'S COTTAGE **(269) 623-8340 • Email: midlakes@mei.net**
KATIE OR CHRISTY **PRIVATE COTTAGE**

Lovely 3-bedroom, 2-bath lakefront cottage on private Wall Lake. Located in a quiet section on Beechwood Point. Beautifully furnished. Fireplace, sauna, TV/VCR, full kitchen with dishwasher. Available year around. Near Richland/Hickory Corners/Hastings/Grand Rapids/Kalamazoo/Battle Creek. No pets/smoking.

Weekly $1,400 - $1,550

DOWAGIC

SHADY SHORES RESORT **(269) 424-5251**
COTTAGE RESORT

On Dewey Lake, 20 miles east of Benton Harbor. Furnished and equipped housekeeping cottages have elecric ranges refrigerators, heat, private bath, blankets and cooking/eating utensils. Includes boats, bicycles, playground, badminton, shuffleboard, croquet and tennis. Safe swimming on sandy beach.

Weekly $400-$600

JONES

SANCTUARY AT WILDWOOD **(800) 249-5910 • EMAIL: info@sanctuaryatwildwood.com**
DICK & DOLLY BUERKLE **BED & BREAKFAST/COTTAGES**

★ EDITOR'S CHOICE ★

Lodge and cottages rest on more than 98 acres of woods and meadows. The

Sanctuary provides security for 2 herds of whitetail deer as well as many waterfowl that visit the pond. Nature is emphasized throughout the lodge. Private decks/balconies. Each room or cottage with private baths, fireplace, Jacuzzi and refrigerator. Jeniaire kitchenette available. Heated pool. Close to ski areas and winter activities. Special romantic, canoe or golf packages. Deluxe breakfasts served. Conference room available. *Website: www.sanctuaryatwildwood.com*

Nightly $159-$219 (2 night minimum. Weekday rates Sun.-Thurs.)

Editor's Note: Lovely setting, beautiful rooms, a true "Sanctuary" ...highly recommended.

KALAMAZOO

HALL HOUSE   (269) 343-2500 • (888) 761-2525
DAVID & CATHY GRIFFITH   BED & BREAKFAST
"Experience the Difference". Premier lodging in National Historic District. Guests enjoy the exceptional craftsmanship, polished mahogany and cozy fireplaces of this 1923 Georgian Revival City Inn. Six large guest rooms offer private bath, CATV, VCR, in-room phone, and A/C. Romantic Jacuzzi suite. Smoke free. *Website: www.hallhouse.com*
Nightly $89-$180

LAWRENCE

OAK COVE RESORT   (269) 674-8228 • Email: info@oakcove.com
                          HISTORIC LODGE/COTTAGE/HOME RESORT

Modified American Plan resort...sumptuous breakfasts and dinners served daily. Historic property nestled on 16 beautiful wooded acres with 500' of sandy beach on sparkling Lake Cora. Units recently updated and include A/C, microwaves, refrigerators. Linens provided. Enjoy the heated pool, bicycles, paths in the woods, rowboats, canoes and paddleboats. 18 holes of FREE GOLF, daily. Other activities include shuffleboard, badminton, horseshoes, volleyball and gameroom. Nearby antique shops, flea markets, wineries, horseback riding, go carts, movies and bowling. *Website: www.oakcove.com*

*Weekly $940(lodge)   *$1,010 (cottages/homes)
*Per couple, children's rates vary/Plus tax and gratuity
Editor's Note: This traditional cottage resort offers a beautiful lake view, friendly owners, great food and plenty to do. A/C is a nice addition to cottages.

MENDON

MENDON COUNTRY INN **(269) 496-8132** • EMAIL: vasame@aol.com
GEFF & CHERYL CLARKE **BED & BREAKFAST**

Overlooking St. Joseph River, this romantic country inn has antique filled guest rooms with private baths. Free canoeing, bicycles built for two, fifteen acres of wood ps and water. Restaurant and Amish Tour guide. Featured in Country Living and Country Home magazines. 9 Jacuzzi suites w/fireplace. 18 rooms.

Nightly $79-$169

Editor's Note: Charming historic inn. For those seeking contemporary styling, the Creekside Lodge rooms (in the back of the lot) make for one romantic stay.

NEW BUFFALO

SANS SOUCI EURO INN & RESORT **(269) 756-3141**
ANGELIKA SIEWERT EMAIL: **sans-souci@worldnet.att.net**
 SUITES/HOME/COTTAGE RESORT

This gated nature retreat offers 50 acres of towering trees, groomed landscapes, and a myriad of wildlife on a shimmering, secluded lake. Tendering vacation homes, getaway suites, and lakeside cottages, all with whirlpool baths and wood burning fireplaces. *Website: www.sans-souci.com*

Nightly $160-$220/bedroom (Call for off-season and weekly rates)

SAUGATUCK

BEACHWAY RESORT & **(269) 857-4321** • EMAIL: info@beachwayresort.com
BAYSIDE INN **SUITES/PRIVATE COTTAGES & HOMES, B&B**

Located on the banks of the Kalamazoo River, Beachway Resort is next to the award-winning Oval Beach. It includes luxury units with a diverse range of amenities. Outdoor pool. Their B&B, once a boathouse, is a charming home located on the water in downtown Saugatuck. Private decks and baths.

Nightly $70-$450

BEECHWOOD MANOR B&B AND COTTAGES **(269) 857-1587**
JAMES & SHERRON LEMONS **BED & BREAKFAST/COTTAGES**

The historic inn of Beechwood Manor. Privately owned and fully restored. Built for a diplomat in the 1870's, on National Register. Private baths. Additional features include boat slips, tandem bikes, off-street parking. Private cottages are also available.

B&B Nightly $125-$150 Cottages Weekly $995 (and up)

Editor's Note: B&B maintains that Old-world ambiance. Located on a residential side street.

BRIAR-CLIFFE (269) 857-7041 • EMAIL: briarcliffe@macatawa.com
DAVID & SHIRLEY WITT GUEST SUITES

★ EDITOR'S CHOICE ★

Luxury suites on a scenic bluff overlooking the sandy shores of Lake Michigan. Comfortable sitting room with fire-place, TV/VCR. 5 acres of woods. Queen sized canopy beds. Ceramic bath with Jacuzzi for two. Refrigerator, microwave. Stairway to private sandy beach.

Website: www.lakemichiganbnb.com

Nightly $150-$225

Editor's Note: Classic styling combined with antique-filled rooms and a very quiet setting make this a nice place for that special getaway.

GOSHORN LAKE FAMILY RESORT (800) 541-4210 • (269) 857-4808
RIC GILLETTE COTTAGE RESORT

★ EDITOR'S CHOICE ★

22 housekeeping cottages, some with wood burning fireplaces. All with A/C, equipped kitchens, picnic tables and BBQ grill. Sandy, private swimming beach, volleyball, horseshoes, basketball, fire pit area and rowboats. Outdoor swimming pool. Near Saugatuck, Lake Michigan beaches and golf. No pets. *Website:www.glresort.com*

Weekly $750-$1,200

Editor's Note: Refreshing changes and expansions! We recommend the newest cottages, which are well designed with contemporary comforts. Spacious grounds with small but sandy beach area.

HERITAGE MANOR INN (269) 543-4384
ROSS & DIANE HUNTER EMAIL: rdhunter@heritagemanorinn.com
B&B AND TOWNHOUSES

Lovely, country-style B&B near Lake Michigan and Saugatuck. Indoor pool, whirlpool. Rooms with private baths, some with Jacuzzi, fireplace. Full breakfast. 3 furnished townhouses also offered with full kitchens and living rooms. All include A/C, CATV, some VCR's.No pets/smoking. *Website: www.heritagemanorinn.com*

Nightly $75-$250 Weekly (townhouses): $1,000-$1,200

MASON HOUSE   (847) 498-2938 • EMAIL: patkresq@msn.com
PATRICIA ROTCHFORD   PRIVATE COTTAGE

★ EDITOR'S CHOICE ★

Beautifully landscaped, upscale 4-Seasons home in quiet residential area, 1/4 block to town and Lake Michigan. Newer home sleeps 8-10. Two baths, dining room, living room, laundry room, full kitchen with extras such as dishwasher, popcorn popper, cappuccino maker. Two bedrooms,

sofa sleeper and blow-up bed. Florida room with sleeper, deck with grill and sink, two sitting garden rooms, fenced yard, shared inground pool, fuel fireplace, central A/C and heat. Towels/linens included. TV, VCR, telephone/computer hook up. Open year round. Ask about pet policy.

Weekly $750* and up
Weekends   from $345* (*off-season rates)

Editor' Note: Immaculate home, delightfully styled, located on a quiet street. Very nice choice.

PARK HOUSE B&B & COTTAGES   (800) 321-4535 • (269) 857-4535
LYNDA & JOE PETTY   BED & BREAKFAST & COTTAGES

★ EDITOR'S CHOICE ★

On National Historic Register. Saugatuck's oldest residence (1857) hosted Susan B. Anthony. Eight rooms, queen beds, private baths. Four cottages with equipped kitchens, TV/VCR. All include A/C. Two luxury suites, two cottages offer jet tubs, fireplaces. Close to town, beach, ski trails. *Website: www.parkhouseinn.com*

Nightly $95-$225

Editor's Note: Inviting ambiance retains the style of its period with the added comforts today's guests appreciate. Lovely choice for the area.

THE KINGSLEY HOUSE   (269) 561-6425 • EMAIL: garyking@accn.org
GARY & KARI KING   BED & BREAKFAST

In Fennville, minutes from Saugatuck, 1886 elegant Queen Anne Victorian B&B. Featured in Innsider Magazine, rated as a "Top Fifty Inn" in America by Inn Times. AAA approved. Near Holland/Saugatuck. Private baths, whirlpool/bath. Special getaway suite. Beautiful surroundings, family antiques. Homemade breakfast. A/C. 8 rooms.

Nightly $85-$175

Editor's Note: Well appointed rooms and welcoming proprietors...very nice.

THE KIRBY HOUSE   (800) 521-6473 • EMAIL: info@kirbyhouse.com
RAY RIKER & JIM GOWRAN   BED & BREAKFAST

The most popular bed and breakfast in the Saugatuck/Douglas area. Furnished with antiques. Private baths, air conditioning and fireplace rooms available. Pool, Jacuzzi and bicycles. Full gourmet breakfast buffet. Close to shopping and lake Michigan. Reservations imperative. Major credit cards accepted. *Website: www.kirbyhouse.com*

Nightly $100-$175

WICKWOOD COUNTRY INN   (269) 857-1465
JULEE ROSSO-MILLER & BILL MILLER   BED & BREAKFAST

★ EDITOR'S CHOICE ★

A charming European-style Inn located in the beautiful Victorian Village of Saugatuck on the Eastern Shores of Lake Michigan. Owner Julee Rosso-Miller, serves up breakfast and hors d'oeuvres daily using recipes from her four best selling cookbooks. "The Silver Palate", "The Silver Palate Good Times", "The New Basics" and "Great Good Foods". 11 rooms with private baths.

Nightly $145-$325

Editor's Note: In the heart of Saugatuck. Beautifully decorated rooms. Just a short walk to shops, restaurants and more.

ST. JOSEPH

THE SAND CASTLES   (800) 972-0080 • EMAIL:info@sandcastlecottages.com
                                              COTTAGE RESORT

Located halfway between South Haven and St. Joseph. 11 housekeeping cottages (sleep 2 to 8). Kitchenette or full kitchen. Ceiling fans, A/C, and heat. Larger units have separate bedrooms and living/dining/kitchen areas. Cable w/HBO hookups (bring your own TV). No pets. 4 blocks to Lake Michigan beaches. *Website: www.sandcastlescottages.com.*

Weekly $350-$800

Editor's Note: Traditional cottages with well maintained interiors and some nice extras like ceiling fans and A/C. Sizes range significantly.

SOUTH CLIFF INN BED & BREAKFAST
BILL SWISHER

(269) 983-4881
BED & BREAKFAST

Overlooking Lake Michigan, traditional brick home has luxurious accommodations and relaxed atmosphere. Tastefully decorated rooms with traditional and antique furnishings. The private beach is just steps away. Full buffet breakfast. Room with whirlpool tub /fireplace available. A/C. Seven rooms.
Website: ww.southcliffinn.com
Nightly $85-$225 (Seasonal)

SOUTH HAVEN

A COUNTRY PLACE BED & BREAKFAST & COTTAGE
JOHN & CINDY MALMSTROM

(269) 637-5523
Email: acountryplace@cybersol.com
BED & BREAKFAST/COTTAGE

Restored 1860's Greek Revival furnished with American antiques. Five charming guest rooms with private baths feature English country themes. Full breakfast served daily. Cozy cottage features pine interior, full kitchen, king size bed, and 3 single beds in the loft and porch, Franklin fireplace. Lake Michigan beach access 1/2 block from property. Open year around. *Website: csinet/acountryplace*
B&B Nightly $100-$145   Cottage Weekly $750 (Daily off-season $125)
Editor's Note: Lovely B&B...comfy rooms in a welcoming country ambiance.

GREENE HOMES, LLC

(269) 639-8383
PRIVATE COTTAGES

Weekly vacation rentals on or near Lake Michigan. All homes and cottages are fully furnished. The largest home accommodates up to 19 guests. Rentals offer diverse amenities, TV with VCR or DVD, dishwasher, washer, dryer, AC, fireplace, etc. No pets/smoking. *Website: www.greenehomes.com*
Weekly $650-$2,500

LAST RESORT B&B INN
(269) 637-8943
BED & BREAKFAST/COTTAGE

Built in 1883 as South Haven's first resort inn. Most rooms with view of Lake Michigan or harbor. Penthouse suites provide best views and feature Jacuzzi. A/C. Open April-Oct. 14 rooms/private baths. Also available, cottage for two with view of the harbor. *Website: www.lastresortinn.com*

Nightly $80 (and up)

LOKNATH-CHANDERVARMA, HARBOR'S UNIT #32
(269) 344-3012
PRIVATE CONDO

2 bedroom/2 bath condo (sleeps 7). Elegantly furnished, large master bedroom. A/C, CATV, equipped kitchen, microwave, dishwasher. Panoramic view, private beach, pool, laundry, garage. Provide your own towel and linens. Minimum 7 day stay. Available all year. No pets.

Weekly $1,100 (May-Sept.)

MICHI-MONA-MAC LAKESHORE COTTAGES
(847) 332-1443 • (269) 637-3003
COTTAGE RESORT

Watch spectacular sunsets from the private, spotless beach. One and 2 bedroom cottages with new kitchens, private baths. Beachside rooms with lovely bay windows and fireplace. Open all year. No pets/smoking. Great family vacation or romantic getaway.

Weekly $800 (and up)   Off-Season, Nightly $115 (and up)

Editor's Note: The beach is small but lovely with incline taking you to water's edge. Units are linked together apartment style. Small but well maintained.

NORTH BEACH INN & PIGOZZI'S
(269) 637-6738
INN

1890's Victorian styled B&B overlooks Lake Michigan Beach. All rooms offer private baths. Restaurant, Pigozzi, serves full breakfasts, lunch and dinners.

Call for Rates

RIVERBEND RETREAT
(269) 637-3505 • EMAIL: riverbend@i2k.com
PRIVATE COTTAGES

★ EDITOR'S CHOICE ★

Two cozy cedar cottages on beautiful Black River. Enjoy the peacefulness. In-ground heated pool, boat dock, canoes, boat, private hot tub, stone fireplace, central air. Fully equipped for 12 people, including towels and bedding, phone, TV, VCR, dishwasher, laundry. Open year around. Off-season priced for couples or groups. No pets.

Weekly $2,100-$2,300 (in-season, 12 people)

Editors Note: Luxurious vacation homes ... many amenities. Set back from the road on a spacious lot overlooking the Black River. Highly recommended!

THE OAKLAND   **773-388-3121**
LYNN & BOB BRUNO   **PRIVATE HOME**

Historic landmark resort built in 1927. Immaculately maintained and fully equipped for 8-10 people. Steps away from South Haven's North Beach providing beautiful views of the harbor, lake and sunset. A/C, CATV, VCR, W/D. No pets/smoking. *Website: wwww.megsint.net/~kmb/oakland.html*
Weekly $2,200 (June-Sept.); Nightly (off-season) $50 (per person)

Editor's Note: This spacious home offers plenty of room PLUS it's right across the street from one of South Haven's fabulous beaches. See our review in this edition.

THE SEYMOUR HOUSE   **(269) 227-3918 • EMAIL: seymour@cybersol.com**
FRIEDL SCIMO   **BED & BREAKFAST/LOG CABIN**

Enjoy the unsurpassed beauty of this 1862 Victorian mansion on 11 wooded acres. Picturesque 1-acre pond. Trails through the woods. Minutes to Saugatuck, South Haven, beaches, restaurants, galleries, horseback riding, golf and orchards. 5 rooms/private bath, fireplaces, Jacuzzi. Guest log cabin. A/C, gourmet breakfasts *Website:www.seymourhouse.com*
Nightly $80-$145

Editor's Note: Scenic backyard, nature trails and a well maintained historic home combine for a relaxing stay.

SLEEPY HOLLOW RESORT   **(269) 637-1127**
                       COTTAGE/APARTMENT/DUPLEX RESORT

★ EDITOR'S CHOICE ★

This 58 years old Art Deco style resort provides the "all in one" family vacation. Six tennis courts, volleyball, Olympic-size pool, children's activities on the resort promises to keep you busy. Cottages and apartments include partial to full kitchens, private baths. Open May 1-Oct. 7.

Weekly $1,550-$3,440 ($440-$2,380 off-season)

Editor's Note: Amazing transformations have occurred at this long-time resort. Newly renovated/re-built cottages are definitely leaning towards upscale. Highly recommended. See our review in this addition.

SUNSET HAVEN   (269) 639-7140
LYNNE VANLEERDAM   PRIVATE HOMES

Several furnished homes offered for your vacation comfort. Ideally located 1-2 blocks from Lake Michigan, an easy walk to downtown. Amenities include AC, equipped kitchens, CATV, VCR. Available year around. No pets/smoking.
Website: www.sunsethaven.com

Weekly $650 - $1,800 (June-Aug.)   Nightly $125-$225 (Sept.-May)

Editor's Note: We visited several of Lynne's homes ... all were well maintained and very comfortably designed with nice amenities. Most rentals are just a block or two from the lake.

TANBITHN   888-304-5894
MAC & RAE LEE HOWARD   PRIVATE COTTAGE

Two bedroom (sleeps 5) cottage on North Shore Drive. Features CATV, VCR ceiling fan and room A/C. Linens provided (bring towels). Light and airy interior. Only 1/2 block from beach, 1 block from marina. Fall/winter rates negotiable. No pets.

Weekly $975 (June-Aug.)   Nightly $140 (Sept.-May)

Editor's Note: Small but bright and appealing interior and decor. Sits right off the sidewalk ... fun for people watching.

THOMPSON HOUSE   (269) 637-6521 • EMAIL: JLT_KT@cybersol.com
JOYCE THOMPSON   PRIVATE HOME

Charming home, sleeps six. One block to South Beach, Riverfront Park. Great garden, umbrella table, wraparound porch and deck. Enjoy all the modern conveniences including CATV, microwave, dishwasher, laundry, central air, electronic air cleaner, a water purifier and whirlpool bathtub. No pets.
Website: www.thompsonhouseofsouthhaven.com

Weekly $1,000

Editor's Note: Well maintained home, simply furnished, on a quiet side street. A nice place to be away from the maddening crowds.

VICTORIA RESORT B & B   (800) 473-7376 • (269) 637-6414
BOB & JAN   BED & BREAKFAST/COTTAGE RESORT

Three acre resort located 1-1/2 blocks from Lake Michigan. Close to downtown. Some rooms and cottages feature fireplaces and whirlpool tubs. Outdoor pool, bikes, tennis and basketball courts. Winter packages include: two-night stay, dinner, breakfast in bed, and more. *Website: www.victoriaresort.com*

Cottages, Weekly $1,260 and up

Editor's Note: Comfortable and very clean accommodations for family fun.

YELTON MANOR BED & BREAKFAST
ELAINE HERBERT & ROB KRIPAITIS

(269) 637-5220
EMAIL: elaine@yeltonmanor.com
BED & BREAKFAST

★ EDITOR'S CHOICE ★

"Top of the crop in luxury B & B's". On the sunset coast of beautiful Lake Michigan. 17 guest rooms with private baths. Some have Jacuzzi, fireplace and private decks. Extravagant honeymoon and anniversary suites. Gourmet hors d'oeuvres, fabulous breakfast and daylong goodies. A true make-yourself-at-home, luxurious geta-way. Take a tour at our *website: www.yeltonmanor.com*

Nightly $90-$220

Editor's Note: A premiere resort for executive retreats. No direct view of the Lake, but still a great way t o forget about the...STRESS.

STEVENSVILLE

CHALET ON THE LAKE

(269) 465-6365
CHALET/CONDO RESORT

51 A-frame duplexes on Lake Michigan, 7 miles south of St. Joseph. Includes 2 bedrooms (sleeps 8) will full kitchen, dining area, living room, CATV. Resort features volleyball, 5 tennis courts, 2 pools and a large private beach. Bring towels. Open year around. No pets.

Weekly $865-$1,200 (plus tax)

UNION CITY

VICTORIAN VILLA INN
RONALD J. GIBSON

(800) 34-VILLA • (517) 741-7383
BED & BREAKFAST

19th Century Italianate inn. Fourth floor tower offers birds-eye view of the town. "Victoria's" restaurant offers 7-course champagne candlelight dinners. Private baths. 7 bed chambers, 3 suites (2 with fireplace, 1 with hot tub). Credit cards. Outdoor smoking.

Nightly $85-$120 (Sun-Thurs); $125-$160 (Fri./Sat, holidays)

UNION PIER

GARDEN GROVE B&B — (269) 469-6346 • (800) 613-2872
PAULA & JERRY WELSH — BED & BREAKFAST
Pamper yourself with comfort and beauty at a vintage 1925 inn. Decorated with colorful flair and botanical style; we bring the garden indoors year-round. Deluxe accommodations. Jacuzzi-whirlpools, fireplaces, balconies, private dining. Everything the discriminating inn guest expects: Charm, romance, hospitality, scrumptious breakfast. Outstanding area: wineries, beaches, shopping.

Nightly — $90-$200

THE INN AT UNION PIER — (269) 469-4700
BILL & JOYCE JANN — BED & BREAKFAST
Harbor Country's premier bed & breakfast...just 200 steps from the beach! Choose from 16 spacious guest rooms, most featuring woodburning fireplaces and porches or balconies, 2 Jacuzzi suites. Relax in the outdoor hot tub and sauna. Gourmet breakfast and complimentary refreshments. Bicycles. Corporate retreats. *Website: www.innatunionpier.com*

Nightly — $150-$225

Editor's Note: Large B&B with comfortable rooms, uniquely styled. Located on quiet side street.

RIVER'S EDGE BED & BREAKFAST — (269) 469-6860
KEITH & PRUDENCE — EMAIL: sindelarkp@earthlink.com
— BED & BREAKFAST
On 30 acres of wooded trails and orchards, bordering a half mile of the Galien River, you'll find peaceful River's Edge. Eight large rooms all feature double size jacuzzis, fireplaces, TV/VCR/CAB, ceiling fans, and unique beds styled by artisan Andy Brown. Bikes, cross-country skis, and canoe available to guests, and only one block to Michigan's beaches. A full hot breakfast is served every morning. *Website: wwwriversedgebandb.com.*

Nightly — $99-240 (in-season)

Editor's Note: Plenty of land with the home featuring a distinct contemporary, country flavor. Very nice retreat.

PINE GARTH INN   **(269) 469-1642 • (888) 390-0909**
NESSA & DENISE   **BED & BREAKFAST/COTTAGES/HOME**

★ EDITOR'S CHOICE ★

Beautiful lakefront estate and guest houses located on 200 ft. of private sugar
sand Lake Michigan beach. B&B has 7 rooms, spectacular lake views, queen
beds, private baths and VCR. Guest houses are charming with 2 bedrooms, full
kitchens, fireplaces, hot tubs, grills, private decks and some screened porches.
Carriage House is romantic and the Villa House is 4,000 sq. ft. of heaven with
beautiful lake views, screened porches, unbelievable kitchen; perfect for families or adult getaways. Open year around. *Website: www.pinegarth.com*

Nightly $155-$210 (Rooms)*; $250-$280 (Cottages)*
* Call for off-season rates and Villa House rates.

*Editor's Note: Lovely B&B with beautiful lake view. Well-styled cottages are lo-
cated on the quiet street behind . Excellent sandy beach accessed down stairway.*

VICTORIAN VILLA INN   **(800) 34-VILLA • (517) 741-7383**
RONALD J. GIBSON   **BED & BREAKFAST**

19th Century Italianate inn. Fourth floor tower offers birds-eye view of the
town. "Victoria's" restaurant offers 7-course champagne candlelight dinners.
Private baths. 7 bed chambers, 3 suites (2 with fireplace, 1 with hot tub).
Credit cards. Outdoor smoking.

Nightly $85-$120 (Sun-Thurs); $125-$160 (Fri/Sat, holidays)

Michigan Wineries & Casinos Map

$$\boxed{\$ = \text{Casinos} \qquad \text{\textcommabelow ♀} = \text{Wineries}}$$

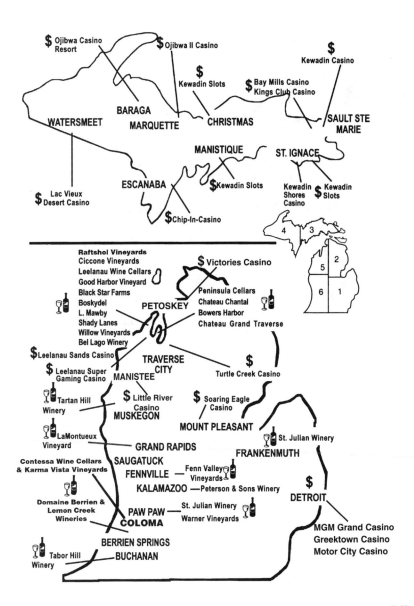

$ Ojibwa Casino
Resort

$ Ojibwa II Casino

$ Kewadin Casino

$ Kewadin Slots

$ Bay Mills Casino
Kings Club Casino

BARAGA

WATERSMEET

MARQUETTE

CHRISTMAS

SAULT STE MARIE

MANISTIQUE

ST. IGNACE

$ Lac Vieux
Desert Casino

ESCANABA

$ Kewadin Slots

Kewadin
Shores
Casino

$ Kewadin
Slots

$ Chip-In-Casino

4 3
5
6 1
2

Raftshol Vineyards
Ciccone Vineyards
Leelanau Wine Cellars
Good Harbor Vineyard
Black Star Farms
Boskydel
L. Mawby
Shady Lanes
Willow Vineyards
Bel Lago Winery

$ Victories Casino

Peninsula Cellars
Chateau Chantal
Bowers Harbor
Chateau Grand Traverse

PETOSKEY

$ Leelanau Sands Casino

$ Leelanau Super
Gaming Casino

**TRAVERSE
CITY**

MANISTEE

$ Turtle Creek Casino

Tartan Hill
Winery

$ Little River
Casino

MUSKEGON

$ Soaring Eagle
Casino

MOUNT PLEASANT

LaMontueux
Vineyard

GRAND RAPIDS

St. Julian Winery

FRANKENMUTH

Contessa Wine Cellars
& Karma Vista Vineyards

SAUGATUCK

FENNVILLE

Fenn Valley
Vineyards

Domaine Berrien &
Lemon Creek
Wineries

KALAMAZOO

Peterson & Sons Winery

PAW PAW

COLOMA

St. Julian Winery

Warner Vineyards

$ **DETROIT**

BERRIEN SPRINGS

BUCHANAN

MGM Grand Casino
Greektown Casino
Motor City Casino

Tabor Hill
Winery

Michigan Wineries

Nestled along Michigan's shorelines in some of our state's most scenic areas, wineries are flourishing. Boasting a unique collection of wines, our winemakers continue to receive national and international recognition.

An enjoyable part of any Michigan experience is a leisurely drive through beautiful wine country. Visit our tasting rooms and see why Michigan wines have gained international attention.

Of course, be responsible. We want you to have a *safe* and *enjoyable* Michigan vacation.

REGION 1

FRANKENMUTH, MONROE & PARMA

St. Julian Winery

989-652-3281
Monroe: 734-242-9409
Parma: 989-531-3786
One of Michigan's oldest and largest wineries. Family-owned and operated since 1921.

REGION 5

CEDAR

Bel Lago Winery

6530 S. Lakeshore Dr.
231-228-4800
Produces wines taken from grapes grown in family-owned vineyards. Provides Pino Grigio, Chardonnay, Pino Noir and a variety of sparkling wines. Tasting room treats visitors to a panoramic view of Lake Leelanau.

LAKE LEELANAU

Boskydel Vineyards

2881 S. Lake Leelanau Dr.
231-256-7272
Small winery preparing limited but very nice dry and semi-sweet table wines ... presented in a unique tasting room. We understand during Christmas you can also pickup your holiday tree here.

Good Harbor Vineyards

34 S. Manitou Trail
231-256-7165
Excellent wines come from this 50-acre, well-tended vineyard. Known for Chardonnay, Pinot Gris, Riesling, Pinot Noir, Seyval and champagne.

OLD MISSION PENINSULA

Chateau Chantal

15900 Rue de Vin
231-223-4110
Operating B&B and vineyard. Impressive, Old World-styled winery. Known for Chardonnay, Pinot Gris, Pinot Noir, Merlot, Riesling and Gewurztraminer, Ice Wine and champagne. Several

award winning specialties. Incredible views of East and West Grand Traverse Bays.

Chateau Grand Traverse

12239 Center Road
231-223-7355
Williamsburg: 231-938-2291
Traverse City: 231-941-4146
Large wine-making facility grows and produces award-winning, premium varietal wines. Estate-grown. Excellent Riesling, Pinot Noir, Merlot, Cabernet Franc and Ice Wine. Also a variety of area specialties like Spiced Cherry Wine, Cranberry Riesling, to name a view. Overlooks Grand Traverse Bay.

Peninsula Cellars

18250 Mission Road
231-223-4050 • 231-223-4310
Using the finest grapes in the area, wines are estate bottled with limited production. Specialties include Chardonnay, Dry Riesling, Raftshol Red and a variety of dessert wines.

OMENA
Leelanau Wine Cellars

12683 E. Tatch Road
231-386-5201
Very nice selection of dry to semi-sweet wines ... barrel-fermented, aged Chardonnays and Reislings. Also produces a variety of seasonal and fruit wines. Tours available.

SUTTONS BAY
Black Star Farms

10844 E. Revold Rd.
231-271-4884
South of Sutton's Bay. State-of-the art wine producing facility. European vinifera varieties. Lovely estate with trails winding through woodlands and orchards. Elegant, fully operational B&B. Impressive equestrian center also operated on the estate.

Chateau de Leelanau

5048 Wouth West Bay Shore
231-271-8888
One of the Leelanau Peninsula's newest wineries. Noted for being Michigan's first winery owned by women. Specializes in still and sparkling wine made from Chardonnary, Gewurztraminer and Cabernet Franc.

Ciconni Vineyards

10343 East Hilltop Road
231-271-5551
Operated by Silvo (father of rock star, Madonna) and his wife, Joan. Noted for dry Gewurz-traminer along with Cabernet Franc, Pino Noir, Chardonnary, Pino Grigio and rose de Cabernet. New tasting room.

L. Mawby Vineyards

4519 S. Elm Valley
231-271-3522
Original vines date to 1973. Limited but pure winemaking production ... barrel-fermented made with simple machinery. Specializing in white table wines and methode champenoise sparkling wines. Most wines taken from estate.

Raftshol Vineyards

1865 North West Bay Shore Dr.
231-271-5650
Opened November 1999. Specializing in Bordeau varietal reds, including Merlot and Cabernet Sauvignon and white wines, including Chardonnay.

Shady Lane Cellars

9580 Shady Lane
231-947-8865
On historic 100-acre farm Maintains more than 10,000 vines. Gold medal award winners producing excellent methode champenoise sparkling wines along with Pinot Noir, Riesling and Chardonnay. New tasting facility.

Willow Vineyards

10702 East Hilltop Rd.
231-929-4542

Est.1992. Panoramic views of West Traverse Bay enhance the ambiance of this vineyard. Producer of premium Chardonnay, Pinot Noir and Pino Gris all estate or regionally grown.

TRAVERSE CITY

Bowers Harbor Vineyards

2896 Bowers Harbor Road
231-223-7615

Small but delightful winery offering a beautiful overlook of Bowers Harbor. Chardonnay, Riesling and sparking wines plus specialty fruit wines.

Peninsula Cellars

11480 Center Road (M-37)
Winery: 231-223-4050
Tasting Room: 231-933-9797

Family operated. Wines are estate bottled using the area's finest fruit. Known for Chardonnary, Dry Riesling, Raftshal Red, Apple, White Cherry and Jubilee dessert wines.

St. Julian Winery

(Main winery in Paw Paw)
Traverse City: 231-933-6120

REGION 6

BERRIEN SPRINGS

Lemon Creek Winery

533 E. Lemon Creek Road
269-471-1321

Producer of the first commercial, entirely Michigan-grown Cabernet Sauvignon. 11 white/9 red wines. Home winemakers can purchase picked grapes or grape juice.

Domaine Berrien Cellars

398 E. Lemon Creed Road
269-473-WINE (9463)

Opened in 2001. All wines made from grapes grown on their vineyard. Nice selection of red and white wines. Tasting room and tours available.

BUCHANAN

Tabor Hill Winery

185 Mt. Tabor Road
800-283-3363
Bridgman: 269-857-6566
Saugatuck: 269-857-4859

Numerous award-winning wines, sparkling wines and non-alcoholic juices. Gift shop. Fine meals served in rustic dining room overlooking the vineyards. Their 'Classic Demi-Sec' is the only Michigan wine served at the President's table in the White House.

COLOMA

Contessa Wine Cellars

3235 Friday Road
269-468-5534

Newly opened, just off Exit 39 on I-94. Beautiful facillity with exceptional wines. Tasting room and tours from 12-5.

Karma Vista Vineyards

6991 Ryno Road
269-468-WINE (9463)

Also off Exit 39 on I-94. Premium wines include Carbernet Franc, Riesling and Chardonney.

FENNVILLE

Fenn Valley Vineyards

6130 122nd Avenue
269-561-2396

Known for estate-bottled Reislings, Champagnes, Pinot Gris and barrel-aged red wines. Barrel fermented white made from a new variety of Chardonel. Winners of numerous awards and honors.

KALAMAZOO

Peterson & Sons Winery

9375 East P. Avenue
269-626-9755
Producer of wines without use of chemicals or preservatives. Over 30 variety of Michigan-grown fruits and grapes.

PAW PAW

St. Julian Winery

716 S. Kalamazoo
616-657-5568 • 800-732-6002
Union Pier: 269-469-3150
Michigan's oldest and largest winery (since 1921). Producer of over 40 wines. Fine dining also available at the Apollo Restaurant.

Warner Vineyards

706 S. Kalamazoo
269-657-3165
Family-operated for over 30 years. Located in an historical structure built in 1898. Produces a variety of sparkling, table and dessert wines. Self guided tours.

Michigan Casinos

Oh, Lady Luck you done me wrong, but I keep coming back for more.

REGION 1

DETROIT

Greektown Casino
555 E. Lafayette Blvd.
888-771-4386

MGM Grand Detroit
1300 John C. Lodge Service Dr.
313-393-7777 or 877-888-2121

MotorCity Casino
2901 Grand River Ave.
877-777-6711

REGION 2

MT. PLEASANT

Soaring Eagle Casino
6800 Soaring Eagle Blvd.
888-7EAGLE7 or 989-775-7777

REGION 3

BRIMLEY

Bay Mills Resort & Casino
11386 W. Lake Shore
888-422-9645 or 877-229-6455

Kings Club Casino
12140 W. Lake Shore
906-248-3241

CHRISTMAS

Kewadin Slots
105 Candy Cane Lane
906-387-5475

HESSEL

Kewadin Slots
Three Mile Road at M-134
906-484-2767

MANISTIQUE

Kewadin Slots
Route 1
906-341-5510

ST. IGNACE

Kewadin Shores Casinos
3039 Mackinac Trail
906-643-7071

SAULT STE. MARIE

Kewadin Casino
2186 Shunk Road
906-632-0530

REGION 4

BARAGA

Ojibwa Casino Resort
797 Michigan
906-353-6333

ESCANABA

Chip-In-Casino
W399 Highway 2 & 41
906-466-2941
800-682-6040

MARQUETTE

Ojibwa II Casino
105 Acre Trail
906-249-4200

WATERSMEET

Lac Vieux Desert Casino
N5384 US 45
906-358-4227

REGION 5

MANISTEE

Little River Casino
2700 Orchard Highway
(Corner of US 23 & M22)
231-723-1535 or 888-568-2244

PETOSKEY

Victories Casino & Entertainment
1967 US 131 South
231-439-6100 or 877-4-GAMING

SUTTONS BAY

Leelanau Sands Casino
2521 NW Bayshore Drive
231-271-4104
800-922-2946

Leelanau Super Gaming
  Palace
2649 NW Bayshore Drive
231-271-6852
800-922-2946

WILLIAMSBURG

Turtle Creek Casino
7741 M-72, E
231-267-9574
888-777-8946

MICHIGAN FALL COLOR TOURS

Our Faavorite Fall Color Tours

BEST COLOR VIEWING TIMES

Mid-September to Early October

What fall time experience is complete without a leisurely stroll or relaxing drive among the vivid colors of Michigan's beautiful landscapes?

Late September to Mid-October

Early to Mid-October

Mid to Late October

EAST LOWER PENINSULA (Region 1 & 2):

- *The River Road, National Scenic Byway.* The tour begins three miles south of Oscoda on River Road Scenic Byway. Follow this scenic, 22 mile road which runs along the bluffs above the Au Sable River. This drive offers panoramic views of the river, its forested banks and islands. You'll find outstanding fall colors and the Lumberman's Monument (only 20 minutes west of Oscoda on River Road Scenic Byway) which offers a wonderful overlook. Then, just 1-1/2 miles west of the Monument's Visitors Center, is the *Eagles' Nest Overlook* which has been the home to families of eagles for over 10 years. The overlook also offers a photographer's dream view of Cook Pond and the river valley.

- *AuSable River Vista. Listed as a National Forest Scenic Overlook*, this beautiful vista has breathtaking, vibrant colors in the fall and offers a 20-mile stretch of the AuSable River Valley and Alcona Pond. To begin this tour, go north on M-65 and turn west on F-30 in Glennie. Continue three miles to AuSable Road and turn right. This vista is about four miles north of AuSable Road. Enjoy the view.

- *Irish Hills Tower.* The lovely hills make this area a choice spot for any driving tour. The variety of trees found here create a beautiful bouquet of fall colors. The Tower (one mile west of US 12 and M-124) offers an excellent, panoramic view of northern Lenawee County.

UPPER PENINSULA (Regions 3 & 4):

The truth is, just about anywhere in the Upper Peninsula is a perfect spot for fall touring. Just taking a quiet side road may bring you to one of the UP's many scenic views or majestic waterfalls highlighted by brilliant fall colors.

If you're not into impromptu exploration, however, here are a few "planned" routes that offer plenty of great scenery with a wonderful blend of autumn colors.

- *Porcupine Mountain National Park & Lake of the Clouds Scenic Overlook* (approx. 170 miles). You can enjoy the colors from your car but will need to do a little hiking if you want to truly experience panoramic views of fall's beauty on this trip. One such view is the Lake of the Clouds Scenic Overlook. It's a 1/4 mile hike up a rather steep hill. However, this is a view you don't want to miss. At the top you'll find yourself perched high above the lake. You'll be awed by the spectacular view of the Porcupine Mountains, filled with vivid colors of green, gold and red, reflecting off the still waters of the lake. From Baraga, take 41 north to Chassell, west to Painesdale. Take 26 north to the Highway 38 intersection and go west to Ontonagon. Take 64 west to Silver City and the Porcupine Mountains State Park. You'll return to Baraga on Highway 38.

• *Seney National Wildlife Refuse & Tahquamenon Falls* (approx. 88 miles). Again, the beauty here is only enhanced by the vivid colors of autumn. From Grand Marais, go South on 77 to Seney National Refuge where you'll want to explore nature at its finest. Then continue east on 28 to Newberry, north on 123 to Paradise (gateway to the Whitefish Point Lighthouse, Whitefish Point Bird Observatory, and Tahquamenon Falls). To return, follow 123 to 28 and go west, back to 77.

NORTHWEST LOWER PENINSULA (Region 5)

• *Old Mission Peninsula* (38 miles): Combine stops at roadside fruit stands, charming restaurants and shops with this relaxing fall color tour. This is a delightful trip through the peninsula which divides Grand Traverse Bay into East and West Arms. Take M-37 (Center Road) north from Traverse City's Garfield Road. Stay right where M-37 and Peninsula Drive fork, continue north to the tip of the peninsula. Backtrack on M-37. Turn right on Peninsula Drive, along the West Bay shore to Traverse City.

• *Leelanau Peninsula* (approx. 93 miles): Touring through Michigan's "little finger" has been a popular fall experience for generations. It's an easy and beautiful tour which takes you along shorelines, through quaint villages including Suttons Bay, Omena and Northport with homey restaurants and shops. Feeling lucky? Stop by the casino. Then, on to the tip of the little finger. Tour the Grand Traverse Lighthouse, the view is outstanding.

More brilliant colors can be seen as you continue along the western coast through Leland, Glen Arbor and Sleeping Bear Dune where you'll find spectacular colors along the 7-mile Pierce Stocking Scenic Drive. You'll want to checkout the Dune Climb for a little *exercise* before your return trip. To take this tour, follow M-22, from Traverse City, along the coast to Northport (to get to the "little finger" take M-201 to C-629). M-22 continues south from Northport through Leland into Glen Arbor, then M-109 brings you to the Pierce Stocking Scenic Drive at the Sleeping Bear Dune National Lakeshore. M-109 will meet up with M-22 and M-72 for your return to Traverse City.

• *Interlochen/Benzie County* (approx. 98 miles): Let the sounds of nature mingle with the sounds of music from the Interlochen Center for the Arts. This premiere music education center is open all year and features well-known professional entertainers as well as student performances. On natural grounds, the Center offers inviting pathways through the trees and natural shrubbery which will surround you in the brilliant colors of fall. Then onto your exploration of Benzie County where you'll find fine art and craft galleries and plenty of small town ambiance.

Follow US-31/M-37 south from Traverse City to the M-37 and US-31 intersection. Turn right on US-31, then left on M-137 to C-70, and right in the town of Karlin, then right on County Line Road. This will take you through Thompsonville. Take a right on M-115 and travel to Benzonia and Beulah to loop back onto US-31 south. A left turn at Chum's Corners will return you to Traverse City.

• *Tunnel of Trees* (50-110 miles, depending on tour route): This is a wonderful drive at any time of the year, but it's really impressive during the fall. We should note this drive is a bit trickier than the others because there are no road shoulders. The driver will have to stay focused on the road.
From the Harbor Springs, go north along M-119. We recommend exploring the Thorn Swift Nature Preserve on lower Shore Drive. Pass Cross Village and continue a few more miles to the stop sign, turn left following Lake Shore Drive to Lakeview Road. At Sturgeon Bay explore the dunes and beach. Continue on Lakeview which changes to Gill Road.

From here you can take two different routes, depending on your time and interest. The shorter tour will take 1.25 hours with the longer taking 2.5 hours. The shorter one is as follows: Take Gill Road for 3 miles toward Bliss and the Pleasantville Road (C-81) junction. Continue on Pleasantville Road back to M-119 and take a right to return to Harbor Spring.

Here's the long tour: Gill Road to Cecil Bay Road (5 miles). Go left and continue to the road's end, then right on Wilderness Park Drive (if you want to visit the Park, take a left). Continue north passing Colonial Fort Michilimackinaw and pass under I-75 at the base of the Mackinaw Bridge. You'll begin the Cheboygan County Scenic Route on US-23 and continue south along US-23 into Cheboygan. Take a right at the M-27 junction. Continue on M-27 passed Mullett and Burt Lakes which will take you through Indian River to the junction of M-68. Turn right to Alanson and then left on US-31 to Petoskey. Head north on M-119 which will take you back to Harbor Springs.

SOUTHWEST LOWER PENINSULA (Region 6):

• *Lakeshore Drive from Grand Haven to Holland* (approx. 22 miles): This beautiful drive on Lakeshore is a photographer's paradise. Stop at Kirk Park and Tunnel Park to enjoy the crisp air as you take in the surrounding brilliance of autumn at its best. This drive is a simple one—just start in Grand Haven and go south on Lakeshore Drive.

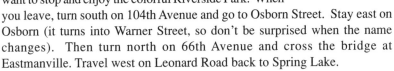

• *Grand River Basin* (approx. 40 miles): Scenic bayous and brilliant colors combine to make this tour a fun experience. To begin, start in Grand Haven (Robbins Road) and go east to Mercury Drive (continue east). You'll pass a few Grand River bayous and will want to stop and enjoy the colorful Riverside Park. When you leave, turn south on 104th Avenue and go to Osborn Street. Stay east on Osborn (it turns into Warner Street, so don't be surprised when the name changes). Then turn north on 66th Avenue and cross the bridge at Eastmanville. Travel west on Leonard Road back to Spring Lake.

• *P.J. Hoffmaster State Park to Muskegon* (approx. 20 miles). Here's another nice tour we recommend because of the dunes and nature center along the way. Just go west on Pantaluna Road to Lake Harbor Road. P.J. Hoffmaster State is where we highly recommend you explore the dunes area and the Gillette Nature Center. Then head north on Lake Harbor Road to Muskegon.

FAVORITE GOLF COURSES

In 2004 Golf Digest ranked Michigan as the *12ᵗʰ Best Golf Destination* in the World. Most recently, Michigan hosted the 2004 Ryder Cup PGA Golf Tournament. With over 850 golf courses in our state you can be sure there is something to appeal to the novice or the pro. We have selected some of our favorite courses throughout the state that are definitely worth a visit when you are in that region.

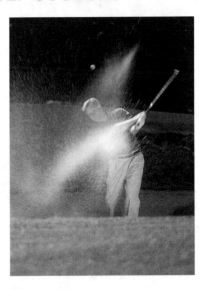

REGION 1

Oakland Hills Country Club, Birmingham
Holes: 2-18s, Par: 72 • Yardage: 7108
Telephone: (248) 644-2500
A very challenging course that has mellowed nicely. It owes it's reputation to Robert Trent Jones renovation from the original Donald Ross design. Many of the greens are fairly severe with a variety of slopes and grades.

The Legacy, Ottawa Lake
Holes: 18 • Yardage: 6840/4961, Slope: 134/115
Telephone: (313) 856-1977
Given a 4 1/2 star rating by Golf Digest, this is another successful course designed by Arthur Hill. The beautiful course has tree and water lined fairways and includes #8, a par 3 island hole. Bring all your clubs.

Timber Ridge Golf Course, East Lansing
Holes: 18, Par: 72 • Yardage: 6497/5048, Slope: 137/129
Telephone: (517) 339-8000, 800-233-6669
Scenic, hilly course. Fairly difficult with forced plays, some to small landing areas. Shotmaking rewarded.

REGION 2

Huron Breeze Golf & Country Club, Augres
Holes: 18, Par: 72 • Yardage: 6806/5075, Slope: 128/120
Telephone: (989) 876-6868
Golf Digest ranks this course 15th Best in the State. Not for the average golfer. Rewarded for accuracy. Difficulties include, double doglegs, long distance from tee to green, and forced carries. Wildlife abounds.

Treetops Sylvan Resort Jones Course, Gaylord
Holes: 18, Par: 71 • Yardage: 7060/4972, Slope: 146/124
Telephone: (888) Treetops • (989) 732-6711
Golf Digest ranks this as 27th in 75 Best Resort Courses in America. Well-maintained course for the better golfer. Beautiful vistas. Also try their Fazio and Smith courses.

Michaywe Hills Golf Club, Lake Course, Gaylord
Holes: 18, Par: 72 • Yardage: 6508/5000, Slope: 141/130
Telephone: (989) 939-8911 • (800) 322-6636
Interesting, tough course, difficult greens where every hole is a unique problem. Also try their Pines with a great layout.

The Natural at Beaver Creek Resort, Gaylord
Holes: 18, Par: 71 • Yardage: 6355/4850, Slope: 128/117
Telephone: (877) 295-3333 • (989) 732-2459
A 4 star Jerry Matthews designed 18-hole championship course, with rolling fairways and mature trees and rolling terrain. It's a beautiful course that is also a wildlife sanctuary so don't be surprised to see deer or wild turkey cross your path.

Thunder Bay Golf Course and Resort, Hillman
Holes: 18, Par: 73 • Yardage: 6677/5004, Slope: 131/127
Telephone: (800) 729-9375
Good course for players at all levels. Tight layout with several doglegs and contoured greens. Extremely well maintained.

The Grand Hotel, The Jewel, Mackinac Island
Holes: 18, Par: 67 • Yardage: 5445/4212 Slope: 110/106
Telephone: (906) 847-3331
Comprised of two separate courses, the Grand 9 and Woods 9. A specially designed horse drawn carriage takes you from one course to the other. Courses have unparalleled beauty. Challenging links type course with plenty of sand bunkers and sand traps. The 7th hole of the Grand 9 is a peninsula on the lake.

REGION 3

The Rock, Drummond Island
Holes: 18, Par: 71 • Yardage: 6830, Slope: 140/126
Telephone: (906) 493-1006, (800) 999-6343
A resort that offers secluded beauty and an enjoyable round of golf. Designed by Harry Bowers and opened in 1989.

A-Ga-Ming Golf Club, Kewadin
Holes: 18, Par: 72 • Yardage: 6663/5125, Slope: 129/118
Telephone: (616) 264-5081, (800) 678-0122
Very pretty course with scenic vistas, tall pines and trees lining the fairway. Hilly, fast greens and many blind shots. This resort has made some major improvements to go from a 2-1/2 star rating up to a 4 star.

REGION 4

TimberStone Golf Course, Iron Mountain
Holes: 18, Par: 72 • Yardage: 6937/5077, Slope: 144/132
Telephone: (906) 776-0111
Course received 4 1/2 Star rating from Golf Digest 2000-2001. It's the perfect blend of golf and nature. You play while ascending Pine Mountain and each hole is benched. A very interesting course to play.

REGION 5

Shanty Creek Resort, The Legend Course, Bellaire
Holes: 18, Par: 72 • Yardage: 6764/4953, Slope: 135/119
Telephone: (231) 533-8621 • 533-6076, 800-678-4111
Golf Digest ranks this as 19th in America's 75 Best Resort Courses. Panoramic vistas with lots of trees, hills and creeks meandering through. Excellent golf experience. It is a Palmer and Seay design with no parallel fairways.

Boyne Mountain Resort, Alpine Course, Boyne Falls
Holes 18, Par: 72 • Yardage: 7017/4986, Slope: 129/114
Telephone: (800) Go-Boyne • (231) 549-6000
Wonderful panoramic scenery while playing down a mountain. Try their other (2) very scenic courses.

Grand Traverse Resort, The Bear, Acme
Holes: 18, Par: 72 • Yardage: 7065/5281, Slope: 149/138
Telephone: (800) 236-1577
A Jack Nicklaus design that is best for above average golfer. Terraced fairways, tiered greens, lakes and streams. Ranked in "America's 75 Best Resort Courses" by Golf Digest.

Little Traverse Bay Golf Club, Harbor Springs
Holes: 18, Par: 72 • Yardage: 6865/6191, Slope: 131/125
Telephone: (231) 526-6200
Fantastic views and surroundings. Extremely well-maintained. Golf at it's best!

Heather Course, Harbor Springs
Holes: 18, Par: 72 • Yardage: 7210/5263, Slope: 131/111
Telephone: (231) 526-2171, (800) 462-6963
In the Top 75 of Golf Digests "America's Best Resort Courses". A Robert Trent Jones Design. A true test of skills. Course is carved out of a birch, maple and cedar forest with undulating terrain, sand traps, ponds and small lakes.

Crystal Mountain Resort, Mountain Ridge, Thompsonville
Holes: 18, Par: 72 • Yardage: 7007/4956
Telephone: (800) 968-7686
Panoramic views over a twisting, high elevation course with pine-framed fairways. Also try Betsie View featuring ponds, streams and meadows. Tough course, tight with lots of blind shots and small greens. With pros, Brad Dean and Elaine Crosby, Crystal was named as one of the "Nation's 25 Best Golf Schools".

REGION 6

Grand Haven Golf Club, Grand Haven
Holes: 18, Par: 72 • Yardage: 6789, Slope: 124/119
Telephone: (616) 842-4040
Accuracy rewards on this scenic course. Holes are tight with lots of trees and dunes lining fairways.

Double JJ Resort, Thoroughbred Golf Club, Rothbury
Holes: 18, Par: 72/72 • Yardage: 6900/4851, Slope: 147/126
Telephone: (231) 893-4653 • (800) DoubleJJ
Fast greens and more than one signature hole. A thinking game for the patient.

Hawks Head Golf Club, South Haven
Holes: 18, Par: 72/72/72 • Yardage: 7050/6665/6295, Slope: 137/130/125
Telephone: 269-639-2121
An Arthur Hill designed course, which is another gem. The scenery and layout of the greens are wonderful.

The Sun Is Setting.

It's time to return to daily living. But you'll
remember the excitement, the challenge,
the peace and serenity of green forests,
rolling hills, crystal waters and snow white valleys.
And you'll dream of the things yet to come.

For you are the dreamer, and I am your
dream maker ... the vacation
land for all seasons.

Michigan

by: C. Rydel

Until We Meet Again ...
Your Friends at the Michigan Vacation Guide

INDEX

Want to catch up on past property reviews... or need another copy of our current MVG? Send your check for $14.95 plus $2.00 (shipping/handling) for each copy, along with the name(s) edition(s) to the below address. Direct on-line purchase is available at our Website (www.MiVG.com).

1993-94, MVG 2nd Ed.   1995-1996, MVG, 3rd Ed.
1997-98, MVG 4th Ed   1999-2000, MVG 5th Ed
2001-02, MVG 6th Ed.   2003-2004 MVG 7th Ed.

CURRENT: 2005-06, MVG 8th Ed.

TR Desktop Publishing
P.O. Box 180271 • Utica, MI 48318-0271
586-228-8780
Email: info@mivg.com

Visit our family of on-line properties at:
www.MiVG.com

Michigan Vacation Guide

Cottages, Chalets, Condos, B&B's

Eighth Edition

2005-2006

Editor/Writer: Kathleen R. Tedsen

Associate Editor: Clara M. Rydel

Writer/Photographer: Beverlee J. Rydel

Business Manager: Christian Tedsen

Cover Photographs:

Front Cover: Anchorage Cottages, Oscoda
Back Cover: (top) **Lodge at Oak Pointe,** Caseville;
(lower left) **Lusky's Lakefront Resort**, Lexington;
(lower right) **Ellis Lake Resort**, Interlochen

3 9082 10255 8890

For information, contact:

TR Desktop Publishing
P.O. Box 180271
Utica, MI 48318-0271
(586) 228-8780

Email: info@mivg.com

PRINTED IN THE UNITED STATES OF AMERICA

ISBN: 0-9635953-6-9